COLLEGE SUCCESS STRATEGIES

FOURTH EDITION

Sherrie Nist-Olejnik
Professor Emeritus, University of Georgia

Jodi Patrick Holschuh
Texas State University

Boston   Columbus   Indianapolis   New York   San Francisco   Upper Saddle River
Amsterdam   Cape Town   Dubai   London   Madrid   Milan   Munich   Paris   Montréal   Toronto
Delhi   Mexico City   São Paulo   Sydney   Hong Kong   Seoul   Singapore   Taipei   Tokyo

Editor in Chief: Eric Stano
Senior Acquisitions Editor: Nancy Blaine
Editorial Assistant: Jamie Fortner
Marketing Manager: Kurt Massey
Senior Supplements Editor: Donna Campion
Project Coordination and Electronic Page Makeup: Integra
Cover Designer/Manager: Wendy Ann Fredericks
Cover Photo: Copyright © Andrew Paterson/Photographer's Choices/Getty Images
Photo Researcher: Rona Tuccillo
Senior Manufacturing Buyer: Roy L. Pickering, Jr.
Printer and Binder: R. R. Donnelley and Sons Company-Harrisonburg
Cover Printer: R. R. Donnelley and Sons Company-Harrisonburg

For permission to use copyrighted material, grateful acknowledgment is made to the copyright holders on p. 271, which is hereby made part of this copyright page.

Library of Congress Cataloging-in-Publication Data

Nist-Olejnik, Sherrie,
   College success strategies/Sherrie L. Nist-Olejnik and Jodi Patrick
Holschuh.—1st ed.
     p. cm.
   Includes index.
   ISBN-13: 978-0-134-05185-7
   ISBN-10: 0-134-05185-8
     1. Study skills.   2. Learning, Psychology of.   3. Academic achievement.
4. College student orientation.   I. Holschuh, Jodi.   II. Title.
LB2395.N545 2012
378.1'70281—dc23

                                                          2011026310

Copyright © 2014 by Pearson Education, Inc.

2 3 4 5 6 7 8 9 10—DOH—18 17 16 15

PEARSON

ISBN-13: 978-0-134-05185-7
ISBN-10:   0-134-05185-8

To my family with love—my husband, Steve Olejnik, and my daughter, Kama.

—S.N.O.

To my family—my husband, Douglas, my daughter, Maia, and my son, Samuel.

—J.P.H.

contents

We decided to write a fourth edition of *College Success Strategies* largely because of the ideas that evolved as we taught students to be flexible learners. We realized that students need to know more about the underlying principles of becoming an effective college learner, as well as more about how to use technology to maximize learning. They also need to better understand the importance of task as they study and learn in a variety of disciplines. Such knowledge leads students to be more independent learners. Finally, we believed that we could enhance the writing activities in the book because we firmly believe in the importance of students needing to use all of their senses if they are going to be efficient and effective learners. Thus, with these new additions and streamlining some of the material from the third edition, we think that this new edition is even more effective at helping students become the college students they hope to be.

What's New in the Fourth Edition?

In the fourth edition of *College Success Strategies*, we have concentrated our efforts in three key areas. First, we made the importance of task more explicit. If students do not understand what their professors expect of them, they will have difficulty in selecting the appropriate strategies to use. Therefore, we combined Chapters 4 ("Interacting With Your Professors") and Chapter 5 ("What Is It I'm Supposed to Do, Anyhow?") into one chapter, titled "Professors, Tasks, and You" (Chapter 4). We believe this helps make the connection stronger between what professors "do" and what professors want students "to do."

The second major change is that we have added a new chapter on technology titled "Using Technology To Learn" (Chapter 15), in addition to retaining the **Networking** sidebar. On most campuses today, understanding how to use technology is a necessity, not a luxury. Many professors will expect students to submit work and communicate with them via email, make PowerPoint presentations in class, use course management systems such as Blackboard, download podcasts, and even take computerized exams. And while *College Success Strategies* does not necessarily teach how to do these things, it does remind students of the importance of learning how, and it also provides suggestions for becoming an active learner by using technology.

Finally, we listened to reviewers' suggestions to add more opportunities for students to engage in writing activities. Thus, the **On Your Own** sidebar has been revamped to include a written component as students respond to the strategies presented in each chapter and reflect on what they have learned. We believe that the responses to the On Your Own sidebars when combined with the **Add to Your Portfolio** exercises will help students more fully understand the strategies they have learned.

Continuing Features from the Third Edition

Although we have tweaked *College Success Strategies,* the major premise behind the book remains rooted in the importance of academics. As such, the majority of the text continues to focus on the four key academic factors that must interact if learning is to be maximized: (1) characteristics of the learner; (2) the tasks learners must complete in each class; (3) the strategies that help learners read, understand, and remember what the professor expects them to learn; and, finally, (4) the texts with which learners interact.

We have retained much of the excellent features from the third edition of *College Success Strategies.* Each chapter still contains the following sidebars:

- **Add to Your Portfolio** allows students to apply each strategy presented in the book. By creating a portfolio over an entire term, students will have tangible evidence of the progress they have made in their thinking, learning, and studying.
- **Get Going** focuses on tips and strategies for gaining motivation and overcoming procrastination.
- **Timely Tips** centers on strategies for time management. It also discusses how many of the strategies have practical application beyond the classroom.
- **Studying Smarter** provides quick and easy tips or inspirational quotations to help students get a jump on their learning and studying.
- **Networking** focuses on using technology for learning actively. Some are activities students can try and others are suggestions for incorporating technology to enhance learning.
- **Success at a Glance** depicts key information in a visual way to help students remember it better.

Additionally, each chapter begins with a **Self-Assessment** and concludes with the **Real College** scenarios and **Add to Your Portfolio** activities. The Self-Assessments help students to assess and reflect on their own learning before reading the chapter. Each Real College scenario features a college student who has a problem related in some way to that chapter. By helping these college students solve their problems, students will be able to further apply the ideas and strategies discussed in the chapters. We believe that students may see part of themselves in many of the scenarios. These scenarios, by the way, are based on real issues that our students consistently face as they work toward becoming active learners. The Add to Your Portfolio activities ask students to apply what they have learned to their other courses and help them see how much they have grown as learners as they progress through the term. Finally, Appendixes A and B are psychology and history chapters, as in the previous edition. *College Success Strategies* is designed for students to apply the strategies learned in Chapters 9–14 to each of these chapters. We continue to believe that in order to truly understand the full benefit of the strategies presented, it is important to apply them to full pieces of text rather than to shorter excerpts.

Using *College Success Strategies*

College Success Strategies was designed not only to get students reading about what it takes to learn actively but also to start them thinking and talking about it. The Self-Assessment activities at the beginning of each chapter provide students with a snapshot of their strengths and weaknesses related to the topics discussed. The activities at the end of each chapter ask students to discuss important questions with classmates, to think critically, and to reflect on academic issues. We believe that active learners use numerous senses as they go about learning in college. They read, they write, they discuss, and they visualize. Interacting with information in a variety of ways encourages active processing, and active processing leads to academic success.

As students read and discuss the chapters in the four parts of *College Success Strategies*, they can apply the strategies learned to the textbook chapters in the appendixes. One chapter, titled "Cognition and Intelligence," is from a psychology text; the second, titled "The Nation Divides: The Vietnam War and Social Conflict, 1964–1971," is from a history text. These two chapters will be especially helpful in providing practice as students engage with Chapters 12–14, but they can (and should) be used in any of the other application activities throughout *College Success Strategies* as well. Applying the strategies to longer pieces of text will give students practice that simulates regular college classes. As students preview, annotate, rehearse, and review the material, they learn how to monitor their learning to know their level of understanding. *College Success Strategies* teaches students to be active learners in charge of their own understanding.

The text boxes in *College Success Strategies* provide students with important information and should not be overlooked. From these boxes students can pick up quick and easy studying tips, learn more about using technology, improve their motivation and time management skills, and overcome procrastination. All of this information focuses on helping students become more self-confident and successful.

Finally, as students work through *College Success Strategies*, they will build a portfolio showcasing their newfound skills. At the end of each chapter, students can apply the strategies to a content-area course (e.g., psychology, biology, history, geography, and so forth) as a way of seeing if they can transfer strategy use to college learning. Ultimately, this should be the goal. Once students use the strategies as part of their daily academic life, they are well on their way to being active learners.

acknowledgments

There are many individuals who contributed directly or indirectly to the fourth edition of *College Success Strategies*. Certainly it is important for us to acknowledge the students whom we continue to have the privilege to teach. As is always the case, our students help to ground our writing in reality—the reality of the many pressures currently faced by today's college students and the reality of just how important life-long learning has become. We continue to be struck by the major impact that technology has on students' learning. Today's students are truly the first generation of college students who are expected to know and keep abreast of new technological advances that can enhance learning. We have a hard time keeping up with them!

In addition to our students, our thanks go out to the numerous professors and graduate students on the University of Georgia and Texas State University campuses and beyond who have willingly shared their concerns and their expertise about learning and what it takes to be successful in their particular disciplines. This text would not have been nearly as effective without their valuable insights. A special thanks to Denise Pinette Domizi, Eleanor Pardini, Daniel Forbes, and Gretchen Pettis for their suggestions and willingness to share the parallel note-taking strategy in *College Success Strategies*; and thanks also to Audrey Haynes for the use of Web notes from her political science class.

Certainly, we acknowledge our respective families—our spouses, parents, siblings, and children—who always offered their continuous support, and sometimes even additional insights, as we sometimes turned our attention from them to work on this book. As always, we appreciate their understanding, support, and advice.

The authors would like to acknowledge the major support we have received from the Pearson staff, including Editor-in-Chief Eric Stano, Senior Acquisitions Editor Nancy Blaine, and Editorial Assistant Jamie Fortner. We appreciate their encouragement and enthusiasm as we crafted the fourth edition of this book. We also wish to thank our reviewers: Kim Zernechel, Minneapolis Community & Technical College; Karen S. King, Montgomery College; Joseph Scalise, The University of Georgia; Ann Becks, University of Florida; Stacy Kirch, Orange Coast College; and Dr. Marian Smith, Chippewa Valley Technical College. Everyone's patience, attention to detail, and helpful suggestions made working on this book an enjoyable experience.

SHERRIE NIST-OLEJNIK
JODI PATRICK HOLSCHUH

Now That You're Here

READMENT THIS CHAPTER TO ANSWER THE FOLLOWING QUESTIONS:

- How does studying in college differ from studying in high school?
- What special situations can you expect to encounter in college, sooner or later?

SELF-ASSESSMENT

DIRECTIONS: On a scale of 1 to 5, with 1 being "strongly disagree," 3 being "somewhat agree," and 5 being "strongly agree," respond to each of the statements below. This should give you a good idea about how much your college experience differs from what you experienced in high school.

	Strongly disagree ⟷ Strongly agree
1. My college professors seem to expect much more of me.	1 2 3 4 5
2. My college classes move at a faster pace.	1 2 3 4 5
3. My college classes require more than just memorization.	1 2 3 4 5
4. My college classes give me few chances to earn extra credit.	1 2 3 4 5
5. My college classes require me to spend more time studying.	1 2 3 4 5
6. My college professors give less frequent exams.	1 2 3 4 5
7. I have more freedom in college.	1 2 3 4 5
8. I often feel anonymous in college.	1 2 3 4 5
9. I have experienced motivation problems in college.	1 2 3 4 5
10. Managing my time effectively is more challenging in college.	1 2 3 4 5

Now add up your score. The higher your score, the more differences you are experiencing in making the transition from high school to college. The more differences you experience, the more time it may take you to make the adjustment. But don't despair! The skills you will learn in *College Success Strategies* will help you make this transition.

Starting college! You may feel as if you have been preparing for this day forever. You've taken a college preparatory curriculum in high school, you've talked with friends or siblings who are already in college, and you may have visited several campuses before deciding which school to attend. Or you may be returning to college after several years of working, having already gone through careful life assessment and financial budgeting. Regardless of your situation, you are probably excited about what the next few years have in store for you. And some of you may even be a little wary and unsure of yourselves as you begin down the college path.

Studying Smarter

Avoid the need to cram! Pay some attention to every class every day.

In this chapter, we will discuss some of the ways in which college differs from high school. In addition, we will present eight situations that you are sure to encounter in college sooner or later and will offer suggestions about how you might deal with them. Keep in mind as you read this chapter that campuses differ in size and in the expectations they have of students. For these reasons, some of the generalizations and solutions offered here might not apply exactly to your particular situation.

How Does College Differ from High School?

How many times since high school graduation have you heard one of your relatives say something like this: "Oh _____ (insert your name)! Enjoy these college years. They will be the best of your life." Although this statement is probably true—college is enjoyable and memorable—it is also demanding and, in many instances, just plain different from high school. It's a time in your life when you will go through many changes as you prepare for the world of work that follows. In this section we will discuss some of the reasons why high school and college differ.

■ **Reason 1: College Requires Greater Independent Learning.** Your high school teachers may have been willing to give you lots of test preparation help. They may have prepared study guides or even provided the exact questions that would be asked. Although college instructors also want you to be successful—we have never met a professor who wants students to fail—they don't give students as much study help. Sure, most professors will answer questions about course content and things you don't understand, but they will not provide you with a variety of supplementary learning materials, and they certainly will not give you test questions. They expect that you know effective and efficient study strategies, and if you don't know how to study for their courses, they expect you to learn how.

TIMELY TIPS

Learning How to Learn

Did you know that learning how to learn on your own may be one of the most important benefits of going to college? As you move into the world of work, most employers will expect you to do a considerable amount of learning on your own. Employees who need lots of guidance in learning new things aren't nearly as valuable as those who are self-starters. So one of the most important skills you want to foster early in your college career is the ability to learn on your own. In fact, you should make mastering this skill one of your top priorities in college.

■ **Reason 2: College Courses Move at a Faster Pace.** If you ask first-year college students about the differences between high school and college, one of their most common responses would be that college courses move much faster than high school classes. What might have taken a full year to cover in high school will probably be covered in a semester in college. It's not uncommon for college professors to move through three, four, or more chapters in a week, expecting you to keep up. In addition, more topics are generally covered in greater detail. However, college professors may go into detail on just a few points and expect you to fill in the rest of the details on your own.

■ **Reason 3: College Courses Require You to Think Critically.** In your high school classes, perhaps you were required to memorize lots of facts for exams. You may even have been discouraged from questioning either your high school textbooks or your high school teachers. But as you proceed through college, you will find yourself in classes where your professor wants you to do more than memorize. You might have to critique an essay on gun control, read and respond to a historian's view of the Vietnamese conflict, or compare and contrast conflicting scientific theories. All of these tasks require you to think critically because you need to go beyond memorization to applying or synthesizing the information.

■ **Reason 4: College Classes Have Few Safety Nets.** Usually on the first day of a college class your professor will give you a syllabus. The syllabus outlines the course requirements and also generally tells you how your grade will be determined. Something that will become clear as you read your syllabus is that many of the safety nets that you had in high school, such as extra credit assignments or other bonuses to improve your grade, have all but disappeared. This means your course grade will be determined by the grade you earn on a limited number of tests or papers. So you'll need to give every assignment your best effort.

■ **Reason 5: College Requires You to Study Longer and More Effectively.** You will probably find out pretty quickly that both the amount of time you put into studying and the way you study in college will have to change if you want to earn high grades. Many of our students tell us that they really didn't have to study in high school. "Studying" was reading over a study guide or reading over class notes for about a half hour. Many students begin college without ever having had to read their texts, and some have never taken essay exams. It is important to realize that studying in college requires not only more time but also having a variety of study strategies at your disposal.

■ **Reason 6: College Provides Fewer Chances for Evaluation.** In high school, it may have seemed as though you were always taking tests or writing papers. Chances are you were tested over small amounts of material (only one or two chapters) and you had numerous chances for evaluation. If you did poorly on one test, you could usually make it up on the next one. In college, on the other hand, you will probably have fewer chances to be evaluated. At first, the idea of taking fewer tests per course in a term may seem appealing. But think about the big picture. If you have only three exams, you are going to be held responsible for much more information at one time than you were in high school. What at first seems to be an advantage—fewer tests, homework that goes unchecked, a longer period of time between exams—may actually work against you, unless you know how to stay on top of things.

GET GOING

Keeping Up with Assignments

Many students enter college thinking that if there is no test coming up that week, they have nothing pressing to do. But, because you may have four or five chapters on each exam (or even more), you will need to stay on top of your reading each week. Don't procrastinate on your reading because you will need time to process all of the material.

■ **Reason 7: College Gives You Greater Freedom and Greater Responsibility.** Legally, you become an adult at age 18, which just happens to be about the same time you graduate from high school. In college, no one makes you stay on top of your schoolwork or keeps track of your comings and goings or checks to see that you have done all of your reading and studying before heading out for a night on the town. This freedom comes with a tremendous amount of responsibility. It is your responsibility to prioritize the tasks you *have* to do against the things you *want* to do.

■ **Reason 8: College Provides Greater Anonymity.** If you attend a moderate-sized to large college or university, you will be faced with being somewhat anonymous—and in some cases, very anonymous. By *anonymous* we mean that you can become just another face in the crowd. Most of you probably attended high schools where you got to know your teachers and classmates fairly well. Your teachers not only knew your name but also were concerned about whether or not you were learning and understanding the information presented in their classes. For the most part, in college, your professors have few opportunities to get to know you well. All is not lost, however. Most of the time, students are anonymous only if they want to be, regardless of how large or small their campus may be. You can become more than a "face" to your professors by making appointments to talk with them. You can join clubs that have faculty sponsors. You can take part in a variety of campus activities with other students who share your interests.

■ **Reason 9: College Requires You to Be Proactive.** Being proactive means that it's your responsibility to take the initiative in a variety of situations. In high school, either your teachers or your parents may have insisted that you get help if you were having problems with a particular course. And you may have followed their advice reluctantly. In college, however, it becomes your responsibility to know the resources that are available on your campus, so that if you do run into difficulties or need the services of some office, you'll know how to find the information you need or where to go for assistance. If you are proactive and find out a little about them before you need their services, it will save you time in the long run. Don't wait until you are in dire need of these resources before seeking them out. Some of these services may include:

■ **The Library.** In addition to providing resources, the library is a great place to study, to do research online, or to meet your study group. Most campuses have library orientations that help students learn to navigate large and complex systems.

■ **The Learning Center.** The campus learning center can be an excellent source of assistance because it generally offers a variety of services, from academic counseling to assistance with writing, studying, and mathematics.

■ **Tutorial Services.** Like learning centers, most campuses offer tutorial services for a broad range of courses. Generally, tutoring is provided by undergraduate students who earn top grades in the areas in which they tutor. This tutoring is usually free, but appointments are often necessary.

■ **Health Services.** Because getting sick enough to need the services of a doctor is inevitable, know where your campus health facility is and what the rules are to be able to see a medical professional. Don't wait until you feel as if you're on your deathbed. Find out where to go and what to do early on.

■ **Counseling Center.** More and more students are enlisting the help of a trained professional from their campus counseling center. If you find that you have problems that are getting in the way of your academic success, you should seek out help. Sometimes talking with a friend works. If it doesn't, find out more about the services offered through the counseling center.

■ **Student Center or Student Union.** On most campuses, the student center is the hub of campus where you can meet friends, but most also offer a wealth of resources. Sometimes campus organizations and clubs have offices in the student center. Social event and concert tickets can be purchased there. You can get general information about the campus, such as bus schedules, campus maps, and event schedules. Often, the campus bookstore is located in or near the student center. When you don't know where else to turn, the student center is a good place to start if you need information about your campus.

NETWORKING

Your School's Web Site

Access the Web site of the college or university you are currently attending. Search the Web site for information about some of the services discussed in this chapter, such as the learning center, health center, or counseling center. What did you find out about these services that you didn't know before? What other services did you find?

Check your syllabi to see if any of your professors list their e-mail addresses. If they do, write a brief e-mail to introduce yourself or to ask a question. Also, if any of your professors have personal Web pages, check them out.

So, college is different from high school in many ways. You must think differently about the expectations, learning conditions, level of responsibility, and studying methods than you did in high school. This is not bad. It simply means you will have to make some transitions in the way you learn and study in order to be successful.

SUCCESS AT A GLANCE

How High School Differs from College

	High School	College
Independence	Less independence	Greater independence
Pacing	Slow	Fast
Level of Critical Thinking	Less critical thinking	Greater critical thinking
Safety Nets	Teachers provide many	Professors provide few
Study Effort	Limited and sporadic	Greater and more effective
Evaluation	Many opportunities	Limited opportunities
Responsibility	Rests on others	Rests on you
Anonymity	Little	Lots
Importance of Being Proactive	Low	High

ON YOUR OWN

Reflecting on What You Have Read

Reflect on the reasons we discussed about how college is different from high school. Write brief responses to the following questions: Which differences seem to be impacting your college career so far? Write about two additional differences from your own experiences. What do you wish you had learned in high school that would have better prepared you for college? Finally, write about two ways in which college and high school are not so different.

What Special Situations Can You Expect to Encounter Sooner or Later?

Now that you have seen some of the ways in which high school and college differ, let's examine this transition from another perspective. We'll present eight situations that most college students will encounter sooner or later, and we'll also examine how you might cope with or handle each situation. All of these situations will be addressed again throughout this text, so you will be able to explore these ideas in greater detail.

In a perfect world, none of the following situations would occur. All students would go to class every day, distribute their study time over several days, stay on top of their reading, and make the dean's list every term. However, the world of college is an imperfect place. So, let's discuss some of the situations that you might encounter in college, some for which you might not be prepared. As you read each section, think about how you might handle the situation and what additional information might help you cope better.

■ **Professors Who Take Roll.** Someone may have told you that the only time you really *have* to show up for classes in college is on test days, or that if you can get the information on your own, professors don't really care whether you are in class. Although many professors don't take attendance, eventually you will run across one who does, and, in reality, most actually do want you present in class. Many professors truly believe that attending class will help you learn. We believe this as well; so even if your professor does not take roll, it's still a good idea to attend class.

■ **An Early Morning Class.** Most college students are not morning people. In fact, there's even scientific evidence to indicate that the biological clocks of college-aged people are preset to stay up late at night and to sleep late in the morning. However, the college officials who determine the times of class periods evidently are unaware of this research. Unfortunately (for most college students), a time will come when you will have to take an early morning class. If you do have that early class, try to juggle the rest of your schedule so that you can go to bed earlier than usual. Additionally, try to take one that meets only two or three days a week, thus allowing you a little more flexibility on other days.

■ **A Course or Professor You Don't Particularly Like.** It's sad but true—there will be courses you don't like and professors with whom you fail to connect. Even if you have a wide range of interests and you can get along well with almost everyone, at some point you'll probably have to make it through a rough class. You can take one of two routes when this happens.

Route A: You can think of every excuse imaginable not to do the work or go to class. You can blame your attitude on the professor or the boring material that you are expected to learn.

Consequences of Route A: You could receive a poor course grade, develop a bad feeling about yourself, or have to work doubly hard in another course to bring up your overall grade point average.

Route B: Acknowledge that you really don't care much for the course or the professor. It's one course, however, and you can make it through. Study with someone who seems to like the course. Try to motivate yourself with small rewards. Tell yourself that this is temporary and the course will soon be over.

Consequences of Route B: Perhaps you will not earn an A in the class, but you will emerge with your ego and your grade point average intact.

■ **Cramming for a Test.** Imagine you have a big test in a couple of days (or worse yet, tomorrow) and you've done very little preparing. Now it's *cram time!* We've never met a student who didn't have to cram at some time. And cramming occasionally probably isn't a horrible thing, but it shouldn't become the way you live your academic life. If you have to cram occasionally, try to use the strategies you'll learn in this book to study to your advantage. And, as soon as possible, regroup so that you don't have to cram again.

■ **Difficulty Maintaining Motivation for Academics.** Most college students experience motivation problems at some time or other. It usually doesn't last long, but for some students the decline in motivation is long enough and severe enough to interfere with their schoolwork. Other students experience a lull in motivation in just one class—generally a class with which they are experiencing difficulty. Still others begin the term with good intentions, yet quickly develop general motivation problems in every class. If you are having motivation problems, try setting some specific, reachable goals. Whether your lack of motivation is concentrated in one particular course, occurs at a specific period of time (such as around midpoint), or is generalized across all your academic courses, goal setting can help you stay focused and improve your motivation to learn.

■ **Personal Problems and/or Illness.** No one plans on getting sick or having serious personal problems, but at some point you will likely experience both predicaments. However, there are some things you can do to salvage even a bad situation. First, as you plan your schedule for the term, build in some flexibility, just in case. If everything goes according to plan, the worst thing that can happen is you'll have some extra time to study, work, or play. Second, as mentioned earlier, use the services that are available on your campus. Third, develop a set of reliable peers who can be there for you in times of illness or other problems. Often, knowing that some other person can help you makes all the difference in the world.

■ **Frustration.** It's a given that you will experience frustrations and stressful situations, but it's how you deal with them that makes the difference. Try not to let things build up to the point where you can't cope. As much as possible, deal with frustrations as they arise. Evaluate all the alternatives. And try not to become stressed by things you have no control over. So...take a walk. Go work out. Spend a few minutes venting to a friend. In time it will work out.

■ **Juggling Too Many Responsibilities.** College students tend to be busy people—going to class, studying, attending meetings, working, exercising, taking part in campus organizations, and the list goes on. Add to all of this family responsibilities, social interactions, and some good old time to play, and you can easily become overcommitted. Although you certainly want to get the most out of your college experience, try to think about how new responsibilities will affect you. Remember that your primary job in college is to be a student. Then you can ask yourself: "What other kinds of responsibilities can I take on?" Will you have so much to do a month from now that you will constantly feel stressed out and frustrated? If you can think about this in advance and learn to say "No" when you find yourself maxing out, you will be able to keep all those balls in the air and be a much happier student.

■ **Having Problems Organizing Course Materials Even If You Are a Very Organized Student.** With all of the advances in technology, more and more professors are making students responsible for a wider variety of materials from a broader range of sources. Rarely will you have just a textbook in your courses. The more likely scenario is that you will be responsible for information from not only one or more texts and lectures but also any or all of the following: online course management systems, CD-ROM supplements, on-line materials, workbooks, computerized homework assignments, and lab manuals. Being responsible for learning materials from a variety of sources in the same course requires you to keep up with a lot. You may have to be creative and find new ways to organize so that you can keep it all straight.

Studying Smarter

I will study and get ready, and perhaps my chance will come.

—Abraham Lincoln

Real College

Wanda

DIRECTIONS: Read the following "Real College" scenario and respond to the questions based on the information you learned in this chapter.

Wanda was a pretty good student in high school. She earned good grades and "studied as much as she needed" to make As and Bs. She just naturally assumed that she would earn similar grades in college. But here it is, only three weeks into the fall semester, and things aren't going as planned. She didn't do well on her first chemistry test because she had to cram and asked the professor for an extra credit assignment. Her professor chuckled and shook his head no. Then there's the pace. Things seem to be moving so fast. She's having a difficult time keeping up. From her perspective, she's studying about the same amount of time as she did in high school, but her efforts don't seem to be paying off. In addition to these academic problems, she feels alone and isolated. She likes her roommate and would like to get to know her better, but her roommate knows a lot of people already so she's not around much. It seems so hard to make new friends.

1. What advice do you have for Wanda?
2. What could she do to help herself academically? Socially?

ADD TO YOUR PORTFOLIO

1. Sometimes professors can seem intimidating, especially when you first begin college, but most college teachers are personable people who enjoy interacting with students. In order to get to know one of your professors a little better, make an appointment to talk with her. You might discuss course expectations, ask for studying pointers, or discuss your past successes or problems with similar courses. Write up a one-page summary of your conversation.

2. Find out where you can get help with academic problems. Is there a learning center on your campus? If so, what services does it offer? How do you go about making an appointment in the learning center? Jot down this information for future reference.

3. Find out where you can get counseling assistance. Is there a counseling center that can help you make the adjustment to college? What if you just need someone to talk with? How do you go about making an appointment to see someone? Jot down this information for future reference.

CHAPTER

Active Learning: What's in It for You?

READ THIS CHAPTER TO ANSWER THE FOLLOWING QUESTIONS:

- How do active learners differ from passive learners?
- What are the benefits of active learning?
- What are the four factors that influence learning?
- What is the holistic nature of active learning?

SELF-ASSESSMENT

DIRECTIONS: On a scale of 1 to 5, with 1 being "rarely," 3 being "sometimes," and 5 being "most of the time," evaluate how active you are as a learner.

	Rarely ⟷		Most of the time

1. When I read my texts, I can make connections with what I have read earlier in the course.   1 2 3 4 5

2. After I read my texts, I can restate the key ideas in my own words.   1 2 3 4 5

3. After lectures and when I am finished reading my texts, I can clearly state what I don't understand.   1 2 3 4 5

4. I can take meaningful and organized notes for a full class period without losing concentration.   1 2 3 4 5

5. When I prepare for tests, I use my time wisely.   1 2 3 4 5

6. I seek out help when I am having problems understanding the material presented in a course.   1 2 3 4 5

7. I use different strategies for learning, depending on the course and the type of exams.   1 2 3 4 5

	Rarely ← →		Most of the time		
8. If information I hear or read fails to fit with what I already know, I try to examine the issue from a variety of viewpoints.	1	2	3	4	5
9. When I enter a testing situation, I have a good idea of how I will do.	1	2	3	4	5
10. I am motivated to learn in most of my classes.	1	2	3	4	5
11. I feel confident about myself as a learner.	1	2	3	4	5

Now, add up your score. The higher your score, the more active you are as a learner. The lowest score you can receive is 11; the highest score is 55. Your score gives you an overall picture of how much work you have to do and also lets you know which areas of active learning you need to work on.

What Do Active Learners Do?

You hear it all the time, read about it in magazines and newspapers, and even watch television programs dedicated to one theme: ACTIVITY! Be active, exercise. It's good for your health. It seems as though everywhere you turn there's another piece of research or another claim about the importance of being active. Let's take the premise that you are tired of being out of shape. You take the big step and join a fitness club or gym so that you can work yourself back into shape. Such good intentions! But what if you went to the gym and merely watched other people exercise? Would you become fit? Of course not, because you would not be an **active** participant. Learning works in the same way. If you are not an active participant in learning, you won't become mentally fit, nor will you maximize your performance in the classroom.

To define active learning, we'll discuss the differences between active and passive learning by examining seven characteristics of active learners and contrasting them with the characteristics of passive learners. Active learners:

■ **Read with the Purpose of Understanding and Remembering.** We'd bet that no one deliberately sits down to read with the purpose of *not* understanding the text. However, we're certain that you have been in situations where you "read" an assignment, closed the text, and thought, "What in the world was that about?" When you respond to a text in that manner you are reading passively. Active readers, on the other hand, set goals before they read and check their understanding as they read.

Studying Smarter

When trying to change your study habits, be open-minded and try new approaches.

13

When they finish, they can explain the main points and know that they have understood what they have read.

■ **Reflect on Information and Think Critically.** Being reflective is an important part of active learning because it means that you are thinking about the information. In other words, you are processing the information. You may make connections between the new information and what you already know, identify concepts that you may not understand very well, or evaluate the importance of what you are reading. An active learner reflects constantly. In contrast, passive learners may read the text and listen to lectures, and even understand most of what is read and heard, but they do not take that crucial next step of actually thinking about it.

■ **Listen Actively by Taking Comprehensive Notes in an Organized Fashion.** We are always amazed at the number of students who engage in activities other than listening and note taking in their lecture classes. We've seen students reading the campus newspaper, doing an assignment for another class, working crossword puzzles, or chatting with a classmate. Perhaps the all-time winner for passive learning, however, is a student who regularly came to class with a pillow and blanket and fell asleep on his girlfriend's shoulder. Unlike these students, active learners are engaged learners. They listen actively to the professor for the entire class period, and they write down as much information as possible. To be an active note taker, you must be more than simply present. You have to think about the information before you write.

■ **Know That Learning Involves More Than Simply Putting in Time.** Most students know about the importance of having good time-management skills and expect to invest time in studying in order to be successful. But just putting time into studying is not enough. It is the quality of that time—what you actually do with it—that makes the difference. In college, effort does not count—performance does.

NETWORKING

Going Online

There is so much information and misinformation available to you on the Internet that it takes an active learner to be able to sift through it. To practice your skills as a critical thinker, go online to your local newspaper or to a news magazine and use the search function to find a current article that interests you. Try to actively engage in the article to find out the author's intent. Question the author as you read. Does any of the information seem suspect or unsupported? Does it agree or disagree with what you already know about the topic? Use the answers to these questions to help you reflect on the information you find.

- **Get Assistance When Experiencing Problems.** Because active learners are constantly monitoring their understanding, they know when their comprehension breaks down, and they ask for help before they become totally lost. In addition, active learners can often predict the courses (or even particular concepts within courses) that may give them trouble. They have a plan in mind for getting assistance should they need it. Active learners may hire individual tutors, take advantage of free peer tutoring, or seek assistance from their professors. Although passive learners may seek help at some point, it is often too little, too late. In addition, because passive learners do not reflect and think critically, they often don't even realize that they need help.

- **Accept Much of the Responsibility for Learning.** Active learners understand that the responsibility for learning must come from within, while passive learners often want to blame others for their lack of motivation, poor performance, time-management problems, and other difficulties that they might experience. When active learners don't perform as well as they'd hoped, they evaluate why they didn't do well and change those studying behaviors the next time. Passive learners, on the other hand, often approach every course in the same manner and then get angry with professors when their performance is poor. It is only when students accept the responsibility for their own learning that they can truly be called active learners.

- **Question Information.** Active learners question information that they read and hear, while passive learners accept both the printed page and the words of their professors as "truth." Active learners don't question *everything*, but they do evaluate what they read and hear. When new information fails to fit with what they already know, they may differ in the conclusions they draw or in the inferences they make.

Benefits of Active Learning

As you can tell by reading the last section, being an active learner involves having both *skill* and *will*.

- By **skill**, we mean that you have the tools to handle the studying and learning demands placed on you. You have a variety of study strategies that you consciously employ, and these strategies change depending on the text, the task, and your own personal characteristics as a learner, as we will discuss further in the next section. In addition, you know how to manage your time, you know when and where to get assistance if you are having difficulty, and you can monitor and evaluate your learning.

SUCCESS AT A GLANCE

Differences Between Active and Passive Learners

	Active Learners	Passive Learners
Reading	Read to understand and remember.	Read but may not understand or remember.
Reflecting and Thinking Critically	Make connections between what they already know and new information in texts, in lectures, and from studying with peers.	Don't think about and process information that they read and hear.
Listening	Are engaged during lectures and take organized notes.	Pay little attention during lectures and take unorganized or incomplete notes.
Managing Time	Put in quality study time.	May put in a lot of study time, but not quality time.
Getting Assistance	Realize when they need help and seek it early.	Seek too little help too late.
Accepting Responsibility	Understand they are responsible for their own learning, analyze weak performance if it occurs, and change the way they study accordingly.	Blame others for poor performance, approach every course in the same way, and fail to learn from their mistakes.
Questioning Information	Question new information that doesn't fit with what they already know.	Accept what they read and hear in lectures as true and don't question.

■ By **will,** we mean that you have the desire and motivation to follow through. Skill is nothing without will. For example, you may have a friend, relative, or peer who is knowledgeable but not motivated in the classroom. Even though he reads widely and can intelligently discuss a variety of issues, he does little work associated with school and rarely studies. Teachers may say that this person is "bright but lazy," or "… isn't working up to his potential." In other words, students such as these may have the skills to do well; for some reason they simply do not have the will. And because skill and will go hand in hand, unmotivated students—those who do not have the will—may experience difficulty in college and end up dropping out or being "asked" to leave.

It's much easier to teach students the skills needed to be active learners than it is to give them the will. Skill is something that can be developed only if one has the will to do so. Think about the example used earlier in the chapter pertaining to exercise: If you go to the gym to develop skill, and you have the will to put in the effort to persist in developing your athletic skill, you'll be successful. But if you work out for two weeks, then only sporadically, then not at all, you seemingly lack the will to be successful, even though you might have the skills to do so. No one can force you to go to the gym, just as no one can force you to study effectively, to plan your time, or to go to class. All of that is a matter of will, no matter how much skill you have.

GET GOING

Developing Will

One way to develop the will to learn is by setting your own purpose for learning. Many students seem unaware of what they hope to get out of their courses, so it is no wonder they are not motivated to learn. For one of your courses this semester, figure out what you hope to accomplish by the end of the class. If you make your plan for a course you don't particularly enjoy, it just may help you find your will.

Active learning, then, has numerous benefits, both in terms of academic and psychological payoffs.

■ In terms of **academic payoffs,** active learning leads to higher grades, increased time to pursue extracurricular and social activities, and, most importantly, gained knowledge. Active learners tend to earn higher grade point averages, seek more involvement with their professors, and like to learn new things. And while all active learners certainly don't believe that they are studying simply for the "love of learning," they are more apt to find learning new things more of a challenge than a chore or a bore.

■ The **psychological payoffs** of active learning may even outweigh the academic benefits. Have you ever heard the saying "Success begets success"? This saying means that being successful motivates you to do what it takes to have greater success. In other words, once active learners experience academic success, they want to continue along that path. Being successful will make you feel good about yourself, create

Studying Smarter

The difference between a successful person and others is not a lack of strength, not a lack of knowledge, but rather in a lack of will.

—Vince Lombardi

greater self-confidence about learning, generate positive feedback from family, and often influence your future goals. Everyone knows that it's much easier to continue to use the skills you have acquired if you get positive feedback about how you have applied those skills.

Four Factors That Influence Active Learning

As you can see, active learning is a complex process. Part of the complexity of learning is caused by the many factors that you have to consider. Cognitive psychologists, those who study how people learn, suggest that there are four key factors that influence learning:

1. Your own characteristics as a learner;
2. The tasks your professors ask you to do;
3. The texts with which you interact; and
4. The strategies you select.

We briefly cover each of these factors here, but we will discuss each factor in greater detail in later chapters.

Factor 1: Characteristics of the Learner

As a student, you bring a variety of unique characteristics to each learning situation. These characteristics play a key role in how well you will perform, your interest in the material, and the strategies you will select to learn the course content.

■ **Motivation** is one of the most important characteristics you can bring to a learning situation. Without motivation, you would find it hard to get out of bed each morning. And you will probably experience frustration and failure as a student. General interest in the topic being studied helps, but if you are open to learning new things and expanding your interests, you will be more successful. Motivation is discussed in Chapter 6.

■ **Background knowledge** plays a role because the more you already know about a topic, the easier it is to learn. This means that it might be a good idea to select at least some courses during your first semester or two that you know a lot about. Using the knowledge you already possess is discussed in Chapter 3.

■ Your **ability to concentrate** on what you are reading or studying also affects your learning. Everyone has times when his mind wanders and concentration is difficult. But if you frequently leave class or finish reading a chapter feeling that you got little or nothing out of it, learning may be difficult. There are things you can do to improve your concentration, however. Attention and concentration are discussed in Chapter 10.

■ Your **beliefs about knowledge and learning** are a characteristic that is rarely discussed, but is very important. What do you believe knowledge is? Do you believe that knowledge consists of information that is transmitted from your professor to you? Or do you believe that you can be a part of creating knowledge? How you answer questions such as these influences the way you learn. Beliefs about learning are discussed in Chapter 7.

These characteristics and others not only help determine what you will learn but also how you will study course material. Active learners understand the importance of being aware of these characteristics as they approach learning tasks, whether the tasks are easy or difficult.

TIMELY TIPS

Getting to Know You

Figuring out your own characteristics as a learner can help you with more than merely succeeding in your classes. Once you know yourself, you can begin to make changes regarding relationships with others, how you manage your time, how you keep track of your obligations, and even how to meet your goals for your future. This is because you are learning all the time—not just in your classes—and your learning characteristics will impact your existence outside of the classroom and into your life. As you read *College Success Strategies*, think about how you can apply these concepts to your life.

Factor 2: The Tasks

Simply put, tasks are what your professors ask you to do. You can think of them as daily tasks, such as reading your text before you attend lectures, or larger tasks, such as preparing for various kinds of tests or writing papers. Most professors are pretty clear about what the tasks are. They will let you know the number of tests you will have and the kinds of tests they will be (e.g., essay, multiple choice, etc.), as well as their expectations about papers, lab participation, and library work. Some will even let you examine copies of old tests or student papers so that you can see the kinds of questions they will ask or what their writing expectations are. Others will give you example test questions so that you can get an idea of how the questions will be asked.

But some professors aren't so clear in defining course tasks. Some may even give you conflicting messages. Therefore, it is important to try to get your professor to be as clear as possible about the tasks you must undertake. If you don't know what is expected of you, then you can't select the proper learning strategies or the most effective way to approach your texts. We discuss issues relating to tasks in many of the chapters in this book but most directly in Chapter 4.

Factor 3: The Texts

Texts are crucial to learning in college. In fact, it has been estimated that 85 percent of all college learning involves reading. Students often think of texts as simply **textbooks.** Certainly textbooks are a major source of information in many of your college classes, but texts also come in other forms. **Periodicals, newspapers, novels,** and **essays** are printed texts. Another type of text that is being used more often on university campuses is **computer text,** sometimes called nonlinear text or hypertext. You may even be required to view films or documentaries, which are **visual texts.**

In addition to textbooks, **lecture notes** are the other most frequent type of "text" with which college students must interact. Strategies for note taking are discussed in Chapter 10.

Whatever types of text you are expected to use, you should know how the particular text is organized. In most textbooks, each chapter is usually organized in the same fashion. In addition, your professor's lectures probably follow the same pattern each day. Even visual texts have organizational patterns. Once you have determined how your text is organized, learning the material becomes a much easier task. Like learner characteristics and tasks, texts are an important part of the learning puzzle. Texts are discussed in more detail in Chapters 9 and 10.

Factor 4: The Learning Strategies

The final, and perhaps the most complex, factor that influences learning consists of the strategies that you choose. It is important to realize that strategies should be chosen based on your characteristics as a learner, the tasks you have to do, and the texts used. Thus, a large portion of this text—Chapters 11, 12, 13, 14, and 15—is devoted to learning strategies.

Strategies for active learning have several features in common.

1. Once you learn them, you can use all of these strategies on your own. Because studying is mostly a solitary activity, it is important to be able to use strategies without guidance from someone else—a professor or a friend, for example.

2. These strategies have specific underlying processes that research has consistently shown to lead to better performance. For example, all of the strategies you will learn have a self-testing component, which immediately tells you whether you understand the information.

3. The strategies require participation on your part in the form of critical thinking and reasoning. They will help you to think beyond the text and to analyze, synthesize, and apply the information.

4. The strategies are flexible. You can modify them according to your own learning preferences, the tasks, and the texts.

The Holistic Nature of Active Learning

Active learners possess three different kinds of knowledge about the strategies they use during learning. It's not enough just to know how to use a particular strategy; in order to be an efficient and effective learner, you need to have declarative, procedural, and conditional knowledge (Paris, Lipson, and Wixson 1983).*

1. **Declarative Knowledge.** Declarative knowledge is *knowing what*—what you need to do and what strategy you need to use. For example, if you are in a history class and the task is to get ready for an essay exam in which you need to synthesize information, declarative knowledge enables you to select the proper study strategy that matches the task. You might say to yourself, "I need to begin by predicting some questions, and then I need to practice answering those questions."

2. **Procedural Knowledge.** Procedural knowledge involves more than knowing what you should do. It is *knowing how* to do it. Returning to our history example, you have to know how to go about predicting questions that are likely to be on your test. You might search your lecture notes for hints your professor gave about important ideas, look to see what she spent a lot of time on in class, think about the larger themes that were discussed, or look for overlap between your lecture notes and your text. Once you have predicted your questions, then comes the practice. You need to have a

---

*Paris, S. G., Lipson, M. Y., & Wixson, K. K. (1983). Becoming a strategic reader. *Contemporary Educational Psychology, 8,* 293–316.

plan—sketch out an outline of the key points you want to include in your answer, say those points to yourself, and practice writing out the answers to one of the questions you predicted. You might even show it to your professor if she is willing to give you feedback. As the term *procedural knowledge* suggests, you have "procedures" to follow once you have identified the appropriate strategies.

3. **Conditional Knowledge.** Conditional knowledge means knowing under what conditions to use certain strategies—*knowing when and why*. Using our history example again, you would know that you have to use test preparation approaches that lead to synthesis, since that is what the task requires. Therefore, you will not want to use strategies that encourage only memorization. When you achieve conditional knowledge, you will know how to apply the most appropriate learning strategies for all of your courses.

Becoming an active learner, especially if you have been a passive learner, takes some time and effort. It doesn't happen overnight. Most students, especially first-year students, are located somewhere in the middle of the active–passive continuum. That is, rarely are students totally passive or completely active learners when they begin college. Becoming an active learner is a sort of work in progress.

Look back at your score on the self-assessment at the beginning of this chapter. Your score probably was not 11, the lowest possible score, nor 55, the highest. You probably fell somewhere in between. But by thinking about the factors that influence learning, and about the three types of knowledge, you are already on your way to becoming a better learner.

Real College

Malcolm

DIRECTIONS: Read the following "Real College" scenario and respond to the questions based on what you learned in this chapter.

Meet Malcolm. Malcolm has a good attitude about being in college, but he's having a little trouble academically. Perhaps Malcolm does not understand that numerous factors must interact in order for him to be an active learner.

Malcolm decided after the first week on campus that he was made to be a college student. He has signed up for volunteer work, joined two campus clubs, and found several local hangouts where he can socialize with friends. He has discovered that he loves his freedom—the fact that he can come and go as he pleases. He never knew that a day could go by so quickly. Because he is often up late trying to study while lying on his bed or just hanging out with his roommate, he has trouble getting up for his 8:00 A.M. math class. Some days he is late; on other days, he never even hears his alarm. His other classes also present problems. He hates his history class because there is so much to read, and English, well ... who cares about iambic pentameter?

Malcolm is stressed out because he wants to do well, but he has already missed two math quizzes because of oversleeping and made a D on the first test. He thought he should have done much better because he did most of the homework, which is about as much as he had in high school math classes, and he made As and Bs then. In English, he made a C on his first writing assignment, which he felt was good for him. In history, he has no grades yet because there is only a midterm and a final, but he is far behind on the reading assignments. Right now, things don't look promising for Malcolm!

Based on what you read in this and other chapters in this book, what advice do you have for Malcolm? As you are thinking about this advice, remember what we said earlier about the following four factors of active learning: (1) your characteristics as a learner; (2) the tasks you must complete; (3) the texts you use; and (4) the strategies you select. How might Malcolm consider each of these factors in order to become a more active and effective learner?

ADD TO YOUR PORTFOLIO

Write down at least two things you can do right now to move toward becoming a more active learner. They can be small things, such as sitting closer to the front of the classroom to help you focus better and take better notes. Or you might try reading a section of one of your text assignments and then stopping to reflect on what you remember. Both are little changes, but if you make two small changes this week and two small changes the next, and so on, you will be well on your way to becoming an active learner. Monitor your progress for two weeks by keeping a daily journal. As you go through the semester, continue to add to this list of activities. By the end of the term, you will be pleasantly surprised at how far you have come.

How You Learn

READ THIS CHAPTER TO ANSWER THE FOLLOWING QUESTIONS:

- What role does memory play in learning?
- How do the two major theories of learning differ?
- How can you stretch your memory?
- How can you use your senses to be a more effective learner?

SELF-ASSESSMENT

DIRECTIONS: Respond to these questions to determine your knowledge about how memory works.

1. T F Researchers know how human memory works.

2. T F Most people attend to all the sensory information around them.

3. T F If you want to remember something forever, you should store it in short-term memory.

4. T F Short-term memory holds only five to nine pieces of information at one time.

5. T F Usually, to move information from short-term to long-term memory you must rehearse the information.

6. T F Information processed at deep levels will be remembered for a long time.

7. T F Using mnemonics can hinder memory processing.

8. T F Creating acronyms can improve memory processing.

9. T F A person with a visual learning style can learn only by seeing things.

10. T F To remember more you should learn using all of your senses.

Have you ever heard a student comment that he doesn't do well on tests simply because he has a bad memory? Does it seem to you that the older the person, the poorer the memory? And why can you remember some things very easily, while other information needs to be pounded into your head? The answers to all of these questions have something to do with the way memory operates. Because researchers can't actually "see" memory, no one knows for sure exactly how memory operates. But scientists do know that certain sections of the brain are responsible for certain types of memories. Although there are different theories about how information gets into and is retrieved from memory, the theories do have commonalities. As you read about the two most common theories, keep in mind that they are just that: plausible explanations about how memory works.

Studying Smarter

Rehearsing class information daily increases your memory of it by at least threefold.

The Role of Memory: Two Theories

The Parts Theory

According to what we will call the parts theory, there are three different types of memories, or what we refer to as parts. It is easiest to think of memory as sort of a flowchart that might look something like this:

Sensory Store   →   Short-Term Memory   →   Long-Term
                         (STM)   Memory (LTM)

The first part, the **sensory store,** serves as a kind of filter. That is, your senses are often bombarded with information, much of which you can't remember. For example, if you are looking up a number in the telephone book, you don't look at every number. You run your finger down a specific page until you find the number you are looking for and then you use that piece of information in some way. For the most part, you probably have no recollection of the other names, addresses, or telephone numbers that were in that column. Your sensory store has filtered that information for you. Likewise, it is very likely that as you walked to class this morning you saw many other students but can't recollect the faces of the ones that you passed. That's your sensory store at work as well.

Although your sensory store can never be filled up, it can overload. Think about a situation in which your senses have been overwhelmed. It may have been at a place like Disney World, where there are so many sights and sounds that it is difficult for your sensory store to take them all in. It may have been when you were trying to study for a history exam but your roommate had the TV on, your next door neighbor was listening to loud music, a fire truck was blaring its siren, and dogs were barking in the distance. When too much vies for your attention, it's difficult for the filter to function in your best interest.

Under normal circumstances, however, when you identify a piece of information that you need to remember, your sensory store filters out what you don't need and you actually are not even aware of the process. What happens to the information that you need to remember? According to the parts theory, your **short-term memory (STM)** takes over. STM holds the information for a brief period of time—less than 30 seconds—unless you do something to retain it. In addition, short-term memory can hold only a small number of items, from five to nine pieces of information; this limit is sometimes referred to as 7 ± 2 pieces of information. Let's return to the phone number example. You have just looked up the number of the campus health center. Phone numbers are seven digits, so it is within the capacity of STM. You pick up your phone to make the call just as your roommate walks in with a brief question. You answer her question and begin to dial the health center. But you can't remember it. Only about a minute has passed, but the number didn't stay in short-term memory long enough for you to use it.

You can do two things to increase the amount of time that information stays in STM. You can rehearse the information by saying it several times or by writing it down, or you can "chunk" the information to reduce the number of pieces you have to remember. When you **chunk** information, you group it together so that you are learning fewer pieces of information. For example, grouping the numbers in a phone number into two groups—531-2958—rather than thinking of it as seven separate numbers—5-3-1-2-9-5-8 makes it easier to remember and helps hold the information in STM. Likewise, it is easier to remember your Social Security number in three chunks—000-00-0000—rather than as nine separate pieces of information.

But what if you need to remember the information longer than a minute? Then your **long-term memory (LTM)** takes over. LTM has an unlimited capacity; it never gets full, which is why you can remember things that happened when you were a small child. In fact, older people can often remember things that happened decades ago but have difficulty remembering things that happened last week because the older the memory, the more firmly it is fixed in LTM. In order to get information into LTM (like information that you study for an exam) you have to rehearse. Just as rehearsal will help you hold information in STM, it also helps you put information into LTM so you can remember it for an indefinite period of time. Therefore, if you write it, repeat it several times, listen to it over and over again, and/or talk it through with someone, you will be able to remember it later. (You'll learn more about rehearsal in Chapter 11.) According to the parts theory, the number and variety of ways you rehearse will influence how much information you can remember and for how long.

TIMELY TIPS

The Importance of STM

Although most students rarely think about how memory influences their learning, it is a crucial part of being able to retain information over time, something that you must be able to do if you are going to be an effective learner. It is interesting to think about the different parts of memory and what would happen if one of the parts failed to function properly, or not at all. That is the premise of the movie *Memento*. In this film, the main character loses his short-term memory as a result of a head injury. In order to remember things and to track down the individual who raped and killed his wife, he tattoos himself and takes photographs as ways of recording what he has learned. If he doesn't do this, every minute of his life and all the information he "knows" will be forgotten. Although this is certainly an extreme case, it drives home just how crucial STM is to learning and remembering.

Some things seem to get into LTM without rehearsal. For example, years from now when you are sitting around with friends, the September 11, 2001, date might come up. Many will remember where they were and what they were doing when they heard that two airplanes had crashed into the World Trade Center in New York City. Tragic or personally traumatic events somehow are easily etched into our LTMs without effort.

Think for a minute about how this theory of memory applies when you are taking a test. For example, throughout a multiple-choice exam, your sensory store must filter out distractions, such as the hum of the air conditioner, the noise from the hallway, or the person behind you with a persistent cough. Your STM must hold each question while you think about the correct answer. Finally, you must retrieve the information you need from your LTM in order to answer the question.

The Levels of Processing Theory

Not all psychologists agree that the parts theory explains how memory works because they do not believe that there are separate systems in the brain. Another plausible explanation is what is called the *levels of processing theory.* Scientists who purport this theory believe that the degree to which you can remember and retrieve information depends on the level or depth to which you have processed the information: Material that is processed at a shallow level cannot be remembered very well or for very long, but information that is processed at a deep level is remembered considerably better.

According to the levels of processing theory, it's not important to process everything at a deep level. In fact, if we did that we often would be wasting our time. For example, if you simply want to remember the phone number long enough to call the health center to get an appointment, repeating the number several times or writing it down in an attempt to process it deeply would be a waste of time. You would still need to rehearse the information, but for just long enough to make the call. This type of rehearsal is called **maintenance rehearsal**—engaging in just enough rehearsal to process the information shallowly so that you can use it for a brief period of time and then forget it. This is not the kind of rehearsal you would want to use when studying for an exam.

On the other hand, if it was important for you to remember that telephone number for a long period of time so that you could retrieve it quickly a few days later, you would need to engage in **elaborative rehearsal**—making the information meaningful and rehearsing to the point where the information is at your fingertips. For example, you might note that the last four digits are the same as your grandmother's address. Usually, when you use elaborative rehearsal, you are engaging in deep processing because you want to use or retrieve the information easily at some time in the future. If you were studying for an essay exam in history, for example, it would be important for you to use elaborative rehearsal in order to have access to the information at test time. Elaborative rehearsal includes writing the information in an organized way, repeating the material, or personalizing it in some way to make it easier to remember.

ON YOUR OWN

Reflecting on What You Have Read

Think about the two theories of memory you have just read about—the parts theory and the levels of processing theory. Reflect and write about the following questions: Sometimes events get into long-term memory with little effort. Why do you suppose this happens? Why is it sometimes difficult to get information into long-term memory? How can knowing about these theories help you learn in college?

Stretching Your Memory

Although you will have to do more than memorize in most of your college classes, we are not suggesting that the role memorization plays is trivial. In just about every course you take, you will have to do some memorization of information. When you are trying to memorize, there are ways to stretch your memory to make it easier to learn and retrieve material. **Mnemonic devices** help you stretch your memory, and you most likely already use them but may not be aware of their names.

GET GOING

Who's Who?

In the past few weeks you have probably met quite a few new people. Have you found that you just can't remember all of their names? To remember names, it is important to engage in memory techniques. At the very least, you must be motivated and make a concerted effort to remember by saying people's names several times to yourself. But you can also use mnemonics to help. When you meet someone, repeat the name and form a mental image (Amy—Amy has red hair—I picture a fire on Amy's head), or use an association (Holly—just like the holly at Christmas time). It might also help to use the method of loci by recalling an object in the place where you have met this new person and associating the name with the object (Mark—dartboard). Try it yourself. As odd as it may sound, it really works.

In general, mnemonics encourage the personalization of information so that you have easy access to it at some future date. Mnemonics are good for learning lists of items or for learning sequences of events or processes. They can be visual to help you create images, or they can be a string of letters or a nonsense sentence—anything that enables you to remember information better. Even if you are unfamiliar with the term *mnemonics*, you have probably used them without knowing it. For example, you may have learned the rhyme "use *i* before *e* except after *c*, or in words sounding like *a*, as in neighbor and weigh." This mnemonic is known by almost every elementary school child.

Try out the following techniques to stretch your memory.

■ **Acronyms.** You can use mnemonics to learn a list by creating an acronym. This means taking the first letter of each item you are trying to memorize and making them spell something. Your mnemonic device doesn't have to make sense to anyone but you. In fact, the more outrageous the memory device, the easier it generally is to remember. For example, if you needed to remember the parts of the forebrain, you might use this mnemonic: 4brain = TLC. This mnemonic works since you are probably already familiar with the letters "TLC" being used together, as in tender loving care. In this case, *TLC* stands for Thalamus, Limbic (system), and Cerebral (cortex). You could then create other mnemonics that would help you remember the parts of the midbrain and the hindbrain or the functions each of these portions serves.

■ **Imagery.** Forming images is another powerful way to help you remember when you review. Like other mnemonics, images can be very personal and don't have to make sense to anyone except the person forming the images. Images work best when the information you are trying to learn is concrete rather than abstract. In other words, it is difficult to make images for concepts such as courage, democracy, or freedom, and it is much easier to make images for ideas such as cell division, presidential elections, or chamber music. Images work well because they give you both verbal and visual labels for things. A simple example may help you understand this idea. The three letters *d-o-g* together form a very familiar word—dog. Few people would have trouble understanding this word when they saw it in print. But what would happen if you asked each person who read that word to tell you his or her image of a dog? Would everyone describe *dog* in the same way? Of course not. Your image of a dog would be based on some experience you have, whether it's a dog you currently own or one that bit you when you were a child.

■ **Method of Loci.** In the method of loci technique, you imagine a place that is familiar to you such as your living room, the street where you live, or your residence hall. Then you walk down this path through your memory. As you proceed, you attach a piece of information you have to learn to different places and objects to help you remember it. Remember, the path markers can be as strange as you want (and the stranger the better) because that will make it easier for you to visualize. One of the authors uses a simplified version of the method of loci to remember who attended certain meetings. She visualizes the room and the table where the meeting was held, starts at one end, and mentally walks a path around the table, visualizing where each person was seated.

We realize that some of these techniques may sound strange, but we guarantee that they help stretch your memory under the right circumstances. And they can be fun to create, which also helps you remember information.

The Role of Learning Styles

When students talk to us about their difficulty remembering information, they often mention learning styles as a reason why memory sometimes breaks down. However, when we use the term *learning styles*, we are referring to how students learn best. Researchers who study this issue suggest that there are three main kinds of learners:

■ **Visual learners,** or those who learn best by watching or seeing. Visual learners like to be shown how to do things and often learn best through diagrams or by using imagery. If you are a visual learner, when someone asks you how to spell a word, you probably have to write it down first rather than simply trying to spell the word in your head or out loud.

■ **Auditory learners,** or those who learn best by listening or speaking. Auditory learners can learn easily through listening to lectures or by talking information over with a peer. If you are an auditory learner, you probably rarely miss a class lecture and you may participate in study groups for many of your courses. You may rehearse information by saying it over, either to yourself or out loud.

■ **Kinesthetic learners (also called tactile learners),** or those who learn best by touching or movement. Kinesthetic learners generally learn best through writing or even typing things out. If you are a kinesthetic learner, you may rehearse information by writing it several times. You also may enjoy lab courses where there is a hands-on approach to learning.

Sometimes in study skills classes, instructors will have students take a learning styles inventory to find out how they learn "best." We believe these tests oversimplify the complex task of college learning. We are not the only ones who share this view. In their review of the research on learning styles, Professors Pashler, McDaniel, Roher, and Bjork (2009) conclude that "at present, there is no adequate evidence base to justify incorporating learning styles assessments into general educational practice."* These tests often pigeonhole students into one of the three categories and then give them suggestions for learning and studying based only on that particular style. But there has been no evidence to support this way of learning. Moreover, students can feel trapped when their preferred mode cannot be used in a particular course. For example, it is hard to learn kinesthetically in a philosophy course. Additionally, even in this day of technology, the fact remains that most colleges use the traditional classroom structure where students must read texts, listen to lectures, take notes, and take exams. Therefore, you need to tap as many of these learning styles as possible if you are to be successful in college. That is why we suggest that rather than relying on one particular learning style, which may actually impede your learning, you use strategies that incorporate them all. We call this learning through your senses.

*Pashler, H., McDaniel, M., Roher, D., & Bjork, R. (2009). Learning styles: Concepts and evidence. *Psychological Science in the Public Interest, 9,* 105–119.

Using Your Senses to Learn

Many first-year students are "one-trick ponies." That is, they prepare the same way for all of their classes, regardless of the type of test they'll have. They study biology the same way they study history. However, in college, it is important to use a variety of strategies and all of your senses to learn. In history, for example, you would want to read your text, listen actively to the lectures, and take a good set of notes. In that way, you would be using your senses to begin to get the information into your memory. You have a record of the important information to study from, and you are actively engaged. As test time approaches, you might study with a group of other students, make time lines as a way of outlining major historical events, and predict and answer essay questions. You would be listening, reading, discussing, and writing as a way of engaging all of your senses. Contrast that approach with simply attending all the lectures. Which preparation method do you think would be more successful?

Although we encourage you to use all of your senses to learn, we also realize that many students prefer one mode of learning over another. That's fine. We always encourage students to go with their strengths while realizing that they can also use strategies and approaches that are related to their weaker modes. In fact, most students have to approach learning in college by using a multiple-sense approach. For example, in the sciences, there are generally diagrams to learn and understand. You can't ignore that task just because you aren't a visual learner. Likewise, just because you learn best visually, you still must attend and listen actively to lectures.

In Chapter 11, we present a variety of strategies that will assist you in learning and remembering information. We have divided these strategies according to the three major types of learners:

■ **Visual learners** learn best by seeing information. When they read their texts, they often visualize what the page looks like. They like to create diagrams,

---

Studying Smarter

Computers have become a necessity on college campuses, a "luxury" that no student can do without. In fact, many colleges now require freshmen to purchase or lease a computer before they begin their first semester. Although many students come to campus computer savvy, few actually use their computers as part of the learning and studying process. Try to think about ways the computer can make you a more efficient learner. Learn how to use the online library. Take your laptop to class to take and then reorganize your notes. Create diagrams and flowcharts for scientific material and summarize key points. These are just a few ways to use your computer to help you learn.

flowcharts, concept maps, or concept cards. They also tend to use imagery to remember information.

■ **Auditory learners** learn best from listening or hearing information. They may be able to actively listen to lectures, but they may take horrible notes. They like to study with others so they can hear what others say. They also like to say information out loud.

■ **Kinesthetic learners** learn best by doing. They learn best through writing and may write information in an organized way as a method of rehearsal. They like to be shown how to do things rather than having to figure it out through reading or listening.

Real College

Leo

DIRECTIONS: Read the following "Real College" scenario and respond to the question based on what you learned in this chapter.

Leo knows he is a kinesthetic learner. He loves to work on cars and has learned everything he knows by having hands-on experience at his uncle's body shop. Now that he is in college, he finds that he is having a lot of trouble remembering the material in his classes. The professors talk so fast, and he has never been a good note taker. Although he is not sure how this would work in some of his classes, he wishes there were more opportunities to try out some of the things his professors are presenting—to use his kinesthetic abilities.

To remember what was discussed in class, Leo tries to memorize all of the key terms. He writes the information on cards and repeats it over and over again until he thinks he has it down cold. However, sometimes he finds that he can't remember even the simplest definitions on exams. Although Leo finds this really disturbing, he chalks it up to a bad memory.

Using what you have learned about how memory works—how to stretch your memory—and using your senses to learn, how would you suggest Leo modify his approach to maximize his learning?

ADD TO YOUR PORTFOLIO

1. Think about yourself as a learner and assess the learning style that seems most like yours. You can either take one of the online assessments or, better yet, assess your own learning style by writing down how you think you learn. Summarize what you learn about yourself.

2. Try some of the mnemonic methods for stretching your memory the next time you prepare for an exam. Write down at least one mnemonic per method. Evaluate the effectiveness of each method. What worked and what did not work for you?

Professors, Tasks, and You

READ THIS CHAPTER TO ANSWER THE FOLLOWING QUESTIONS:

- What is a professor?
- What do we mean by *task*?
- How can you figure out what your professor expects?

--- **SELF-ASSESSMENT** ---

DIRECTIONS: Rate the following tasks. Place an *E* beside the tasks you consider the easiest, an *M* beside the tasks you consider of middle-level difficulty, and a *D* beside the tasks you consider the most difficult.

1. _____ Taking a matching exam in history

2. _____ Analyzing a chemical process for a chemistry lab

3. _____ Writing a persuasive essay for English class

4. _____ Evaluating and drawing a conclusion about several articles presenting conflicting accounts of an event for political science

5. _____ Taking a multiple-choice exam over two psychology chapters

6. _____ Taking an exam over the bold-faced terms for biology class

7. _____ Debating a controversial issue in sociology class

8. _____ Giving an informational speech for speech communications class

9. _____ Solving calculus problems on a mathematics exam

How you rated these tasks probably has something to do with your own personal background and interests. For example, if you love mathematics you might have thought solving calculus problems was easy. However, there are some overarching ideas that you will learn about in this chapter that make numbers 1 and 6 the easiest tasks; put numbers 2, 5, 8, and 9 somewhere in the middle; and make numbers 3, 4, and 7 the most difficult tasks.

In Chapter 2, when we introduced the idea that there are four factors that impact learning, we briefly discussed the role that task understanding plays in being an active learner. Because much of your success as a college student rests on your ability to interpret the task, we talk about it here in greater detail. We firmly believe that unless you can figure out what your professors expect, you will run into difficulty in selecting the appropriate way to go about studying. It follows, then, that determining tasks is crucial to your success in college.

There's more to studying and being a successful student than meets the eye, and studying hard is not always studying smart. Your ability to understand what professors do, what your professor wants you to do, and the way you are supposed to do it goes a long way in making you a more efficient and effective student. Why? To answer this question, we'll begin by trying to help you understand your professors a bit. Then we'll explore two important aspects of task: what we mean by "task" and how you can figure out what the task is.

Studying Smarter

Be sure you understand what your professor expects from you. Ask questions. Knowing the task right from the start enables you to select the appropriate strategies.

What Is a Professor?

Take a minute to consider the characteristics that you believe define a professor. Did you think about words or phrases such as smart, well-educated, reads a lot, well informed? When college students are asked to complete this task, they generally write down descriptors that have to do more with the education a professor has rather than terms that focus on other traits. For example, when we carry out this activity with our students at the beginning of the term, we rarely get comments such as fair-minded, cares about students, helpful, or energetic; nor do we get comments such as mean, unapproachable, distant, or unfair. The point we want to make here is that most students seem to lump all professors in the same bag: Professors are smart, they have a considerable amount of education, and they are *the* source of knowledge in the classroom. But it is important to know a little background about these people who are teaching you because it will also help you to understand why they have you do the things they do—why they ask you to do certain tasks.

Most professors have what are called advanced degrees. The degree required generally depends on the type of postsecondary institution in which an individual teaches. For example, a community college may require teachers to have a minimum of a master's degree, while a four-year college or university would expect a doctoral degree. It is becoming more and more common for colleges to prefer or require the professors they hire to have a terminal degree—a doctor of philosophy, or PhD for short. A person can have a doctor of philosophy in botany, English literature, history, education, or just about any other discipline you can think of. Usually, it takes an individual three or more years after he or she has completed a master's degree to earn a doctorate.

A professor who has a brand-new PhD under her belt usually will be hired at the **assistant professor** level. Each new assistant professor receives guidelines from her institution that outline what she must do in order to get promoted to the next level, which is **associate professor.** Depending on the type of post-secondary institution, the criteria for promotion may be weighted heavily on the professor's ability to teach, but it might also be determined by the research she publishes, the committees she serves on, and the service projects in which she participates. Often, faculty must be evaluated as having superior accomplishments in two of these areas—teaching, research, and service—in order to get promoted. It takes between four and seven years to reach the associate professor level.

The next rank, **full professor,** is reserved for those who are able to sustain exemplary teaching, research, and/or service records for another several years, because college teachers usually must hold the rank of associate professor at least five years before being promoted to full professor. Full professors generally have high status because they have outstanding track records.

The ranking system of professors is quite complex and unlike that of any other profession. One of the more interesting aspects of the promotion system that college faculty go through is that at every level they are judged by their peers. That is, a committee of faculty who have already been promoted to the associate professor level examines the credentials of those who are trying to advance to that level. Those of us who are part of this unique system often wonder how and why it has become so complicated.

We believe that students should be somewhat familiar with this ranking system so that they can better appreciate how much work their college professors must invest in order to be promoted. Some college students believe that all professors have to do is teach for a few hours and then sit in their offices and wait for students to come and ask them questions. Nothing could be further from the truth. Just like you, they have a variety of tasks to do so that they can be successful. And, just like you, college professors tend to be busy people.

Additionally, professors are those who assign and evaluate your academic tasks. To understand your professors is to better understand your college tasks. Let's return to the idea of task by defining in more detail what we mean when we use this term.

What Is a Task?

The task for any course consists of two parts:

1. the type of activity in which you engage and
2. the level of thinking required as you engage in the activity.

NETWORKING

Using the Web to Understand Your Professor and the Task

Find the Web page of one of your professors. See if you can find out some interesting information about him or her. Then look for any information that might help you figure out the task. For example, if you will have multiple-choice exams, look to see whether your professor has put any example test items on the site. Also check out online information about the course. Sometimes rather than putting material concerning tests and other course requirements on their own personal Web page, professors will have a separate page for each course they teach. These pages can provide a wealth of information to help you better understand the task.

Part One: The Type of Activity

The activity you will be asked to engage in is usually a test, a paper, or a project that your instructor will use to evaluate you. But knowing that you have to take a test is not enough information to be able to carefully select an appropriate approach to studying. You need to know the *type* of test you will take.

■ Is it an objective exam, which includes multiple-choice, true/false, or matching items?

■ Is it a more subjective exam that requires answering essay, short-answer, or identification questions?

■ Is it a combination of both types?

Because you should not approach studying for multiple-choice tests in the same way you approach studying for essay tests, it's very important to know right from the beginning the basic type of test you will have. As we will discuss in greater detail later, the kind of reading you do, the way you think about the material, and the strategies you select all have a bearing on the kinds of tasks you are asked to complete in a course.

A situation that occurred to students enrolled in a large lecture history course emphasizes the importance of knowing precisely what your task is. For each test, students were told that they would have "objective items" and two essay questions. On the first four exams, the objective items were always multiple-choice questions. When it came time for the final exam and the professor told students that they would have a test that was part objective and part essay, they assumed that they would once again have multiple-choice questions. Imagine their surprise when the tests were distributed and the objective items were fill-in-the-blank questions. Many students were outraged and went to see the professor when they discovered that they had done poorly on the test. But the professor (he was one of those full professors) wouldn't budge. His definition of task for objective items included fill-in-the-blank as well as multiple-choice questions. The point here is clear: Get as much specific information as possible about the test. Ask the right questions. Just knowing that you will have an objective test is likely to be insufficient information.

If the task in a course consists of papers or projects rather than exams, the same advice holds true. Talk with your professor about specific aspects of the paper, especially if they seem unclear. In some political science courses, for example, students must do a project that consists of several different pieces. First they select a political issue to follow throughout the term. They must sub-scribe to and read the *New York Times* daily and find a minimum of 30 articles concerning their issue. For each article they must write a brief summary. At the end of the term, they complete two additional tasks. First they write a policy statement, and then they write a memo to an influential political figure about this issue. Students who fail to understand how to carry out the numerous pieces involved in this task have severe problems in doing well on a long-term project that can wind up being a large percentage of their course grade.

SUCCESS AT A GLANCE

Thinking About the Task

Type of Task + Level of Thinking = Task Knowledge

■ Matching exam	**Memorization**
■ Multiple choice	**Comprehension, Application, Analysis**
■ Essay/Short answer	**Analysis, Synthesis, Evaluation**

Part Two: The Level of Thinking

Once you have identified the specific activities your professor expects, you're closer to being able to select the best strategies. The other part of task identifi-cation, and perhaps the more important part, is knowing what level of think-ing is required to carry out that task. There are many types of thinking that a professor may want you to engage in.

Have you ever heard of Bloom's Taxonomy?* This classification provides a way to categorize the kinds of questions that students typically encounter in their classes. Knowing the level of questions your professor asks can help you choose appropriate learning and study strategies.

Bloom discusses six levels of questioning:

1. **Knowledge**—includes knowledge of dates, events, major ideas, and bold-faced terms.

---

*Adapted from: Bloom, B. S. (Ed.) (1956) *Taxonomy of educational objectives: The classification of educational goals: Handbook I, cognitive domain.* New York: Longmans, Green.

Question Words: list, define, describe, identify, match, name, what, who, when, where

Examples: When did the Tonkin Gulf incident occur?

What does the term *IQ* stand for?

Define *reliability*.

2. **Comprehension**—includes grasping the meaning, explaining or summarizing, grouping, predicting outcomes, or inferring.

Question Words: summarize, describe, interpret, distinguish, defend, explain, discuss, predict

Examples: Which of the following is an example of a skill that someone with *componential intelligence* might excel in?

Summarize the evolution of the Black Power party.

Explain Gardner's Theory of Multiple Intelligences.

3. **Application**—requires the ability to use the material in a new context, to solve problems, or to use rules, concepts, or theories.

Question Words: apply, demonstrate, calculate, illustrate, show, relate, give an example of, solve

Examples: If a plant with the genotype of BbCcDd were crossed with a plant that was BBCcdd, what would be the chances of producing a plant with the genotype of BbCcDd?

Illustrate how a school system might use Sternberg's Triarchic Theory of Intelligence.

4. **Analysis**—involves understanding organization of parts, clarifying, concluding, or recognizing hidden meaning.

Question Words: analyze, explain, compare and contrast, select, arrange, order

Examples: Compare and contrast the characteristics of short-term memory and long-term memory.

Select the most appropriate method for solving this calculus problem.

5. **Synthesis**—involves creating new ideas, relating knowledge from several sources of information, predicting, and drawing conclusions.

Question Words: combine, create, design, formulate, compose, integrate, rewrite, generalize

Examples: Rewrite the play *The Cherry Orchard* as if it were written by Ibsen.

Design a solution to the current parking problem on campus.

6. **Evaluation**—relies on the ability to make choices based on evidence, to support stance with reasoning, to recognize subjectivity, and to assess value of theories.

Question Words: support, judge, discriminate, assess, recommend, measure, convince, conclude

Examples: How successful would the proposed federal income tax cuts be in controlling inflation as well as decreasing unemployment?

Do you agree with President Johnson's decision to escalate the Vietnamese conflict? Why or why not?

Most objective exams will have questions at each of these levels. Many students fail to think about this part of the task and concentrate their studying on the knowledge level, which often results in lower test grades and frustration. Another mistake that students, primarily first-year students, often make is believing that objective exams don't involve higher-level thinking. That is, they think that multiple-choice and true/false tests are basically memorization tasks. However, on most objective tests, some of the questions will be factual in nature, some will ask for examples, and some will require you to synthesize and analyze. Most essay questions require the highest level of thinking, but other subjective exams, such as identification items, could ask for just factual information. Remember, unless you know the task and the types of thinking expected, you will have a difficult time selecting the appropriate study strategies. In the next section, we will give you some hints about how to get more information about the task.

TIMELY TIPS

Planning for the Tasks After College

There are many tasks that college students have to do in addition to doing well in their courses. For example, to prepare for life after college, many career centers suggest that first-year students do the following three tasks:

1. **Visit the career center.** The staff can help you with choosing a major, planning for the future, exploring job options, and more.
2. **Start a résumé.** Many students struggle with creating a good résumé of their experience. By starting early, you can update it every term and graduate with a helpful tool for your job search.
3. **Find a summer internship.** These opportunities can be a great way to learn more about your field and in the future can set you apart from other applicants.

How Can You Get Information About the Task?

Now that you understand how important it is to know the task for each of your classes, you might ask the obvious question: How do I carry out the task? Because few professors will state the task precisely and completely, it becomes important for you to be able to piece together bits of information from a variety of sources in order to paint the picture for yourself.

1. **Attend Class Every Day.** The best place to begin, of course, is with what your professor says in class, especially in the early part of the term. Some professors spell out the task very neatly and clearly on the first day when they go over the syllabus. Others will give you a big picture of the task early in the term and then fill in the details as the course moves along. Still others, and perhaps most college professors fall into this category, give you a combination of implicit and explicit cues and expect you to pick up on those cues.

GET GOING

Go to Class

One of our favorite quotes comes from E. Jean Carroll who stated, "If Joan of Arc could turn the tide of an entire war before her eighteenth birthday, you can get out of bed." But we would like to add "...and go to class" to this quote. Attending every class is the most important thing you can do to help yourself not only stay on task but also to better understand the specific tasks for each course.

---

2. **Write It Down.** It's just as important to take notes concerning what's expected of you as it is to take notes on the content. Students often think that they will remember how to structure an essay or the types of questions that will be on their exams. However, they discover two or three weeks later that they have only a faint recollection—or worse, no recollection at all—of some important piece of information that the professor had discussed in class. Go to class, listen carefully, and write down what your professor says about the task in your lecture notes.

3. **Consult Your Syllabus.** Read your syllabus carefully at the beginning of the course and then return to it on a regular basis. Look for any statements that tell you about course expectations. Examine your syllabus for the following information:

   ▪ The number of tests you will have or papers you will have to write, and the approximate dates tests will be given or papers will be due.

   ▪ Your professor's office hours and phone number (or e-mail address) so that you know how to make an appointment to talk with her.

   ▪ Your professor's policies on make-up work and the consequences of missing an exam or another deadline.

   ▪ Your professor's attendance policies (if any).

Studying Smarter

If you have exhausted all efforts to figure out the task in a course, run—don't walk—to your professor's office, especially if you have already taken one test and performed poorly. Starting a conversation with your professor by explaining what you are doing and asking her for some advice about how to study may give you a lot more information about how she wants you to think about the course information.

■ Your professor's philosophy on the course. This can give you insight into how your professor will approach the content and can go a long way in helping you define the task.

■ The course objectives. Reading these statements will tell you what the professor hopes you will learn in the course.

All of these factors either directly or indirectly relate to task. Thus it is important not only to read your syllabus carefully at the beginning of the term, but also to refer to it often as the term progresses. If your professor has a course Web site, it may prove to be an additional source of information about the task.

4. **Pay Close Attention When Your Professor Talks About the Test.** Even if you think you have a clear understanding of what the task is, it's always a good idea to pay very close attention when the professor explains what the test is going to be like. Many professors routinely provide example questions before an exam, but others will provide example questions only when asked. Thinking about questions asked on old exams gives you lots of information, especially about the level of thinking required. You want to use these questions as ways of gathering information about the level of thinking, not about the actual content that you should study. Chances are your professor will write the same *types* of questions on future exams but probably will not ask the exact same questions.

5. **Ask Former Students.** Students who have already taken the course will be able to give you details about a course and a professor. But make sure that you ask former students the right questions. For example, asking someone, "Are Professor Smith's tests hard?" is not the best way to pose the question because what is a difficult test to one person may not be difficult to another. Better questions would be: "What kind of tests does Professor Smith give?" "Can you remember examples of some questions?" "What kinds of structure does he expect for essay questions?" "Does he give you much guidance?" Questions such as these invite answers about the task.

ON YOUR OWN

Thinking About Yourself as a Learner

Most college students do not consciously sit down at the beginning of the term and say to themselves, "Gee, before I start doing my reading and studying for this class, I'd better figure out the task!" For students who intuitively understand that it is important to figure out the course demands, it's more of an unconscious effort. Think about yourself as a learner and write a paragraph that addresses the following questions:

- Have you taken the time this term to try to get to know something about your professor? If so, what have you found out that might help you understand the course task better?

- Have you taken time this term to figure out the task in each of your classes? If not, how might you begin to gather that information this term and in future terms?

- Have you ever been in a class where you had a very difficult time understanding what the professor's expectations were? How did you handle that situation? What might you do differently now?

- Can you think of any other sources that might be able to give you task information? (We have mentioned your professor, syllabus, copies of old exams, and students who have already taken the course.)

- How might you organize your notes to draw attention to task information?

Real College

Tina

DIRECTIONS: Read the following "Real College" scenario and respond to the questions based on the information you learned in this chapter.

Tina decided that she could no longer put off taking a required history class, even though she "hates history with a passion." It's not that she hasn't done well in history. On the contrary, her grades in high school history classes were quite good. She sees herself as a good memorizer, and since her high school history experience involved lots of memorization of names, dates, events, and the like, she tended to make good grades. She just doesn't like history—plain and simple.

As Tina looks over her class schedule for the term, she thinks about skipping the first class or two because, from her perspective, two fewer history classes to go to would be a good thing. But her roommate, who has already taken the course, advises her to attend every class—even the first one. Tina reluctantly takes her advice and actually finds the professor to be engaging and humorous.

Obviously, in order to earn a good grade in this course, Tina is going to have to figure out what the tasks are. On the first day, the professor says there will be three essay exams as well as a cumulative final, but he doesn't say much else about the tasks. Think about Tina's situation and respond to the following questions:

1. What additional information do you think Tina needs so that she can have a clearer idea of the task?

2. How should she go about gathering the necessary information?

ADD TO YOUR PORTFOLIO

For each of your classes this term, figure out the tasks.

1. Start by looking at the syllabus, e-mailing the professor, or talking to a teacher's assistant (TA). Think about exams, papers, homework, and any other course assignments.

2. Jot down what the professor expects from you for each course task. What clues did you receive that helped you figure it out?

3. Think about how you will approach each course based on the task. How should you approach studying for each exam? Which strategies will be the most appropriate?

4. Finally, think about how long you anticipate each task to take. How will you budget your time?

Getting Organized
Managing Yourself and Your Time

READ THIS CHAPTER TO ANSWER THE FOLLOWING QUESTIONS:

- Why do I need to manage my time?
- What is self-management?
- How can I create a schedule I can live with?
- How do I plan time to study for finals?

SELF-ASSESSMENT

DIRECTIONS: On a scale of 1 to 5, with 1 being "not at all effective," 3 being "somewhat effective," and 5 being "very effective," respond to each of the statements below. This evaluation should give you a good idea of your current time-management system.

	Not at all effective ◄─────► Very effective
1. How effective is your current system for managing time?	1 2 3 4 5
2. How effective is your current system for balancing your school, work, and social obligations?	1 2 3 4 5
3. How effective is your ability to get things done in an organized way?	1 2 3 4 5
4. How effective is your use of short periods of time (such as the time in between classes) to get things done?	1 2 3 4 5

If you scored mostly 5s, then you are already finding success in your ability to manage yourself and your time. However, if your scores indicate that your current system is less than stellar, read on for some great time-management strategies.

Managing yourself and your time may be two of the most difficult challenges for you as a college student. If you are a returning student who has been in the workforce for a while, or if you are raising a family or holding a full-time job while attending college, you will face new challenges in juggling your many responsibilities. If you are a recent high school graduate, you are probably used to having most of your time managed for you. Your school and parents were responsible for setting a good deal of your daily schedule—you were in classes most of the day, and after school you probably had set athletic, club, or family obligations, or perhaps you had a part-time job.

Studying Smarter

Write it down. Make a study schedule and follow it to help you reach your academic goals.

In college, however, you are in class for fewer hours each day, which leaves you with big blocks of time to manage. The trick is to start out with a plan and not have to scramble to make up for lost time once you are already behind. You want to create a plan that will help you maximize your time so you can get everything done without falling behind.

Managing Yourself

Before you can manage your time effectively, you have to be able to manage yourself. We believe that the key to self-management is being able to organize and keep track of all the things that you have to do. College life is very hectic; you have class assignments to complete, roommates to deal with, and tests to prepare for. If you are a returning student, you may also have a job to help pay your way through college, or you may have daily family obligations. However, no matter what your situation, the secret to getting organized is to create a balance among school, home, work, and social life. In the past, you may have been taught about time management with an approach that suggested giving up your social life to focus only on studying. However, we believe that you should be able to take care of your class obligations and still have plenty of time for things you would like to do. We want you to be able to hang out with your friends and spend time with your family, but we also want you to be able to get the work done for your classes so that you can be academically successful and *stay* in college.

In order to create a balance among all the things you have to do and all the things you want to do, consider the following points:

■ **Treat College Like a Full-Time Job.** If you are a full-time student, academic work should take up about 40 hours each week. So for the next several years, consider college your full-time job. You might be in class only 15 hours per week, but you should spend the other 25 hours studying and preparing for class. If you break it down, it is really not so bad. Each day, you will spend 3 to 4 hours in class and 4 to 5 hours reading, studying, and preparing for your assignments. The rest of the time is left for other activities or a part-time job. The good news is that unlike a full-time job, in college you have more control over when you schedule your classes and your study time. No one says that your studying must take place between 9:00 and 5:00, Monday through Friday; you are free to study whenever you want. In addition, you should think of your 40-hour week as more of a mind-set than as a fixed amount of time. In other words, when you have a full-time job, some weeks may require more than 40 hours to get everything accomplished, but other weeks will require less. On the average, though, you should plan on putting in about 40 hours.

■ **Schedule Your Classes for Your Most Alert Times.** Are you a morning person? A late-afternoon person? An evening person? Are you up with the sun, or are you lucky to be awake by noon? If you know you will never make it to an 8:00 A.M. class, don't schedule a class for that time, if possible. Likewise, if you are totally useless in the afternoon, try to schedule your courses before lunch-time. Many students don't consider their class times as an issue to think about when making their course schedule, but because you have the luxury of creating your own schedule, you should try to tailor it to your needs as much as possible. Certainly there will be times when you don't have the ideal schedule, but when it's possible, schedule your classes during the times you are most alert.

■ **Go to Class.** Although many professors don't take attendance, most still believe that going to class is a very important part of learning. Students who skip a lot of classes miss out on the important information that they can only get in class. For example, some professors consider their syllabus a work in progress and modify it throughout the term. Suppose a professor assigned a paper that was mentioned only in class but was not on the syllabus. You would be responsible for turning in the paper, but the only way you would know it was assigned would be if you attended class. Also, as a bonus, only by going to class each day will you know what the professor emphasized, which will help you when you study. So do yourself a favor and *go to class* every day.

NETWORKING

Using Notes from the Web

Some students believe that they can skip class because their professor puts her class notes on the Web. They think that they will be able to simply download the notes rather than take their own. Be advised that a professor's notes are generally meant to supplement those you take yourself. Sometimes the professor's notes are in skeletal form; you are expected to fill in the gaps during the lecture. So while downloading your professor's notes may be a good idea to supplement your own notes, they do not take the place of going to class and taking your own.

■ **Don't Procrastinate.** Procrastination is intentionally and continually putting off work that needs to be done. This problem may actually be the toughest part of self-management for some students. Because you are in control of your own time, it is tempting to put off work until later. It's just human nature. But you quickly can become overwhelmed by all you need to do when you continually neglect your work. Almost everyone has a friend who has procrastinated until the last minute and must "read" an entire novel and write a five-page English paper all in one night. For some students, procrastination tends to become a bad habit and a way of life. Once you start procrastinating, it is difficult to get back on track. However, the strategies in the next section should help you avoid procrastination by helping you determine what you need to do each day.

TIMELY TIPS

Financial Management

Many campuses offer financial management workshops for students who are often bombarded with offers for credit cards the first month they hit college. We believe beginning to learn the complexity of money management is another way to learn to self-manage. Check out what your college offers before you break in that new credit card.

Managing Your Time

Effective time-management strategies can help you organize your responsibilities and reach your goals. To manage your time effectively you will need to determine three important pieces of information:

1. **What Do I Need to Accomplish?** Consider the classes you must attend each week, your work schedule, social commitments, class assignments, and so forth. One of the hardest problems to figure out is how much time an assignment will take. For example, when writing a paper you have to know if it will take you one hour or considerably longer to find what you need in the library or on the Web. Will you be able to write your paper in two days, or will you need a full week? Some of the ability to know how long things will take comes with experience, but the following general rule may help you plan your time:

    Things always take longer than you think they will.

    Given this basic rule, try to plan more time than you think you will need. When you rush to get an assignment completed, you probably feel frustrated or angry when things take longer than planned. You may even give up without completing the assignment. So plan for things to take longer to avoid this problem.

2. **What Things Do I Currently Do That Waste My Time?** Before you can figure out how to spend your time effectively, you need to find out if and how you are wasting time. To do this, think about how you currently spend your days. Are there some things you do that simply waste large amounts of time? For example, are you playing video games, watching TV, surfing the Net, napping, or hanging out with friends for hours on end? All students need some unstructured time each day to simply do things they want to do. But if you find that your unstructured time bleeds over into your 40 hours of being a student, you should restructure your days.

3. **How Can I Keep Track of What I Need to Do?** Most people who manage their time successfully say that they can't live without their daily planner, calendar, or smart phone calendar. It helps them keep track of appointments, assignments, social commitments, and even important phone numbers. If you don't already use tools to help you schedule your time, invest in one today. Take your planner or cell phone (with ringer turned off) with you to class, and be sure to mark down your assignments. But getting things down is only half the battle; you have to make a habit of checking your schedule every day to see what you need to do. To be really effective, schedule things that you must do first—things such as class time, family obligations, or meetings you must attend. Then schedule your study time. Finally, fill in unscheduled times with more flexible obligations such as doing laundry or going shopping. Because you have so many things to juggle in college, sometimes it is hard to find the time to study if you don't specifically add it to your schedule. Planning study sessions along with the rest of your responsibilities helps you stay on top of your school responsibilities.

Studying Smarter

If you tend to nap for long periods of time as a form of procrastination, try the 20-minute power nap instead. Before you lie down to take your nap, set your alarm clock to go off in 20 minutes. Get up as soon as it goes off and get on with your day. If you find that you have not fallen asleep after 20 minutes, get up anyway. You probably didn't need a nap and will feel better just from lying down. We guarantee that you will feel refreshed and ready to tackle your next task.

Creating a Schedule You Can Live With

Creating a schedule that works is a challenge. Many students start out with good intentions but ultimately end up with an unworkable schedule for a number of reasons. Some students create a schedule that is too rigid, so they don't have the flexibility they need. Others create a schedule that is not detailed enough to be of any use. Still others create a good schedule but don't consult it regularly, so they forget what they need to do. In order to avoid falling into one of the time-management pitfalls, consider the tips in the following "Success at a Glance" box as you create your own schedule.

SUCCESS AT A GLANCE

Characteristics of Good and Poor Time Managers

Good Time Managers	Poor Time Managers
Study when they are most alert	Study whenever the mood strikes (even when they are dead tired)
Spend some time every day on each course	Study the night before each exam
Create a schedule that is specific	Do not schedule study times or do so only in a very general way
Make a reading schedule for each class	Read the night before the exam
Prioritize their work	Do the things they like to do first and put the rest off
Make to-do lists to stay organized	Often find that they don't have assignments completed because they did not write them down
Use the time in between classes to get work done	Don't use small pockets between class times

---

Timely Tips for Following Your Schedule

■ **Plan to Study When You Are Most Alert.** If you find that you are tired or you can't concentrate when you study, you probably are not studying at your most alert time. Try to find some blocks of time that are naturally best for you. Some students study best at night; others study best first thing in the morning. Test several times of the day to find out when you are the most ready to study. Experiment with times that you might not initially think are your best times of day—you just may surprise yourself and be a morning or night person after all.

■ **Spend Some Time Every Day on Each Course You Are Taking.** Even when you don't have an assignment due, plan some time each day to read the text, review your notes, and prepare for the next class. If you are taking classes that require problem solving such as math or chemistry, it is a good idea to work some problems each night. If you are taking a language class, plan to review new vocabulary, work on verb conjugation, or review grammar rules every day. By spending some time every day you won't have to cram for exams because you will always be caught up.

■ **Be Specific.** The more specific you can be when planning your study schedule the better because you will know exactly what you need to do each time you study. When you create your schedule, don't just write down "study." Instead, write "Read psychology text pp. 219–230." By creating a schedule that lists each specific task, you are more likely to remember to get everything done.

■ **Make a Reading Schedule for Each Class.** One of the simplest, yet most effective, ways to manage your time and to stay on top of your reading assignments is to make a reading schedule for each class. To make a reading schedule, simply add up the number of pages you need to read in the next week (some students prefer to add the pages in between each exam rather than each week) and divide that number by five (or six or seven if you will read during the weekend). For example, Robert has the following reading assignments this week:

History	Read Chapters 3–4, 65 pages
Statistics	Read Chapter 5, 27 pages
	Complete 15 practice problems
Music	Read Chapters 4–5, 39 pages
Literature	Read 6 chapters of novel, 90 pages
Biology	Read Chapter 8, 29 pages

This equals 250 pages of text reading, which is about average, according to several college surveys. Thinking about reading 250 pages can be overwhelming, but when Robert divides the reading over five days, he sees that he has only 13 pages of history, 6 pages of statistics (and 3 practice problems), 8 pages of music, 18 pages of literature, and 6 pages of biology to read each day. And that sounds a lot more manageable. If he reads over six or seven days, his daily load is cut even more. To create your own reading schedule, survey your reading assignments (usually found on your syllabus), and divide up the reading in a way that makes sense. Use section breaks or headings to help you determine how to divide the readings so that you are not stopping in the middle of a concept.

■ **Prioritize.** When you make your schedule, it is helpful to prioritize what you have to do. You might want to label your assignments as "high," "medium," or "low" priority. For example, reading your biology text before the lab might be a high priority, but starting on your history research paper that is due in three weeks might be lower. In general, start with high-priority tasks first so that you are sure to get them done. But don't ignore the medium and low priorities. That history research paper may be low priority now, but if nothing gets done in the next three weeks, it will become high priority quickly.

■ **Make To-Do Lists.** Sometimes when students begin to study, they start to think about all the other things they need to do—call home, get a haircut, cancel a dental appointment. All of these thoughts are very distracting. To keep yourself on track and to avoid procrastination, keep a to-do list next to you when you study. Write down all the things you think of, including course work, household chores (such as laundry), phone calls, e-mails to answer, and so forth. Cross items off as you complete them. Your to-do list might look something like this:

Date: Oct. 2	What Do I Need to Do?	Priority (high, medium, low)
1.	Finish revising English paper	High
2.	Do laundry	High
3.	Read math pp. 81–97 and do the problems	Medium
4.	Call home	Medium
5.	Plan spring break trip	Low
6.	Think about topic for final history paper	Low

If you don't want to specify priorities as high, medium, or low, simply try to put your to-do list in order, with the highest priority items at the top and the lowest ones at the bottom.

■ **Set Aside One Hour a Week to Plan.** Our most successful students tell us that it takes them about one hour to really plan out what they hope to accomplish in the next week. We suggest taking some time on Sunday nights to review all of your syllabi as you make your reading schedule and to-do lists for the coming week.

■ **Borrow Time—Don't Steal It.** If you decide to go out for a pizza instead of spending an hour reading your psychology chapter—great. But remember that it's important to just borrow that time. If you decide to go out instead of following your schedule, be sure to add the activity you missed (that is, reading your psychology chapter) to your schedule (or to-do list) for the next day so that you can make up that time. By having a schedule that is very specific, you'll know exactly what you have to do to catch up, and you can easily make up for the lost time.

■ **Use the Time Between Your Classes.** Many times students don't know where all of their time goes—an hour in between classes, two hours between school and work, 15 minutes before classes begin—all of this time adds up and it is useful for getting your work done. You can read for class during hour breaks, review your notes while you are waiting for class to begin and between lunch and class, or even meet with a study group in the laundry room. Plan to use short periods of time when making your schedule so this time does not get lost.

■ **Schedule Study Breaks.** If you plan to study for more than an hour at a time, schedule a 10- to 15-minute break for each hour and a half to two hours of study. You should also plan short breaks when switching from one topic to another to give yourself some time to refocus. When taking study breaks, you should avoid turning on the TV, going online, calling friends, "resting" your eyes, or engaging in any activity that could prolong what is supposed to be a brief break. You might get a snack, stretch, or go for a short walk—anything that will give your mind a brief rest.

■ **Take Some Time Off.** Many students feel guilty when they take time off because they are always thinking about the things they should be doing, such as working on that chemistry lab assignment. But when you have a good schedule, you will be able to reward yourself by taking time off without guilt because you know that you have planned time to get all of your assignments done. So, relax and enjoy yourself after you finish your work—you deserve it. Every schedule should include some free time.

■ **Don't Spin Your Wheels.** If you are having trouble in a course, seek help from a tutor, a professor, or a friend—anyone who might be able to help. There is nothing that gets in the way of managing your time more than worrying rather than being productive—especially in a course that is difficult for you. It's important to get help if you need it and get back on track before you fall too far behind to catch up. We tell our students at the beginning of each fall semester not to wait until Thanksgiving to ask for help. Whether you are on a quarter, trimester, or semester system, Thanksgiving is just too late.

53

ON YOUR OWN

Reflecting on What You Have Read

Think about the schedule you have created, and then write down the answers to the following questions. Have you created a schedule that you can live with? If not, what should you do to make it workable? Also write down the obstacles to efficient and effective scheduling. What obstacles do you have that get in the way of making a schedule that works for you?

TIMELY TIPS

Creating a Workable Schedule

Learning to manage your time is a skill that will help you in college and beyond. Start now, and by the time you enter the world of work, you will be a time-management veteran. Start this week. Consider the tips you just read to create a schedule. Use your schedule book to fill in your plan for the upcoming week in the following order:

1. Enter your class and lab times.
2. If you commute, enter the time it takes to travel to and from campus.
3. Enter your work schedule.
4. Enter your meal times.
5. Enter all of your weekly personal activities (clubs, athletics, exercise).
6. Schedule your study times for each class. Include time for the following:

   ■ Reviewing your notes
   ■ Reading the text
   ■ Preparing for exams, writing papers, working on projects, etc.

7. Keep some time open so that your schedule is somewhat flexible.
8. Add any other things that you have to do this week.

Planning for Midterms and Finals

Every principle of time- and self-management discussed in this chapter usually goes into warp speed when you are preparing for midterms and finals. Generally, you will need to rethink your entire schedule to cope with the added pressures. In fact, you might even need to put in a few hours of overtime on your 40-hour workweek, but don't despair. By following the techniques outlined in this chapter, you should get through it. In addition to the strategies we have already discussed, we add the following suggestions to help you cope with crunch exam time:

■ **Plan Ahead.** Start to rehearse and review your notes and the texts *before* exam week so that you can cut down on your workload for the week. Starting early is essential for classes that have cumulative exams (exams that hold you responsible for topics covered over the entire term) because there is so much information to review.

■ **Cut Down on Work or Other Commitments.** If you work part-time, ask for some time off or for fewer hours at your job and make sure that your family and friends understand that you will be extra busy. Try not to add any new commitments during midterm and final time.

■ **Get Enough Sleep.** Pulling all-nighters for a big exam rarely pays off. Instead, try to create your schedule for exam week in a way that leaves you adequate sleep time (try for at least six hours each night). You won't do well on an exam if you are falling asleep while taking it.

■ **Study with a Partner.** Misery loves company, and this is never truer than during midterms and finals. By the time midterms roll around you may have found a study partner or group that works. Study together to keep each other on schedule and motivated to work.

■ **Don't Panic.** We will discuss this point further in Chapter 8, but to put it simply: Midterms and finals are really just exams. The world will not end because of midterms and finals. If you find that the pressure is getting to you, readjust your schedule to allow more break time, and try to really relax during those breaks. If you find that you have excessive anxiety, get some help before it becomes a stumbling block to doing well.

In this chapter you have learned some strategies for managing yourself and your time. Try to make a schedule and follow it strictly for one week. Then make adjustments to suit your needs. Even if you do not consider yourself a "schedule person," it is imperative for you to find a way of keeping track of what you need to do. At the very least, having a schedule helps you organize and take control of your college career.

Real College

Janice

DIRECTIONS: Read the following "Real College" scenario and respond to the question based on the information you learned in this chapter.

Janice is a college freshman. She loves her new freedom. A new town, her own place, new friends, and a great social life. Gone is the 10:00 P.M. curfew that her parents enforced in high school. Janice is living it up and having the time of her life, but she can't seem to make it to all of her classes and is falling way behind on her work.

Janice is taking five courses this term—American literature, accounting, sociology, history, and a chemistry course that involves lab projects. Her reading load is about 240 pages each week, and she has at least one exam every other week. She never seems to be able to keep up with her reading or to find time to study. In addition, Janice is having trouble making it to her 8:00 A.M. accounting course. In fact, she missed both class periods last week. She has also missed several of her chemistry classes; she really enjoys them, but she just can't seem to make it to class on time.

Another concern is Janice's part-time job at a local video store. Although her hours are somewhat flexible, she always works at least two weeknights and one weekend day. She thinks that the 15 hours spent at her job each week are really getting in the way of her studying, but she needs the money so she can't quit or cut back on hours.

She also finds her new social life to be a problem. It seems that no matter when she tries to study, someone is calling or stopping by her dorm room to ask her to go out. Janice really has a hard time saying no and ends up procrastinating on her work every time. She has never had trouble in school before, but now she is failing several courses, including chemistry, which she wants to major in. She knows that she needs to do things differently, but she just can't seem to find the time to get everything done.

Using the strategies you learned about time- and self-management, what advice would you give Janice to help her manage her time?

ADD TO YOUR PORTFOLIO

For one full week, keep a schedule of what you actually do. In your schedule book, jot down everything you do in half-hour increments. Evaluate your schedule to see if you have used your time wisely and accomplished everything in a timely fashion. Then create a schedule you can live with and follow that schedule for one week. Finally, reflect on your schedule by asking yourself the following questions:

1. Did you find that you accomplished more work?

2. What adjustments would you make to your schedule?

3. Have you left enough flexibility in your schedule for emergencies?

4. Are you studying during your most alert times?

Academic Energy
Motivation for Learning, Attitudes, and Interests

READ THIS CHAPTER TO ANSWER THE FOLLOWING QUESTIONS:

- What motivates people to learn?
- How do you get and stay motivated?
- How do attitudes and interests influence learning?
- How can you change your attitude and develop interest for topics you dislike?
- How can you maintain a positive attitude?

SELF-ASSESSMENT

DIRECTIONS: On a scale of 1 to 5, with 1 being "not at all true of me," 3 being "somewhat true of me," and 5 being "very true of me," respond to the following statements as honestly as you can. This assessment should give you a good idea of your motivation, attitudes, and interests.

	Not at all true of me ←→ Very true of me				
1. I feel motivated for college learning.	1	2	3	4	5
2. I am more motivated to succeed in college than most of my peers.	1	2	3	4	5
3. I set and reach reasonable goals.	1	2	3	4	5
4. I am aware when I have reached my goals.	1	2	3	4	5
5. I have a positive attitude about attending college.	1	2	3	4	5
6. I have a positive attitude about many of the courses I am taking this term.	1	2	3	4	5
7. I tend to have a wide range of interests.	1	2	3	4	5
8. I can motivate myself even in courses I find uninteresting.	1	2	3	4	5

	Not at all true of me				Very true of me
9. I know why I am attending college.	1	2	3	4	5
10. I am motivated to learn in all courses, not only those in my major.	1	2	3	4	5

If you scored mostly 5s, you probably have a positive attitude and are motivated for college learning. If, on the other hand, you scored mostly 1s, you may want to pay extra careful attention to the strategies discussed in this chapter.

You already may have noticed that motivation, attitudes, and interests are tied together. It just makes sense that for courses in which you are interested or have a positive attitude, you will be more motivated to learn. But let's try to separate these three important factors related to active learning to define what they are and how they interact to promote active learning and success in college. We'll begin with motivation.

What Influences Motivation?

Motivation is a combination of several factors including choice, desire for learning, value of learning, and personal control. Motivation is influenced by:

1. **The Amount of Choice You Have About What You Are Learning:** Sometimes your professors will offer you several projects to choose from, or sometimes they will even ask you to choose the topics that will be covered. Choices like these will help to increase your motivation. However, even if you are not given choices about the class content, college offers you many choices about what you will learn. You choose your major, and to a certain extent you choose the courses you will take and your course schedule.

2. **Your Desire to Learn:** It's likely that because you are currently enrolled in college you do want to learn, but sometimes you might be required to take courses that don't particularly interest you. For example, most colleges have a liberal arts requirement for all students, which means that, regardless of their major, students must take courses in humanities, mathematics, and the sciences.

3. **How Much You Value the Subject to Be Learned:** As a general rule, the more you believe the subject to be worthwhile, the easier it will be to become motivated. For example, many colleges require students to take at least one foreign language course. If you believe that it is valuable to learn another language, you will feel motivated—perhaps enough to take a second course. However, if you don't see it as valuable, you may have a harder time motivating yourself to learn in your language course.

4. **The Extent to Which You Are Willing to Take Personal Control of Your Learning:** The degree to which you are motivated to learn depends in large part on knowing the strategies to use and then taking control and applying those strategies. That is the "will" part of the "skill versus will" paradigm (see Chapter 2). Other individuals, such as teachers, peers, and parents, can expose you to skills that will lead to effective and efficient learning, but you must have the will to apply them.

In an ideal setting, you would have all of the components of motivation. However, you can learn successfully without choice, desire, and value; but learning will take more of a conscious effort from you.

Studying Smarter

Reward yourself for a job well done when you meet your goals.

What Motivates People?

You may not realize it, but you are always motivated. No matter where you are or what you are doing, *you are always motivated to do something*, even if it's just sleeping. Focusing your motivation on learning, however, may be challenging sometimes.

It's important to understand right from the beginning that you are responsible for your own motivation, even in courses that you don't like. The current thinking on motivation can be summed up by saying that motivation is not something that is done to you. In other words, no one can motivate you but you. Others can provide you with stimuli—for example, explaining the reasons why it is important to learn about biology even though you plan to major in literature. But in the end, the motivation must come from you. Thus, although an interesting instructor makes it easier for you to stay motivated, no one can directly motivate you to learn. Even though people are always motivated to do something, some students find it difficult to become motivated for learning.

You may have heard the terms *intrinsic* and *extrinsic*, especially as they relate to motivation. **Intrinsic motivation** occurs when the activity is its own reward. For example, some people read for the sheer enjoyment, others calculate numbers for the pleasure, and still others conduct experiments for the thrill of discovery. Think of intrinsic motivation as doing something you choose to do for sheer pleasure, for challenge, or simply because it interests you.

Extrinsic motivation, on the other hand, occurs when your incentive is a reward, such as grades or praise or even money. Did your parents ever pay you to get good grades in elementary or middle school? You may have earned $5.00 for each A and $2.00 for each B. Money can be a very strong extrinsic motivator, as can automobiles or spring break trips for college students. You can think of extrinsic motivation as trying to get a job done for some external reward, rather than for the sake of learning. For example, you may be failing organic chemistry, but when the professor offers an extra credit assignment, you decide to do it even though you are not motivated to learn in the course. In this case, you are extrinsically motivated to earn extra credit points that can boost your course grade rather than by learning organic chemistry for the sheer pleasure of it.

The more you are intrinsically motivated to learn, the easier learning will be for you. The key to becoming intrinsically motivated, even in classes you don't particularly like, is to find *something* about the course that you find motivating and to focus on the positives rather than the negatives of the course. It also helps to focus more on understanding the concepts to be learned than on grades and to have a professor who can set the stage for intrinsic motivation.

TIMELY TIPS

Adjusting Your Sleep Cycle

Some students tell us that their motivation is off kilter because their sleep cycle is out of whack. These students are napping for several hours each afternoon and then staying up until the wee hours of the morning. This cycle of sleeping during the day and then staying up all night leads them to miss a good deal of classes and to feel somewhat unconnected to the topics they are supposed to be learning. If you find yourself in this situation, you will need to give up that long daytime nap to get your awake/asleep cycle back on track. You may be tired for a day or two as your body readjusts, but you should find a vast improvement in your motivation for learning.

Getting Motivated Through Goal Setting

Getting motivated is the first step toward staying motivated. One of the best ways to become motivated is to set learning goals. Your goals should be more than just "I want to make an A in the course," because grades are mainly an extrinsic motivator. In fact, students who focus only on grades to motivate themselves usually have a harder time maintaining their motivation as the term goes on. Students who set goals that focus on learning rather than grades tend not only to be more successful but also learn and remember more.

You probably have set goals before without even realizing it. For example, think about some New Year's resolutions you have made—to exercise more, to stop smoking, or to increase your GPA. How many of your resolutions have you kept? If you are like most people, your resolutions are long forgotten by Valentine's Day because you do not set yourself up to achieve your New Year's goals. People tend to be unrealistic when they make New Year's resolutions.

For example, although a goal of exercising more and getting in shape is a good resolution to make, it is unrealistic to expect to be in great shape right away if you have not been exercising regularly. Individuals who do not set short-term goals on their way to reaching long-term goals will soon find that their resolutions are not easily achievable and will give up on reaching their goals.

In addition, the goals you set should be conscious and deliberate. You should set your goals and make a plan to meet them only after you have given them some intentional thought. New Year's resolutions are easily forgotten because they are generally made with little thought. Most of the time we make a resolution in the middle of a party on New Year's Eve when someone says "So what's your New Year's resolution?" We may say the first thing that comes into our mind, which provides very little incentive to follow through. In order to set goals that can be achieved, your goals should be:

■ **Realistic:** Can the goal be achieved? If not, how can the goal be divided into smaller goals? You should try to have short-term, intermediate, and long-term academic goals. A **short-term goal** is one that you will achieve within the next few days, such as "I will read Chapter 10 of my biology book tonight." **Intermediate goals** are ones that you will achieve within the next few weeks or months, such as "I will compare my notes to the text material each night to prepare for my cumulative psychology exam, which will be at the end of the semester." A **long-term goal** is one that will take longer still, perhaps a few months or even years to achieve, such as "I will begin to learn Spanish this year." An even longer-term goal is, "I want to graduate with a degree in marketing." Most people make the mistake of making only intermediate and long-term goals, but short-term goals are also important because they help you follow the progress you are making and they help you stay on track.

■ **Believable:** Do you feel that you will be able to achieve your goal? Being confident about your ability to learn is crucial to your motivation. If you think that a task is too difficult for you to achieve, your motivation will decrease and you might give up before you even try. Some students believe that they can succeed only in certain disciplines. Students will say, "I'm good at math, but I'm terrible at English," or "I can learn history really well, but not science." These statements tell us that the students are motivated to learn one topic but not another. If you find yourself making these kinds of statements, take a minute to reflect on how they are negatively affecting your motivation to learn in those courses.

■ **Desirable:** How much do you want to reach your goal? When goals are desirable, you can provide reasons why you should work hard toward reaching the goal. Reasoning why it is important to accomplish a task helps to intrinsically motivate you. In order to succeed in reaching your goals, they should be goals that you really desire. Then, learning will be particularly rewarding or enjoyable to you and it will be easier to achieve. Your goal may be to graduate from college within four years and to land a good job in your field, but you must have the desire for success to reach that type of goal.

■ **Measurable:** How will you know whether or when your goal has been met? Some goals are easy to measure. If your goal is to lose ten pounds, you will know whether your goal has been met when you weigh yourself. However, sometimes learning goals are not so easy to quantify, so you need to set some standards to help measure your progress. This may be as simple as taking a few minutes to think about what you have learned after each study session or it may include a more in-depth assessment. In general, you will need more checks of your progress for long-term goals than for short-term goals.

Finally, it is a good idea to make your goals public. By public we mean sharing them with others—those you believe will encourage you to stay the course and might even help you achieve your goals. In addition, the fact that others know your goals, in some respects, holds you more accountable. For example, if your goal is to make the dean's list, share that with your roommate, members of your study group, or your best friend. Ask them to check in with you occasionally to see if you are on track. This puts some pressure on you, to be sure, but sometimes a little pressure can be a plus in helping you work toward your goals.

NETWORKING

Finding Motivation

Many sites on the Internet feature tips for getting and staying motivated. Some good sources include college counseling centers or freshman-year experience sites. Try the following keywords to find at least three motivation sites: motivation, college motivation, student motivation, or learning motivation. What kind of information did you find that will help you become more motivated or maintain your motivation?

Staying Motivated

Getting motivated is one thing; staying motivated is another. We rarely see students at the beginning of a term who are not motivated. Almost everyone is excited about the prospect of a new term and, in a sense, starting with a clean slate. But as the term wears on, it is easy for motivation to wane, especially in courses that are causing you trouble. In order to stay motivated, you should give yourself checkpoints on the way to reaching your goals. These checkpoints might include:

■ Monitor your motivation for learning just as you monitor your comprehension when you read. Each time you sit down to study, ask yourself about your level of motivation for the task. You have an internal body clock, which means that you will find that certain times of the day are more conducive to learning than others. (This idea was discussed in Chapter 5.) Listen to your body clock to find out when you are most motivated (first thing in the morning, late afternoon, evening), and try to plan your study sessions around these times. In addition, try to get a handle on how you feel psychologically and physically when you begin to lose motivation. Because your thought processes tend to change when you lose motivation, you may experience less confidence in yourself and have more of a negative take on your life as a student. Physically, you may experience tiredness or an increased stress level, feelings that are not typical for you. Being in tune with yourself can often help you bounce back sooner and easier from a slump in motivation.

■ Study the subjects you find the most difficult, or are least motivated to learn, first. Then move to the subjects that are easier or those that you enjoy more. In that way you will be more likely to stay motivated to study the subjects you find the most interesting.

■ Plan some breaks in your study time—don't try to study for more than one hour without a short break because you will find it difficult to maintain your motivation. If possible, also try to change the type of tasks you do after each break. For example, if you have just spent an hour reading your psychology assignment, take a five- or ten-minute break, and come back and do the practice exercises for your French class.

But what if you find yourself losing motivation? It's important to have strategies to follow in this scenario as well. It might help if you:

■ Take a break and come back to what you were doing at a later time.

■ Switch topics every hour or so.

■ Work with a study group. One key component of motivation is collaborating with others.

■ Plan to study in the library or another quiet place if you find that your social life is interfering with studying. Find somewhere to study where you will be free from distractions and temptations.

■ Use the best/worst case scenario technique. Imagine what will happen and how you will feel if you get your work done. Focusing on that positive image may help you find your motivation. On the other hand, picturing what will happen if the task is not completed is motivating for others. Thinking about the poor grade, or worse—being placed on academic probation—is enough to get some students moving in the right direction.

Sometimes students find that they lose motivation as the term goes on. Some of this is natural—people are generally more motivated at the beginning and at the end of a term. So, if you experience a slight dip in your motivation toward the middle of a term or during the first nice spring day, you probably

SUCCESS AT A GLANCE

Motivation Checkpoints

When you are setting your goals, remember that achievable goals are:

Realistic

Believable

Desirable

Measurable

DIRECTIONS: For one of your courses this term, answer the following questions.

What do I need to learn? What is the task (exam, paper, presentation, discussion, etc.)?

What sources will I need to use (text, labs, lecture, discussion, etc.)?

What is my level of motivation for beginning the task (high, medium, low)? Why?

What are my goals for completing this project? Include short-term, intermediate, and long-term goals.

DIRECTIONS: For one of your courses this term, answer the following questions.

What is my level of motivation for completing the task (high, medium, low)? Why?

What, if any, adjustments do I need to make to reach my learning goals?

shouldn't be too concerned. Set some new goals to get back on track. However, sometimes losing motivation can be a sign of a bigger problem. If you think your loss of motivation may be a problem, reflect on the reason for your lack of motivation. Can you pinpoint the source of it? Or are you unsure why you are unmotivated? Sometimes students become unmotivated by poor grades in a particular course, or sometimes outside influences (for example, family, roommates, social situations, substance abuse, or health concerns) cause students to lose their motivation.

Another way to maintain your motivation is to figure out all of the tasks that you need to complete in your courses. By listing this information, you should be able to find something in the course that is motivating for you. You will also be able to determine the tasks you find unmotivating, which can help you psych yourself up to maintain your motivation. Before each exam (or paper or project) for each of your courses this term, monitor your motivation by answering the questions in the accompanying "Success at a Glance" box.

Any method you find to renew your motivation is great. Try a few techniques to find out what works best. The motivation checkpoints in the "Success at a Glance" box should help you monitor your motivation in many different situations in all of your courses. It will help you discover the kinds of tasks you find particularly motivating and the kinds of tasks you find less motivating. Once you know the kinds of tasks that fail to motivate you, you can counter with some of the techniques discussed earlier.

Changing Attitudes and Interests

Now that you understand the role that motivation plays in active learning, let's turn to attitudes and interests. As you read this portion of the chapter, reflect on how they relate to one another.

How many times have you dealt with a clerk in the grocery store, a family member, your advisor, a server in a restaurant, or even your best friend and walked away thinking, "Now there's a person with a bad attitude"? Everyone probably has a bad attitude about something at some time, which suggests that attitude, like motivation, is situational. Rarely are people positive about everything; nor are they negative about everything.

Likewise, interest is situational. Students generally aren't interested in everything. In most cases, individuals tend to show great interest in a limited number of areas, moderate interest in a greater number of topics, and low or no interest in many more. Everyone knows people who have a strong passion for something—computers, fly fishing, travel, photography, writing, basketball, history. And, more often than not, these passions are reflected in majors that students select and the careers they ultimately choose. Interests can't help but influence academic decisions students make and how actively they pursue certain goals.

Like motivation, attitudes and interests help define who you are as a learner. Moreover, each of these factors is either directly or indirectly a part of your personality, thus making them a bit more difficult to change than basic study habits.

Although everyone seems to know someone who has an overall bad or good attitude, attitudes actually can be thought of as emotional reactions to specific situations. Think of attitudes as:

■ **Reflexive:** By reflexive attitudes we mean that you experience these attitudes without even thinking about them. For example, if your professor assigns you two extra chapters to read before a quiz on Friday and you already have every minute of your schedule between now and Friday planned, you may have an immediate negative reaction. However, that attitude may not be permanent. Perhaps a professor in another class cancels a test that was scheduled for Friday, or a date that you really didn't want to go on is canceled, causing your initial bad attitude to mellow. The bottom line is that most students' attitudes about things change. What you have a bad attitude about on Tuesday you may see in another light by Wednesday.

■ **An Influence on Your Motivation:** It makes sense that if you are motivated in a particular course, your attitude will be more positive than if you were unmotivated.

■ **Characteristics That Match Your Behavior:** For example, if you have a bad attitude toward learning a foreign language and believe that no matter what, you can't succeed, your behavior will follow suit. You won't work on the material on a daily basis, you won't say much in class, and you even may display a poor attitude toward your professor, even if she is a good teacher.

Types of Academic Attitudes

There are four types of academic attitudes you will encounter in college: (a) attitude toward college; (b) attitude toward your instructors; (c) attitude toward the subject and learning environment; and (d) attitude toward yourself as a learner. As you read about each one, think about yourself as a learner and the attitudes you have.

SUCCESS AT A GLANCE

Attitudinal Directions

Toward college

Toward instructors ← Types of Attitudes → Toward subject

Toward yourself as a learner

Attitude Toward College

Students begin college with different attitudes for many different reasons. Some are happy with their school choice, others aren't, and still others don't care. Obviously, it's better to begin on the right foot—with a positive attitude about the college you are attending—but also remember that attitudes change. We've known many students who started college having one perception about what they would experience only to be either disappointed or elated later on. For whatever reason you chose to attend your current college, know that your general attitude about being in college and your expectations of what that college experience will be strongly influence the attitudes you will have. In turn, these attitudes influence your academic performance. Conflicts often occur when there is not a good match between expectations and the realities of college life. For example, if you attended a small high school where you knew everyone and had small classes and lots of individual attention, you may be overwhelmed by being on a campus with 30,000-plus students. In addition, sometimes college just isn't what students expected it would be. Large class sizes, classes that are difficult to get into, long lines, roommate problems, and homesickness are just a few of the many problems that can sour initially good attitudes.

Attitude Toward Your Instructors

Your attitude about your instructor also influences your academic performance. This is especially true for disciplines you don't particularly like. If you enroll in a mathematics course "hating" math and project that feeling onto your professor, you are probably going to have some problems. On the other hand, if you try to have the attitude that each instructor has something unique to offer, you may have a totally different experience. We suggest that students try to get to know their professors and not feel intimidated about talking with them. We know of a student who, at the beginning of every term, makes an appointment to see all of his professors. He takes only about 15 minutes of their time introducing himself and talking with each of them about how to study in their courses. He says it helps him see his professors in a different light, and although he still has a better attitude toward some professors than others, the experience makes all his professors "human." Rarely does a professor turn down his request for an appointment, and in many cases, this initial contact makes it easier for him to approach a professor if he experiences problems with a course.

Attitude Toward the Subject and Learning Environment

When we think about attitudes toward subject matter, it's difficult to separate attitude from interest and motivation because most students have a more negative attitude toward subjects in which they are not interested and less motivated. For example, if you are strong in mathematics and science and have been successful in those courses in the past, you will most likely enter into these courses in college with a positive attitude toward learning the material.

However, if you have little interest in math and science and fail to see any relevance in these courses to your future career choice, then you are more likely to have a bad attitude toward these classes. In fact, some students try to avoid subjects they dislike until the very end of their program. We know students who have delayed taking their lab science, history, or mathematics requirements until their senior year, only to find out that the course wasn't as bad as anticipated. It's also important to try hard not to have preconceived notions about a course. Even though you may have had an unpleasant experience in a similar course, try to begin each course with an open mind. An open mind can go a long way in changing your attitude, helping you develop your interests and maintain motivation.

Attitude Toward Yourself as a Learner

The attitude that you have toward yourself as a learner may be the most important of the four attitudes because it is the sum total of the educational experiences you have accumulated in your 12-plus years of schooling. If you have had teachers who encouraged you, if you have experienced academic success, and if you have parents who have been actively involved in your learning at home, you probably have a positive view of yourself in learning situations. That's not to say that students who have a positive attitude never doubt themselves. They do. But they know themselves well enough to identify what they will have to change and how they will do it in order to make things improve.

On the other hand, if school was not challenging, if you experienced only moderate academic success, and if your family had little involvement with your learning, you may have a more negative view of yourself and lack confidence academically. Students who fall into this category initially may have a more difficult time adjusting to college, but we have seen such students gain confidence in themselves when they begin to experience academic successes.

Maintaining a Positive Attitude

Few students begin college with a totally negative attitude. Thus, we suggest that your first step is to evaluate what it is you like about college. You may have a great roommate, you may have at least one class that seems or one professor who seems to be enjoyable, or maybe you are simply positive about having a new beginning. Whatever excites you and makes you feel positive should be what you concentrate on, especially during those first few days of a new term. Yes, things will go wrong. The new registration system touted by the registrar's office might crash just when you are finally making some progress in adding a class you want, the bursar's office might lose proof that you paid your tuition, and the lines in the bookstore might go on forever. But you have no control over these things. Take a deep breath, count to 10 (or 50, if need be), and try not to let these negative happenings get in the way of your excitement and positive outlook. We realize that this can be difficult, but it's important to learn early on that you need to develop patience with things in life that you have little or no control over. Don't let those things bring you down. Save your energy for staying on top of what you can control.

Another suggestion that students find helpful in maintaining a positive attitude is not to dwell on past mistakes. For example, if writing has always been a struggle for you, telling yourself, "I'm a terrible writer," will do little to help. Rather, concentrate on the positives such as, "I'm a good learner in general, so writing should not be impossible. I can get help at the writing center if I need it, so I know I can do it." Everyone has strong points and weak points. The secret to maintaining a positive attitude is one of balance. If you lack confidence in writing, for example, be sure to balance that writing course with another course that you will like and that will be less of a struggle for you. Also, try to give each course and each professor a chance. Enter each course with the attitude that you will do your best. In some courses, this may mean that you will not earn the best grade. There's nothing wrong with *earning* a C in a course that is particularly difficult for you. There is something wrong, however, in *settling* for a C because your attitude in that course is negative and you simply do not put in the necessary effort.

In addition, expect to learn something valuable in every course you take. We know that's often a difficult suggestion to follow, but if you try to think that parts of a course might be interesting and valuable, both your attitude and your motivation will be better. It's particularly difficult to follow this suggestion when you are a first-year student because we know that first-year students often get stuck taking leftover courses or core courses in which they haven't much interest. But no matter how uninteresting or boring you might find a course, look toward the positive. Think how you might use some of the information at a later date or how it might be related to other areas that do interest you and for which you already possess a positive attitude. Imagine how you might feel at the end of the term if you do well in a subject that either wasn't your favorite or that previously made you struggle.

ON YOUR OWN

Reflecting on What You Have Read

Think about your attitude in your courses this term and write your response to the following questions: Is there a course that you have a bad attitude about? What small steps could you take to improve your attitude in this course? What might be causing your negative attitude in this course? Is it something you can change or something over which you have no control? How is this attitude impacting your motivation and your interest in this and other courses?

The Role of Interests

As we mentioned earlier, attitudes and interests go hand in hand. If you have an interest in something, you also probably have a good attitude toward it. Likewise, when you're not interested in a topic or course, you may not have a very good attitude about having to learn it.

We have found that many students lack interest in a wide variety of areas, which puts limitations on the courses that they want to take. But not having a wide variety of interests doesn't mean that you can't develop some. As we have suggested, every course has *something* interesting about it or people wouldn't spend their lives studying it. Students who have the most focused interests are usually those who have the most difficult time developing new interests. We have had conversations with students that go something like this:

Student: Why do I have to take this stuff—history, sociology, and drama, for goodness sakes? I'm a computer science major and none of this is important to me. I just want to be able to work with computers.

Professor: Well, I understand that, but you also have to take a series of core courses—courses that help you have a well-rounded education. Besides, they can help to develop other interests. One of the reasons for a college education is to give you a broader view of the world.

Student: (rolling her eyes) Maybe so, but I don't care about any of this. I'll do it because I have to, but I'm not going to like it.

The student shuffles off, unhappy, determined to get nothing from any course that isn't computer related. Chances are that she will get into academic trouble simply because she is already convinced that there is nothing about these courses that could possibly be of interest. How different the scenario might have been if she thought about courses as a chance to develop new interests and learn new things.

There are also students who enter college with no overriding interest in any one particular area. Many of these students have not yet selected a major and hope to find something that interests them as a result of enrolling in general core courses. The best advice we can give to you if you fall into this category is to keep up with assignments. Do the reading, participate in discussion groups, study with others, and seek assistance when the going gets rough. Often a class that starts out slowly turns into an interesting course if you keep on top of things. It particularly helps if you create a study group to talk about the information, and it helps even more if at least one person in the group has more than a superficial interest in the course. What starts out as a way to try to earn a decent grade in a class can turn into an experience that creates an enormous amount of interest in a course.

A final suggestion about developing and maintaining interest in courses: Don't wait until the end of your college career to take all the courses you think you'll hate. Intersperse the good with the bad. Try to balance courses you know you'll be interested in with those that you think you won't. And for those less interesting courses, select your instructors carefully. A good instructor can make or break your interest toward and attitude about a particular course.

It is easy to see that motivation, attitude, and interest are related to one another and difficult to separate. Unfortunately, lack of motivation, a poor attitude, and few interests usually go hand in hand. But everyone can make a conscious effort to develop interests, improve attitudes, and work on motivation.

Real College

Martin

DIRECTIONS: Read the following "Real College" scenario and respond to the question based on the information you learned in this chapter.

Martin is a first-year student. Because Martin did very well in high school and also had high entrance exam scores, he had his pick of colleges and was courted by some of the top schools in the country. Martin's parents, who were very proud of their son's accomplishments, persuaded him to attend a large prestigious school. Martin wanted to go to a smaller school that had a good reputation in the sciences because he had a strong interest in majoring in biology. In fact, although he had been successful in all of his courses in high school, he really didn't want much to do with anything that wasn't in some way related to science. His career goal is to become a veterinarian.

When Martin arrived on campus, he immediately felt overwhelmed. The campus was too big, he didn't know anyone, and his classes were extremely difficult. He had no choice in his courses for the first term because his schedule was set for him. He was enrolled in five courses: World Literature I, Political Science, Calculus, Anthropology, and Computer Applications I. Martin became miserable—fast! For the first few days, he tried to maintain a positive attitude and a high level of motivation, but he kept asking himself, "Why am I here? Why did I let my parents talk me into this?" Before he knew it, he found himself with a generally bad attitude about being in college and zero motivation.

Martin is bright and has long-term career plans, but it is also obvious that he's not motivated to do the work and has a bad attitude about school and his classes that may influence him negatively if he doesn't do something fast. Based on what you have read and what you know about the role that motivation, attitudes, and interests play in learning, what advice would you give Martin?

ADD TO YOUR PORTFOLIO

1. Write down three short-term, one intermediate, and one long-term goal for the rest of this year. Before you begin working on these goals, share them with a classmate or friend to help you determine if your goals are realistic, desirable, believable, and measurable. As the year progresses, periodically evaluate those goals.

2. In each of your courses, monitor your motivation throughout the term. What activities do you find particularly motivating? Which fail to motivate? What strategies do you find helpful in regaining your motivation? How can you use these strategies in other situations to help you get or stay motivated?

Just What Do You Believe, Anyway?

READ THIS CHAPTER TO ANSWER THE FOLLOWING QUESTIONS:

- How is your learning affected by your beliefs?
- What are the five belief components that influence learning?

SELF-ASSESSMENT

DIRECTIONS: Read the following scenario and answer the questions honestly. The purpose of this scenario is to help you to identify and think about your beliefs in terms of the five components of beliefs covered in this chapter. Remember that there are no right or wrong responses.

Chris is taking introductory biology. He studies hard for the class, but he has failed his first two exams. When he studies, he tries to focus on the material covered in the lectures, but he really doesn't read the text. He does try to memorize almost all of the bold-faced terms in the text by writing them on three-by-five-inch index cards and flipping through them until he has memorized the definitions. After the last exam, he tried studying with friends, but he didn't find it helpful because his friends explained the information differently than the professor had. He wasn't sure they knew what they were talking about and didn't want to get confused.

Chris believes that science is really just memorization and that most science problems have only one answer, so if he looks at the material enough he should do fine. Even though he doesn't spend a lot of time studying, he feels that he puts in hard work and effort and, therefore, he should be receiving high grades. Chris thinks his poor grades could be due to the new professor teaching the course. Professor Smith tries to have class discussions, despite the fact that there are 250 students enrolled in the class. She also tries to tell the class about all sides of each issue. When there are competing scientific theories, she is sure to discuss each one because she wants to give an unbiased lecture each time. However, Chris knows that science is based on proven facts and finds all these theories confusing. When Chris went to her office asking which theory is the right one, or which one he needed to know for the exam, she told him that all of the theories have some merit and that he must decide for himself what he will believe. Chris believes that it is the professor's responsibility to make sure that the students learn in class. However, this professor often asks exam questions over topics that were covered in the text but not during the lectures. Chris is beginning to believe that he is failing the class because he is not able to learn science.

	Strongly disagree ⟷ Strongly agree				
1. I agree with Chris that science is based on proven facts.	1	2	3	4	5
2. I agree with Chris that the students should only be responsible for the scientific theories that the professor discusses in class.	1	2	3	4	5
3. Like Chris, I believe that there must be one theory that is more correct than others.	1	2	3	4	5
4. I agree with Chris that the professor is responsible for student learning.	1	2	3	4	5
5. I agree with Chris that if I don't do well on my biology exam it is because I am not able to learn science.	1	2	3	4	5
6. Like Chris, I believe that I don't have to read the text as long as I listen in class because the professor goes over all of the important information.	1	2	3	4	5
7. I agree with Chris that learning competing science theories is too confusing for students.	1	2	3	4	5
8. I agree with Chris that there is usually only one right answer to a science problem.	1	2	3	4	5
9. I believe that some people will do fine in Chris's class because they are good learners, but others have a limited ability to learn science.	1	2	3	4	5
10. Like Chris, I believe that I will only do well in this science class if I can learn information quickly.	1	2	3	4	5
11. Chris's plan of taking good notes and trying to memorize facts should be all it takes to get a good grade in introductory biology.	1	2	3	4	5
12. Chris will be able to understand the complex processes involved in biology if he memorizes definitions.	1	2	3	4	5
13. If Chris tried to understand every theory it would take him too much time to read a chapter.	1	2	3	4	5

		Strongly disagree				Strongly agree

14. Like Chris, I believe that no matter how much time and effort is put into it, some people will never be able to learn biology.
    1 2 3 4 5

15. I believe that if I am going to understand my biology text, it will make sense the first time I read it—rereading will not help me understand any better.
    1 2 3 4 5

To find how the five components of personal beliefs that influence learning apply to you, add your scores to the following questions together.

Component 1: Certain Knowledge   1 _____ + 3 _____ + 8 _____ = _____

Component 2: Simple Knowledge   7 _____ + 11 _____ + 12 _____ = _____

Component 3: Responsibility for Learning   2 _____ + 4 _____ + 6 _____ = _____

Component 4: Speed of Learning   10 _____ + 13 _____ + 15 _____ = _____

Component 5: Ability   5 _____ + 9 _____ + 14 _____ = _____

Source: Adapted from Holschuh, J. L. 1998. *Epistemological beliefs in introductory biology: Addressing measurement concerns and exploring the relationship with strategy use.* Unpublished doctoral dissertation, University of Georgia, Athens.

Assessing Your Personal Theory

Your score on each component can range from 3 to 15. Look at where your scores fall on each component. The way the scale is structured, the higher your score on a component, the more strongly you hold a belief that may get in the way of your academic success. The lower your score on a component, the more strongly you hold a belief that research has shown leads to aca-

Studying Smarter
Take responsibility for your own learning by finding out about your beliefs about knowledge.

demic success. Because no one is completely consistent in his or her beliefs, chances are you hold a strong belief on some components (as indicated by either high or low scores) but are more in the middle on other components.

The Five Components of Beliefs That Influence Learning

Many different kinds of beliefs affect your life every day. People have different religious beliefs, moral beliefs, political beliefs, and so on. You may have thought a lot about those kinds of beliefs, but have you ever thought about your beliefs about learning? Have you ever considered how you gain knowledge or what knowledge is? If you are like most students, you probably haven't thought much about where knowledge comes from, but your beliefs about knowledge do impact what and how you learn.

As you read this chapter, consider your own beliefs about learning. Where do your beliefs fall? How might these beliefs affect your learning in college courses? Remember that to get off on the right foot in college you may need to reevaluate your beliefs and the role they play in your academic success.

Component 1: Certainty of Knowledge

Some students believe that knowledge is continually changing based on current information. When they are in class, they think about what they already know about the topic and may change their beliefs about a topic by adding new information to what they already know. For example, a student might enter a physics class believing that when a bullet is shot from a gun, it falls to the ground faster than a bullet that is simply dropped. However, she might change her beliefs based on new information after learning about the laws of gravity.

Other students believe that there are absolute answers and there is a definite right or wrong solution to every problem. These students approach learning by trying to find the truth in all situations. In the same physics class, another student may have trouble understanding that scientists believe that physics is based on theories, not truth, and that these theories are in a constant state of change based on new research.

Additionally, although experts are continually reassessing what they know, students are often encouraged only to look for the facts in their textbooks. They may approach reading history by focusing strictly on names, dates, and places because that was what was important in their previous experience. But most college courses require you to do more than learn facts. Professors tend to view their disciplines as continually changing over time; to memorize only "facts" would be a waste of time. Instead, most professors not only want you to be able to understand what is currently known but also want to prepare you for future learning. Professors expect students to question what they read and be willing to live with the idea that there may not be a solution or definite answer to every problem or question.

Studying Smarter

What is important is to keep learning, to enjoy challenge, and to tolerate ambiguity. In the end there are no certain answers.

**—Martina Horner,
President of Radcliffe College**

Component 2: Simple Knowledge

Some students believe that knowledge is complex and consists of highly interconnected concepts, but other students believe that knowledge consists of a series of unrelated bits of information. Students who believe that knowledge is complex look for relationships between ideas as they learn. They try to see the big picture and the relationships among the small pieces of information within that big picture.

On the other hand, students who have a strong belief that knowledge is simple tend to break information down into very small isolated parts and never put it back together again. Although breaking information into smaller chunks is a great strategy for some tasks, for example, when learning something you must memorize such as the periodic table of the elements, a student who learns *only* isolated pieces of information will miss the big ideas. If a student in history class only memorizes dates and names, she will be unprepared for an essay question that asks her to compare and contrast ideas about the larger concepts. Likewise, a student who memorizes bold-faced terms in biology will not be able to explain more complex science processes. Because most of the assignments you will experience require you to apply what you have learned, you need to go beyond memorizing small bits of information and begin to see how the information is connected.

Component 3: Responsibility for Learning

Beliefs about knowledge also depend on your perception about who is responsible for your learning in college. Some students believe that it is the professor's responsibility to ensure that all students learn the information. Other students believe that although the professor guides their learning, they are ultimately responsible for their own learning.

GET GOING

Taking Responsibility for Learning

The ability to take responsibility for your own learning is a helpful skill to learn in college and use beyond college. When you enter the workforce you will be expected to draw on your ability to direct your own learning (look at the number of help-wanted ads looking for a "self-starter"), which includes making decisions and creating new solutions. So the next time you find yourself putting the responsibility on others ("I can only learn when I have a good professor," "I didn't do well on the test because my roommate made too much noise for me to study"), think about ways to take responsibility for the situation.

In high school, your teachers probably took a lot of the responsibility for your learning in class. You most likely had little choice in the subjects you studied, what you learned, or the way you were assessed (e.g., tests, papers, labs, etc.). In fact, the teachers may have even gone over all of the relevant information in class, which left you little to learn on your own. However, you may have already noticed that college professors have different assumptions about who is responsible for learning.

Professors expect students to take responsibility for a good deal of their own learning. They expect students to be able to figure out information on their own, and they also may expect students to be able to pull together information from a variety of sources.

Component 4: Speed of Learning

Some students believe that learning is a gradual and ongoing process, but other students believe that if learning is going to happen, it happens quickly or not at all. In other words, some people believe that most things worth knowing take a long time to learn, but other people think that if they don't get it right away, they never will.

Students who believe that learning takes time are better prepared for college tasks, while students who believe that learning should happen quickly are often frustrated in college when they are faced with complex information. Many college students believe that learning should happen quickly because of their experiences in high school (and elementary and middle school, too). In fact, research has shown that in high school mathematics classes, most problems that students answered could be solved in less than two minutes. It's no wonder that many students are unprepared for more difficult tasks in college and why some students get frustrated or just give up when faced with challenging problems.

TIMELY TIPS

Time on Task

Most students hold beliefs about how long it should take to complete a task. For example, the student who has encountered only math problems that can be solved in two minutes will likely believe that all mathematics problems can be solved that quickly. Students have similar beliefs about how long it should take to read a textbook chapter, write a paper, or study for an exam. The next time you find yourself unmotivated or frustrated in your classes, think about your own beliefs about the speed of learning. Are your expectations holding you back from giving the task the time it requires?

Component 5: The Role of Ability

Some students believe that people can learn how to learn, but others believe that the ability to learn is fixed and that they are naturally good at some things but will never be able to do other things. For example, a student may say, "I am good at math and science, but not history or English."

Students who believe that the ability to learn is fixed tend to talk to themselves in a negative way. A student may say, "I will never be able to do this," or "I am too dumb to learn this," when in fact he may be just giving up too easily.

On the other hand, students who believe that people can learn how to learn tend to view difficult tasks as challenges they can meet. Instead of giving up, these students will try different strategies for learning and will ask for help from the professor or their friends if they need it.

There are probably people in your classes who make learning look easy, but students who appear to learn "naturally" most likely spend time and effort in activities, such as reading and reflecting, that promote academic success.

Based on what you have read about beliefs, you probably have figured out that students who believe that knowledge is changeable, that knowledge consists of interrelated concepts, that learning is under the control of the student, and that learning may take time and effort will probably have more success in college than students who hold the opposite beliefs.

SUCCESS AT A GLANCE

The Five Components of Beliefs

Component 1:	Certainty of Knowledge	Can range from the belief that knowledge is fact to the belief that knowledge is continually changing.
Component 2:	Simple Knowledge	Can range from the belief that knowledge is made up of isolated bits of information to the belief that knowledge is complex.
Component 3:	Responsibility for Learning	Can range from the belief that it is the professor's responsibility to ensure that students learn to the belief that it is the individual's responsibility to learn information.
Component 4:	Speed of Learning	Can range from the belief that learning happens fast or not at all to the belief that learning is a gradual process that takes time.
Component 5:	Ability	Can range from the belief that the ability to learn is fixed to the belief that people can learn how to learn.

Source: Schommer, M. 1990. Effects of beliefs about the nature of knowledge on comprehension. *Journal of Educational Psychology*, 82, 498–504.

NETWORKING

Deciding What to Believe

You may have noticed that some of the information you find on the Internet seems to contradict other information. Your personal theory of beliefs will influence how you decide which information to believe. Find three sites that give you different perspectives about the same topic. For example, you might look at three reviews of the same movie or three political essays about an issue from a Democratic, Republican, and Independent perspective. Think about how you will decide which one to believe. How do your beliefs about knowledge affect your decision?

Changing Your Beliefs

After evaluating the components of personal beliefs using the scale at the beginning of this chapter, you may have found that you have some beliefs that need to be altered because they may negatively affect your success in college. This section will present some strategies for promoting change.

Your beliefs about learning influence the strategies you use to study, which is part of the reason why beliefs are related to college performance. For example, if you believe that knowledge is simple, then you will select a strategy that reflects your belief, such as making flash cards to memorize definitions of key terms even when your professor expects you to integrate ideas. Thus, when you have all of the terms memorized, you will feel prepared for the exam. If you do not pass the exam, you may not understand what you did wrong because according to your beliefs about learning, you were adequately prepared. The question, then, is this: If you currently hold beliefs that may make academic success more difficult, how do you go about changing those beliefs?

■ **Be Aware of Your Beliefs.** If you have beliefs that are getting in the way of your learning, consider changing them. However, before you can change a belief, you must first be unsatisfied with your current beliefs about learning. For example, when you find yourself giving up on an assignment too quickly or trying to merely memorize when the task requires you to understand and apply difficult concepts, you can reflect on your beliefs, rethink your approach, and take the time to really learn the information.

■ **Look for the Big Picture.** Instead of just memorizing a lot of separate facts, make a conscious effort to relate ideas to what you already know and to other ideas discussed in class. Many of the strategies in *College Success Strategies* can help you to integrate and synthesize ideas as you read.

■ **Learn to Live with Uncertainty.** It is sometimes difficult to accept that there are no right answers to some questions. For example, in a statistics class, you may want to know the "right" way to solve a problem, and although there are some ways that are better than others, chances are that if you ask three statisticians how to solve the problem you will get three different answers.

■ **Don't Compare Your Ability with That of Others.** Worrying that you are not as good as your roommate in math will not get you anywhere. Focus instead on how to improve your ability to learn in the subjects that you find difficult. You can find a tutor to work with or form a study group to help you learn. It may take you longer to get there, but remember that college learning is more like an endurance sport than a sprint.

■ **Realize That Learning Takes Time.** If you begin your assignments with the expectation that they will take time to fully understand and complete, you are likely to experience less frustration and more understanding. Don't expect to learn complex concepts the first time you encounter them. Instead, plan to spread out your study time so you can review difficult material several times.

Now that you know about how beliefs affect your learning, you can begin to examine your own beliefs in the many learning situations you encounter. Your beliefs about learning will change because of your college experiences, and being aware of your own beliefs can help you learn more effectively.

ON YOUR OWN

Reflecting on What You Have Read

Think about your own beliefs and then write down the answers to these questions. What have you observed about your beliefs that may make learning easier for you? What have you observed that may make learning more difficult for you? Evaluate where you are on each of the components of beliefs: Certainty of Knowledge, Simple Knowledge, Responsibility of Learning, Speed of Learning, and Ability. Then note how your beliefs are influencing how you approach and carry out the tasks in your courses. Are your beliefs leading you toward academic success? Why or why not? Share your written responses with your classmates.

Evaluating Internet Information

One real-world example of how your beliefs about knowledge impact your everyday life is in how you perceive information you obtain online.

You can find it all on the Internet, from world-class thinking to pure garbage to blatant lies. Anyone can put up a Web page that looks good. But a well-designed site doesn't mean that the content is good. How can you decide what to believe? There are several ways to evaluate the credibility and quality of the information you find online. Consider the following criteria each time you surf the Web:

- **Source.** Who is the author of this information? Is the source a noted expert in the field, a high school student doing a report for school, a fan, a business, or an organization? Your answer to this question will tell you a lot about the quality of the information. In general, it is best to trust the information from the authority in the field over a fan or hobbyist.

- **Purpose.** What is the reason for this site to exist? Is it trying to educate and inform, or is it trying to market a product? Although commercial Web sites can sound very persuasive, if they are trying to sell you something, you need to consider this when evaluating the information you find.

- **Corroboration.** How does this information compare with other Web sites? Usually there is a good deal of overlap, but if you find a site that is claiming ideas that no one else is discussing, that should send up a red flag for credibility. Try to check out a few sources to help you determine corroboration.

- **Accuracy.** Is the information you find correct? Several of the criteria on this list should help you determine the truthfulness of the information you are finding. For example, if you are doing a paper on different alternatives to help people lose weight and a Web site claims you can lose 25 pounds in a month using their method, you should probably be leery. If the information sounds too good to be true then it probably is false.

- **Timeliness.** How current is the information? Because the Web is an ever-changing source of information, in general, the more current the source, the better. Most Web pages tell you the last time the site was updated. If no one has updated it in a long time, you might want to visit a more current site.

- **Bias.** Does the information seem to present a particular point of view, or is it trying to present an unbiased view? Most sites will contain some sort of bias. Your job is to use the other criteria on this list to figure out what it is.

Real College

Patrick and Friends

DIRECTIONS: Read the following "Real College" scenario about the beliefs of four college students. Respond to the questions based on what you learned in this chapter about beliefs about knowledge.

Patrick is taking history mostly because it is required. In this history class, he finds that the professor often asks exam questions about topics that were not covered in class. Patrick doesn't think that is fair because he doesn't know how he is supposed to figure out what to study if the professor doesn't tell him what is important.

Alysha believes that she will be successful in biology because she has always done well in science classes. She believes a scientist, if he or she tries hard enough, can find the answers to almost anything. One problem she has is that her professor tries to tell the class about too many science theories, which Alysha finds confusing.

David was a good English student in high school. He was always able to quickly understand concepts and didn't need to spend a lot of time on homework. When he started his literature class, the readings were familiar and he didn't really spend much time outside of class reading or studying. However, he found that he did not do well on the first essay exam and that the new concepts were confusing. He still believes that he should be able to learn the information quickly and is unsure why he is having so much trouble.

Li believes that she is the type of person who can't do math. She sees that some students just seem to get it because they are naturally good at learning calculus. She wishes that the college would understand that some people just can't learn math and that it shouldn't be a requirement for all students.

Answer the following questions and then discuss your responses with a partner or small group.

1. How are these students' beliefs similar to yours? How do they differ?

2. How do you think these beliefs will affect the students' performance in their classes?

3. What advice would you give these students?

Add to Your Portfolio

1. Reflect on your self-assessment scores from pages 73–75. Is this an accurate reflection of you? Why or why not? Which components of beliefs do you think are negatively impacting your academic career? Brainstorm and write down three changes you can make to these components during this semester.

2. At the end of this semester, retake the self-assessment (found on pages 73–75). How have your beliefs changed in the past year? What experiences have helped you make the changes you have had?

3. At the end of the semester, reflect on the three changes you sought to make. How successful have your efforts been? What do you think you still need to work on in the future?

CHAPTER

Dealing with Stress

READ THIS CHAPTER TO ANSWER THE FOLLOWING QUESTIONS:

- What are common sources of stress?
- What is academic stress?
- How do you control or reduce stress?

--------------------- **SELF-ASSESSMENT** ---------------------

DIRECTIONS: Take the following assessment of stressful situations to determine your current stress level. Check the events you have experienced in the past six months or are likely to experience in the next six months. This assessment will help you determine whether you are currently experiencing an unhealthy amount of stress. Remember, some stress is necessary and even productive for everyday life, but if you are experiencing an overwhelming amount of stress, look for ways to reduce it and seek help if necessary.

Student Stress Scale*

1. Death of a family member	_____	100
2. Death of a friend	_____	73
3. Divorce between parents	_____	65
4. Jail term	_____	63
5. Major injury or illness	_____	63
6. Marriage	_____	58
7. Fired from job	_____	50
8. Failed important course	_____	47
9. Change in health of a family member	_____	45
10. Pregnancy	_____	45
11. Sex problems	_____	44
12. Serious argument with a close friend	_____	40
13. Change in financial status	_____	39

14. Change of major	_____	39
15. Trouble with parents	_____	39
16. New girlfriend or boyfriend	_____	38
17. Increased workload	_____	37
18. Outstanding personal achievement	_____	36
19. First quarter/semester in college	_____	35
20. Change in living conditions	_____	31
21. Argument with instructor	_____	30
22. Lower grades than expected	_____	29
23. Change in sleeping habits	_____	29
24. Change in social activities	_____	29
25. Change in eating habits	_____	28
26. Chronic car trouble	_____	26
27. Change in number of family get-togethers	_____	26
28. Too many missed classes	_____	25
29. Change of college	_____	24
30. Dropped more than one class	_____	23
31. Minor traffic violations	_____	20
TOTAL	_____	

SCORING: A score of 300 or higher indicates an extremely high stress life; a score of 200–299 indicates a high stress life; a score of 100–199 indicates a moderate stress life; and a score below 100 indicates a low stress life. If you find that you are having a very high stress life, you might want to seek help from a counselor, friend, or family member.

*The Stress Scale was adapted from: DeMeuse, K. 1985. The relationship between life events and indices of classroom performance. *Teaching of Psychology*, 12, 146–149.

Holmes, T. H., & Rahe, R. H. 1967. The social readjustment rating scale. *Journal of Psychosomatic Research*, 11, 213–218.

Insel, P., & Roth, W. 1985. *Core Concepts in Health*. Palo Alto, CA: Mayfield Publishing.

Sources of Stress

Believe us when we say that as a college student you will experience many different types of stress including social pressures, financial burdens, and academic competition. In fact, stress levels in college tend to ebb and flow—you might feel more stress at the beginning of a term when everything is new, less stress in the middle of the term (until midterms, of course), and more stress again at the end of the term when you have to take final exams. Usually we think of stress as something to be avoided, but actually it shouldn't always be avoided. Stress is a normal part of life, and at least some of the stress you experience in college is helpful and stimulating. Without stress we would lead a rather boring existence. The problem comes when you have an extremely high stress life.

Studying Smarter

Keep your stress levels under control by creating a plan to cope with stressful issues.

Generally, college stress can be broken down into six categories: prior academic record, social influences, family, finances, career direction, and situational problems (such as illness or drug problems). Most students think that stress is caused by outside factors. They might say that a test, a professor, or a paper is "stressing them out." But stress is largely an internal process. Therefore, it's important to recognize the things that are causing your own stress in order to put your reactions to it in perspective. As you read about the six categories of stress, remember that stress is natural, it is internal, it is often an overreaction to a specific situation, and *it can be controlled.*

1. **Prior Academic Record.** Interestingly, both good and poor academic records can cause students to feel stress. Students who have a shaky academic past may believe that they can't succeed in college. On the other hand, students who have a 4.0 average may feel stress to sustain their stellar grade point average. Either way, your past history as a learner affects your stress level.

2. **Social Influences.** You probably have realized that dealing with your friends can often be stressful. A fight with your roommate, feeling lonely, missing your old friends, breaking up with a boyfriend or girlfriend, meeting new people—all of these situations—can be stressful. In fact, even situations we would consider to be positive social factors, such as falling in love or socializing with really good friends, can cause a stressful reaction. Having too good of a social life can cause stress because you may worry about the academic work that is not getting done. Overall, however, having good friends and social support will actually reduce your stress levels because you have someone to confide in.

3. **Family.** You may feel pressure to do well in college in order to make your family proud, you may feel stress because you have moved away from your family, or you may feel stress because of family crises that arise. Returning students may feel stress because college is taking away time that they spend with their family. But, like social influences, your family can also be a source of support to help you when you experience a lot of stress. Let family members know what they can do to help you in these situations.

4. **Finances.** Financial stress usually begins in college because students may take out loans to attend college, get jobs to help pay for college, or have to maintain a certain grade point average to keep their scholarships. Many college students are also responsible for paying bills and are gaining responsibility for their own financial security. In addition, college students get their own credit cards, which can lead to great financial stress if used excessively. We know many college students who graduate not only with a diploma but also with student loans and a stack of credit card debt. All of these things can cause stress, especially for students who are handling their own finances for the first time.

5. **Career Direction.** "So what's your major?" "What the heck are you going to do with a degree in that?" You may have gotten similar questions from friends and relatives. Everyone, perhaps yourself included, wants to know what you will do with your life after college. The less sure you are about your career direction, the more stress you might feel about it. You may even be concerned that you'll never find your direction. On the other hand, students who have already decided on a career might also feel stress because they are concerned about achieving their goals.

6. **Situational Problems.** Certain stresses are unexpected and sometimes devastating. You may become ill during the term, experience the death of someone close to you, realize you have a drug or alcohol problem, or cope with an eating disorder. As with all of the categories of stress, if you feel overwhelmed by situational problems, seek help from a counselor on campus or someone you can talk to about these concerns.

Strategies for Reducing Stress

Now that you know what stress is and what causes stress for most students, you will be happy to know that there are many ways to control or even reduce your stress levels. But it is important to take some sort of action before you start to feel overwhelmed. Consider the following strategies for reducing your stress.

■ **Relax.** You should make relaxation a regular part of your day. If you don't know how to go about relaxing, there are numerous paperback self-help books available that offer great techniques and advice. At the very least, try deep breathing or meditation for a few minutes each day to help yourself unwind. If you find yourself "stressing out," stop whatever you are doing, close your eyes, and focus on your breathing for a few minutes. This should help you relax so that you can return to what you were doing, feeling more in control of the situation.

■ **Exercise.** Working out daily is a great stress buster. Physical activity helps take your mind off of your stress, and the chemicals your body releases during exercise actually boost your ability to handle stressful situations. If you are feeling especially stressed, try taking a walk or a jog to clear your head.

■ **Take Charge.** You are in control of your own situation and you have to accept that responsibility. You can control the amount of stress you feel by remembering that stress is an internal reaction to situations, and it is often really an overreaction. However, if stress gets out of control, you can also take charge of the situation by seeking help.

■ **Put Problems in Perspective.** Sometimes it helps to talk to a good friend or a family member who has been in a similar situation. He or she might be able to help put your problems in a more realistic light. Don't get carried away imagining all the things that could go wrong in a situation; focus instead on the positives. Think about how this particular situation will affect you five years from now. Will it affect your life, or will it really not matter much? Sometimes it helps to simply be in the moment.

■ **Be Flexible.** Everyone makes mistakes, and learning from your mistakes will help reduce your stress levels. But if you are too set in the way you do things or the way you view the world, you may end up causing yourself additional stress. It pays to have an open mind and to try new approaches.

■ **Develop Interests.** Join a club on campus, meet with others who share similar interests, or find some new interests on your own. By experiencing life outside of schoolwork, you will be able to enjoy yourself and relax during your time off from studying. Developing new interests also helps you in the classroom because you tend to do better in subjects that interest you.

■ **Seek Help.** Seek out campus resources to help you through stressful times. In fact, it is a good idea to seek out the people and places that can support you *before* you need them. Often, problems can be solved easily if you ask for assistance before a small problem balloons into a major one.

■ **Enjoy Yourself.** Take a walk, read a good book, see a movie, call a friend. Do something you like to do before you start feeling overwhelmed. Remember, if you manage your life well, you should have plenty of time for studying and engaging in activities for fun.

SUCCESS AT A GLANCE

Strategies for Reducing Stress

Relax

Exercise

Take charge

Put problems in perspective

Be flexible

Develop interests

Seek help

Enjoy yourself

Academic Stress: Anxieties

The stress students feel about college, or what we refer to as academic stress, is due to many different factors and is a part of the general stress you feel every day. You want to do well in your classes, you want to gain valuable experience, and you want to be a success in life. However, there are four common types of academic stress or anxieties that can actually get in the way of these goals: public speaking anxiety, writing anxiety, math anxiety, and test anxiety. If you have experienced one of these stresses, you know how harmful it can be. In this section we discuss the four types of academic stress and strategies for coping with each.

GET GOING

Monitoring Your Stress Level

Many students find that experiencing academic stress impacts motivation for learning. Academic stress leads some students to overcome procrastination and get their work done. Academic stress leads other students to feel paralyzed, and they become unable to concentrate or work well at all. We believe that you should take the time to monitor both your motivation and stress levels for a few days. Does it seem like stress helps or hinders? Which academic tasks seem to cause the most stress for you? By identifying your own reaction to stress, you will be better able to create ways to cope with your academic stress.

Public Speaking Anxiety

Public speaking causes people to react in strange ways. They may find that their hands get sweaty, their mouths are dry, or they forget what they were going to say. In fact, research has found that some people fear public speaking more than death. In college, there will be many times when you are required to speak in public, whether it is making a comment in a large lecture class or giving a presentation or speech to a class.

Coping with Public Speaking Anxiety

The best way to cope with a fear of public speaking is to be prepared. Practice your presentation out loud several times before presenting it to your class. Practice in front of a mirror, or better yet, recruit some friends to listen to your speech. Have them record your time to be sure that you are on track, and ask them to critique your speaking style using the following questions:

■ **Are You Speaking Too Fast?** Sometimes when people are nervous they talk very fast, which makes it difficult for the audience to follow. Don't rush through your talk. Instead, try to use a conversational tone.

■ **Are You Using Good Inflection?** When people are nervous they sometimes speak in a monotone, which is difficult to listen to for an extended period of time. Try to speak confidently and with enthusiasm.

■ **Are You Jittery?** You may find yourself moving from side to side or wringing your hands when you are nervous. It is good to move a little, such as using hand gestures or walking around to include the audience, but too much nervous movement can be distracting to your audience.

■ **Are You Making Eye Contact?** When you are giving your presentation it may help to focus on one or two friendly faces in the room and "present" to them. You should be sure to make eye contact with the other people in the room, of course, but concentrate mostly on those two people. This strategy should help calm your fear of speaking in front of a large group.

■ **Have You Jotted Down Some Notes?** Having some notes to follow during your presentation makes you feel more secure and confident. Even if you have rehearsed your talk and have a good idea of what you will cover, you should have notes to glance at just in case you need a reminder of what you are going to say.

Writing Anxiety

Many students experience a great deal of stress when asked to write something for a class, especially if they are asked to write during class with the added pressure of time limitations. Students might be anxious about having to think up a good idea, flesh the idea out, and then have their writing evaluated by their instructor. They sit staring at a blank page waiting for the words to come. This is sometimes called writer's block, and it is a very frustrating experience. Just about every writer, the authors of this book included, has had an experience when finding the words to write has been difficult. However, writing anxiety becomes harmful when students experience writer's block almost every time they try to write. When students are anxious about writing, they try to avoid it as much as possible because they find it to be such a stressful activity. The problem is that in college (and in most careers after college) you are often asked to express your ideas in writing.

Coping with Writing Anxiety

We offer the following suggestions for dealing with writing anxiety.

■ **Write Often.** Like any skill, your ability to write will improve with practice. You may want to keep a daily journal in which you record you experiences. Or you might want to do some "free writing" by giving yourself a fixed amount of time (perhaps five to ten minutes) to write about whatever you want. Another alternative is to sit on a bus or in a coffee shop and write some character sketches about the people you see.

- **Work from a Plan.** It's helpful to make a list of the points you want to make and then use your list to guide you when you are writing your paper. If you are having trouble organizing the points you want to make, talk to a classmate or a tutor about your ideas. Most campuses have a writing center or a place where students can talk to a tutor about their papers at any stage—from choosing a topic, to reading rough drafts, to critiquing final drafts.

- **For Essay Tests, Predict Questions.** This idea will be covered in greater detail in Chapter 17, but in brief, use your class notes and topics emphasized in the text to predict the kinds of questions that might be asked. You might want to look at your professor's old exams to help you predict possible essay questions.

- **Start Early.** Because students who experience writing anxiety try to avoid writing, they often procrastinate. These students sometimes believe that they can write only under pressure, but they are fooling themselves because they are actually making their stress level greater by waiting until the last minute. If they do not make a good grade on the paper, they tend to blame it on the fact that they have trouble writing instead of on the fact that they churned it out quickly.

Mathematics Anxiety

As with writing, some students feel stress when they encounter anything that has to do with numbers. Students who experience math anxiety usually try to avoid taking math or math-related courses. For most students, math anxiety usually results from previous experiences in math classes. You may have had some trouble with a particular topic, such as word problems in algebra, and have told yourself, "I can't do math" ever since. For some reason, math anxiety seems to be the most traumatic and widespread of the academic anxieties. However, just like any other type of stress, math anxiety is an overreaction to a situation and, therefore, you can change your response to mathematics.

Coping with Mathematics Anxiety

The following suggestions can help you deal with mathematics anxiety.

- **Face It Head-On.** Don't wait until your senior year to take your math courses. Take them early, and overcome your fears. In fact, if you wait until later in your college career, you might find that you have forgotten much of what you learned in high school math classes.

- **Take a Class That Is at Your Level.** Don't try to get into calculus if you have never had a precalculus course. If your college recommends a particular course based on exam scores or placement tests, take that course instead of one that is a higher level.

■ **Read the Textbook and Do the Practice Problems Each Day.** Going to class is not enough. You must be able to apply what you have learned to new situations. Additionally, the more times you work with the material, the better you will remember it.

■ **Talk the Problems Through.** One of the best strategies for learning math is to solve problems with words. That is, explain in words how to solve the problem rather than just trying to plug in numbers.

■ **Get Help Early On.** If you find that you are having trouble learning math concepts, seek help as soon as you need it. Get help from a classmate or the instructor, and plan to work with a tutor weekly if necessary. In math classes, the information you are learning usually builds on itself, so if you don't understand what you learned in Chapter 2, you will have even more trouble learning the material in Chapter 6.

■ **Use Positive Talk.** Don't say "I can't" or "I'll never" to yourself. These thoughts can be self-defeating. Instead, try to focus on the positives. Reward yourself for figuring out a tough problem, and keep trying to do your best.

TIMELY TIPS

Learning Life Skills

Are you wondering why you have to take courses that are not really related to your major? Think about what you really need to learn in college. We believe that the time spent learning in college is more than just mastering academic content. In fact, most employers are looking for people who can speak well, write well, think critically, and problem solve effectively. Work on honing these skills while you are in college—even in those classes you may dislike.

General Test Anxiety

Test anxiety is similar to writing and math anxiety, except it is a feeling of stress when studying for or taking an exam, regardless of the subject. You might worry about the types of questions that will be on the test, forgetting about and missing the test, or studying the wrong material. Students who experience test anxiety are often paralyzed with fear when faced with a test situation, and they can end up missing questions they know.

Many different experiences can lead to test anxiety. It might be caused by past test-taking experiences, such as blanking on answers or failing an exam. It could be caused by inadequate test preparation. If you know that you are not prepared to take an exam, it's natural to be anxious about it. Test anxiety can also be caused by competition with your friends or classmates. If you are focusing on how others are doing, you might cause yourself undue stress. In addition, test anxiety can be caused by a lack of confidence in yourself as a learner. When students believe that they are not good learners, they tend to become more anxious about testing situations. If you find that you are talking negatively to yourself about your ability to learn, you may actually be causing yourself greater anxiety.

Coping with Test Anxiety

To cope with general test anxiety, try the following suggestions:

■ **Be Prepared.** If you monitor your learning to the point where you know which concepts you understand and which concepts are giving you problems, you will feel more confident. Allow enough time for studying so that you are sure you have prepared the best you can. In addition, gather all of the things you need for the test. Do you need a pencil, calculator, student ID, notes, or anything else? Have everything ready to go the night before.

■ **Understand the Task.** Talk to the professor about what the exams will be like. Even better, try to look at some of the professor's old exams if they are available. Examining retired tests will give you an idea of what kinds of questions the professor asks and will also help you become familiar with the professor's questioning style. It is also a good idea to talk to the professor or to students who have taken the class about the content and format of the exams.

■ **Arrive to Take the Test a Bit Early.** Get organized and practice some deep breathing techniques to relax. Take a few deep breaths and think of something you find comforting—the sound of the ocean, a walk in the woods. Concentrate on and relax each of your muscle groups.

■ **Have an Approach in Mind.** If you find you blank out on exams, try to make jot lists as soon as you get the test. Read each question and just jot down everything you know about it in the margin of the test. Don't look at any answers if it is a multiple-choice test; just write everything you know before you blank out.

■ **Focus on You.** Ignore other students who finish the exam before you. Just because they finish earlier does not mean that they know more than you do. It might be that they are done so soon because they *don't* know the answers. But either way, don't worry about what other students are doing.

■ **Get Help in Controlling Your Anxiety.** There are usually several resource areas on campus that can help you. You might need some tutoring on course content, you might benefit from some counseling to deal with your anxiety, or you might be eligible for alternate testing situations, such as increased time for tests.

■ **Visualize Your Success.** Think about how well you will do before you walk into the classroom, and remind yourself that you are well prepared and ready to go as the test is being handed out. The more positive you can be, the less anxiety you'll feel.

ON YOUR OWN

Reflecting on What You Have Read

Think about your own academic tasks (e.g., writing essays, giving speeches, solving mathematics problems, taking multiple-choice tests). Write your responses to the following questions: What kinds of academic tasks cause you to feel the most stress? Why do you think you experience anxiety when faced with those tasks? What can you do to reduce your anxiety in those situations? How can you tell the difference between being really stressed out and having normal, productive stress?

NETWORKING

Plagiarism Taboos

With more and more students gaining access to Internet information, campuses have seen an increase in student plagiarism. We believe that this is partially due to the fact that many students do not have a complete understanding of what plagiarism is. So let's lay it out for you, because being accused of cheating when you did not know it was wrong is extremely stress inducing. Plagiarism is taking someone else's ideas and representing them as your own. This includes a theory or idea, a direct quote, a paraphrase of an idea, or pieces of information that are not common knowledge. To avoid plagiarism, be sure to give credit to the author whenever you use someone else's ideas in your own work.

Of course, plagiarism also includes direct cheating, such as buying a paper online, turning in another person's work as your own, or copying directly out of a text without quoting the author. It is easy to avoid this type of plagiarism: Just don't do it. When you find information on the Internet or from any other source, be sure to report where that information came from.

Three Important Tips for Reducing Academic Stress

In addition to the ways to cope with math, writing, and test anxiety, here are three tips for coping with the general academic pressures that you experience every day.

1. **Don't Procrastinate.** This sounds simple enough, but probably most of the academic stress students experience comes from waiting until the last minute to get their assignments done. As we discussed in Chapter 5, you are

Studying Smarter

An "A" is an "A." We know many students who worry needlessly when they receive anything less than the highest scores. In high school, there may have been a difference between a 99 and a 90, but unless your college uses a plus/minus grading system, both of those scores would be recorded as an "A."

much better off starting early and doing some work each night rather than waiting until right before it is due to begin working on it.

2. **Don't Listen to Other Students Right Before the Test.** Listening to your classmates discuss something you have not studied will just make you more nervous. Simply take your seat, gather your thoughts, take a few deep breaths, and wait for the test to begin. Many students who experience academic stress madly rush through their notes as they are waiting for the exams to be passed out, but this too can increase stress if you find a topic that you don't remember. It is much better to use the time before the exam to relax.

3. **Learn to Say No.** Many students experience academic stress because they have too much to do. Don't take on too many responsibilities beyond your classes. You might be offered some interesting opportunities, but if you wind up with too much to do, your grades and your health could suffer. Learn to say *no* to some things if you find you have too much to handle.

Real College

Andrea

DIRECTIONS: Read the following "Real College" scenario and respond to the questions based on what you learned in this chapter.

Andrea is a first-year college student. She is the first person in her family to attend college. She is trying hard to make her parents proud, but she is worried that she won't make it. Every day she wakes up with a pounding headache, and sometimes she even has trouble sleeping because she is so stressed out. Part of the problem is that she is very homesick for her family and her friends. She is also worried about her relationship with her boyfriend who still lives at home—six hours away. He gets upset if she doesn't come home every weekend, and it seems likely that they will break up soon. In addition, although Andrea is starting to meet new friends in college, they are not like her old friends from high school. She just doesn't have anyone she can really confide in yet.

Another problem is that Andrea was forced to register for a math class because it was the only course open, and she hates math. Every time she studies for an exam, she gets so nervous that her palms get sweaty and she can't really concentrate on what she is doing. She is sure that she will fail the course, but she doesn't know what to do about it because she believes that there is no way she will ever be able to learn math. She is thinking about dropping out of school because she's afraid that she is not smart enough.

Use what you have learned about coping with and reducing stress to help Andrea figure out what to do.

1. List three to five strategies Andrea should use to reduce her general stress about her social and family relationships.
2. How do you think these strategies will help Andrea's situation?
3. List three to five strategies Andrea should use to reduce her math anxiety.
4. How do you think these strategies will help Andrea's situation?

ADD TO YOUR PORTFOLIO

For three to five days this week, keep a stress diary where you record your reactions to stressful events.

- What stresses you out?
- How do you react to this stress?
- What can you do to keep your stress levels in check?

Try to use at least two of the strategies presented in this chapter to help you cope with these stressful situations.

Strategic Reading

READ THIS CHAPTER TO ANSWER THE FOLLOWING QUESTIONS:

- How can you create a positive learning environment?
- Why do you need to gear up during reading?
- What are some strategies for gearing up?
- What are the differences between active and passive reading?
- What are some strategies for concentrating on textbook reading?

SELF-ASSESSMENT

DIRECTIONS: Answer each of the following questions by indicating *yes* or *no*. This will give you an idea of how actively you read your textbooks.

	Yes	No
1. Do you read in an environment that is relatively free of distractions?	____	____
2. Do you set learning goals prior to reading?	____	____
3. Do you skim through your reading and pay attention to chapter headings and boldface terms before you read the chapter?	____	____
4. Do you write in your textbooks when you read?	____	____
5. Do you try to put important text information in your own words?	____	____
6. Do you think about the visual aids in the chapter?	____	____
7. Do you reflect on ideas during reading?	____	____
8. Do you understand most of what you have read?	____	____
9. Do you keep up with your reading?	____	____

If you answered *yes* to most of these questions, you are off to a good start. If you answered *no* to most of the questions, this chapter will help you get on track.

Gearing Up for Reading

As a college student, reading is something that you have to do every day. But are you getting what you need out of your textbook reading, or are you just spinning your wheels? Do you find that much of the time you spend reading is unproductive because you are not concentrating and therefore can't remember what you have read? Do you have a difficult time getting and staying motivated? Do you get lost if the reading assignment is long? If so, maybe the problem is that you have not geared up for reading.

Picture a track meet at a local college. The athletes pile out of a van just as the first race begins. They throw off their sweats and start running. Would that ever happen? Of course not. Just as an athlete would never run a race or even practice "cold," you should not expect to start reading or studying without warming up. Athletes warm up to get their muscles ready to perform. Students, on the other hand, need to warm up their brains so that they will be more efficient and productive and remember more of what they read.

Studying Smarter

Part of studying smarter is not only being an effective learner but also an efficient learner. Previewing helps with efficiency because it gets your mind "wired" for reading and helps you concentrate.

There are several activities you can engage in to gear up for reading. You should:

1. **Create a Good Learning Environment.** Think about the place where you currently read and study by asking yourself the following questions: Do you study in a setting that allows you to concentrate and study effectively? Are you constantly distracted by people, noise, or other diversions? Your learning environment can help you in a positive way when reading or studying, or, if you do not have a good setting, it can actually hinder your efforts. You need to create a place that is free from distractions and allows you to maximize your studying time, so consider these factors:

   ■ **Noise Level.** Some students say that they need complete quiet to study. Even hearing a clock ticking in the background is enough to distract them. Other students say that they study best in a crowded, noisy room because the noise actually helps them concentrate. Some study most successfully when they are in familiar surroundings such as their bedroom; for others, familiar surroundings do not make a difference. Some students like quiet music playing; others do not. The point is, you should know the level of noise that is optimal for your own studying. However, in general, the television seems to be more of a distraction than music or other background noise, so we suggest you leave the TV off when you are reading or studying. In fact, we believe that the fewer distractions the better. This means turning off your cell phone and saving Internet surfing or playing computer games as rewards when you have finished studying. If you are convinced you need noise in order to study, we suggest "white noise"—the hum of an air conditioner or the sound of an electric fan—noise that drowns out more distracting sounds.

■ **Your Special "Learning" Place.** Your ideal learning place is one where the only thing you do there is study. If you have a desk, set it up so that you have everything handy—pens and pencils, a tablet of paper, calculator, your books and notes, and anything else you need to study. If everything is right at hand, you won't have an excuse to get up and interrupt your studying. If you find that you cannot create an effective learning environment in your home because there are too many distractions, try to find a quiet place on campus to study, such as the library or the student union. You will also concentrate better when you read or study in a straight-backed chair, such as a desk or kitchen chair. Keep in mind that the absolute worst possible place to study is on your bed. Students who attempt to study on their bed usually wind up doing more napping than studying.

2. **Survey Your Textbooks.** After setting up your learning environment at the beginning of the term, the next step in gearing up is examining your textbooks for each course. Most textbooks are written and formatted in a way that is very reader friendly. Such textbooks have some or all of the following features:

- An introduction at the beginning of the book that outlines the book's features, organization, and format
- Tips for studying and learning the discipline
- Preview questions or an organizer at the beginning of each chapter to help readers focus on what they are about to learn
- Diagrams, pictures, and figures to give readers a better perspective of the topic
- **Bold-faced** or *italicized* words to emphasize key terms
- Summary or review questions at the end of each chapter
- Large margins so that readers have room to write notes as they read
- A CD-ROM or other supplementary materials

Knowing how your textbooks are formatted and familiarizing yourself with your texts will help you become a more efficient reader. Surveying your texts will help you:

■ **Familiarize Yourself with the Topics to Be Covered.** This way, you can activate what you already know. One of the keys to being an efficient and effective reader is to make links to new information using what you already know. Students who do this are able to concentrate their studying efforts in a more productive manner.

■ **Increase Your Interest in Reading the Chapters.** If you have an idea of what you are going to read, you may be more interested in the material and remember it better in the long term. You can think about tying information to current events and to personal situations.

NETWORKING

Building Background Knowledge

You can use the Internet to help you build your background knowledge of the content for your college courses. For one of your classes this semester, choose a topic that interests you and then visit several sites on the Web to find out more about it. Often, getting some additional information before you even begin to read the chapter will help you understand difficult material and can even help you become more motivated to learn in the class.

■ **Give Yourself Time to Gear Up for Reading Effectively.** Unless you have some information about the average chapter length, difficulty, and format of the text you are going to read, you will not be able to plan your time wisely. Taking a small amount of time to preview each chapter can save you a considerable amount of actual reading time.

3. **Preview Your Reading Assignments.** You have found a quiet place to study and you have all of your study tools at your fingertips. Now you're ready to gear up for the day's reading by previewing. Previewing the chapter doesn't take very long, but just as surveying your entire textbook helps you gear up for each course, previewing what you will read each day will help to activate your prior knowledge and build your interest in the specific topics. Previewing consists of the following general steps. We will discuss specifics about previewing in the humanities, social sciences, and hard sciences in later chapters.

■ **Read the Chapter Title.** The title tells you about the overall topic of the chapter and may clue you in to the author's intent. The title can also help you activate what you know about the topic so that you can begin to make links.

■ **Read the Headings and Subheadings.** The headings and subheadings will tell you about the specific focus in the chapter and may suggest the author's approach to the topic. For example, a subheading in your history text called "The Horrors of War" would introduce very different material than a subheading called "War: Benefits and Advances." The headings and subheadings also provide organization to the chapter to help you understand its flow.

■ **Read the Boldfaced or Italicized Terms.** These terms will clue you in to ideas that will be emphasized in the text and will point out new vocabulary or content-specific terms that will be discussed in the chapter. You can also begin to get a better understanding of which terms go with which headings and subheadings for more efficient studying and learning.

■ **Note the Typographical Aids.** Besides boldfaced or italicized words, many texts use graphs, charts, tables, or illustrations to emphasize key ideas. Read the captions that accompany these text aids as another way of determining what is important in the chapter.

■ **Read the Introduction.** If your textbook offers chapter introductions, it is a good idea to read this section when you preview the chapter. Introductions provide a global idea of what the topic is about and the scope of information that will be covered in the chapter.

■ **Read the Summary.** If your textbook contains chapter summaries, it is a good idea to read this section *before* you actually read the chapter. The summary section outlines the key information you should have learned when reading the chapter and focuses your attention to the most important concepts in the chapter.

■ **Read the End-of-Chapter Material.** This may include study questions, vocabulary lists, or application exercises. The end material will also provide cues about what the author deems as the most important information in the chapter. Look for overlap between the summary and the end-of-chapter material as a way of identifying what you should pay particular attention to when you read the chapter in its entirety.

Although this might sound like a lot to do before reading, previewing actually takes only a few minutes to accomplish because you are not getting bogged down in the details of the chapter. Your purpose in previewing is to get a general idea of the concepts that will be covered in the chapter—not to read and digest it totally. Previewing should serve as your warm-up to reading.

4. **Determine Your Reading Purpose.** It is always a good idea to read with a purpose in mind. When you are reading your textbooks for a class, your primary purpose is to learn the information contained in each chapter. However, this is a tall order. If you try to learn every idea contained in every

chapter, you probably will have a difficult time retaining it all. Therefore, as you preview a chapter, you should begin to think of some questions about the key topics. By asking questions, you are starting to think about the key ideas contained in the text, which will make your reading more effective. What you need to do is identify and learn the key ideas contained in each chapter. A good way to help you determine what's important is to use your class syllabus and lecture notes as a guide.

ON YOUR OWN

Reflecting on What You Have Read

Do a reading tolerance test. For each of your courses you probably have a set amount of time for which you can read without losing concentration. We call this your reading tolerance level. Your reading tolerance level will depend on the course, the textbook, your background knowledge, and your interest in the topic. To build your reading tolerance you must first know your starting point. Make a chart. Then when you read in each of your textbooks this week, time yourself. How long can you go before you lose your concentration? Write down your time for each text. Then, with each subsequent time you read, try to build your tolerance by adding two to five minutes to your total reading time. Even if you lose concentration you can generally get yourself back into it for just another few minutes. Aim to get your reading tolerance to 45 to 60 minutes for each class.

Staying Active During Reading

Have you ever finished reading a text chapter only to realize that you don't remember anything you just read? If so, chances are you were not reading actively. Because reading textbooks rarely tops any student's list of favorite activities, and also because reading textbooks is one of the most common college tasks, it is important to learn strategies that enable you to understand and remember what you read. If you finish "reading" ten pages of text and can't summarize what you have read, you have just wasted valuable time. So where do you begin?

Put Away Your Highlighters

When we ask students how they go about reading their textbooks, many students tell us that they try to pull out key ideas by highlighting or underlining during reading. Although this is a popular strategy, highlighting is actually a very passive activity because students do not always understand the ideas they are highlighting. Many students actually put off reading for understanding until after they have highlighted the text. In other words, they skim the text looking for important information, highlight entire sections that seem important, and plan to return to those sections later when they study for the exam. Or, they do the opposite, highlighting only key words that are already either in bold print or italics. Neither approach is very strategic, and both encourage passive reading.

When students highlight their textbooks, they are not being very selective; sometimes entire pages are highlighted in bright pink or yellow or blue. Students who highlight most everything have not been very discriminating about what to mark. They will have just as much information to cope with when they begin to study—and they will have to go fishing in a pink, yellow, or blue sea in order to find the key points.

On the other hand, some students highlight too little. If these students tried to rely on their highlighting for their test review, they would not have adequate information and would probably end up rereading entire chapters or just memorizing small bits and pieces of information. Our advice is to put away the highlighters because you will need to use strategies that promote more active involvement in reading and learning.

Make a Note of It

As we discussed earlier in the chapter, active readers gear up by previewing; then they are ready to focus on their reading. One way to be sure that you are concentrating on and understanding what you read is to annotate your text, which requires you to write in your books. We realize this might take a bit of adjusting to because most of you were not allowed to write in your textbooks in high school. But in college, you buy your own books. Be sure you get your money's worth and "write on."

What Is Annotation?

In a nutshell, annotation is summing up the important information in your text by briefly writing the key ideas in the margin. Unlike highlighting, which promotes passivity, annotation requires that you understand what you are reading. It requires you to actively make decisions about what is important because you are putting the ideas in your own words. As shown on the following page, an annotated piece of text includes key ideas as well as examples, definitions, and other important details about the concepts.

In order to annotate properly, you need to think about what you read before you write. If you find that your mind is wandering or that you are not concentrating, you have to get back on track. Because you stop reading after a paragraph or two to annotate what you have read, you will be able to reconnect with the reading.

Model Annotations of a Psychology Text

2 types of concepts
① artificial
② natural
def) artificial con.
• clearly defined by a set of rules
Ex) geometry △ = 180°
tomato = fruit
def) natural con.
• no clear set of rules; "fuzzy" but a more accurate reflection of world
• indistinct boundaries
Ex) art, crime, sport
• often based on prototypes (def) = best Ex of the concept
Ex) clothing = shirt or pant, ≠ coat of armor
def) probabilistic strategy = • method of def, fit into natural concept
• closer an object is to others in category, the more likely it is to be included

Artificial Concepts: Concepts that can be clearly defined by a set of rules or properties.

Natural Concepts: Concepts that are not based on a precise set of attributes or properties, do not have clear-cut boundaries, and are often defined by prototypes.

Prototypes: The best or clearest examples of various objects or stimuli in the physical world.

Concept Representation
2 theories
① represented by features or attributes

Artificial and Natural Concepts Is a tomato a fruit or a vegetable? Many people would answer, "a vegetable." Botanists, however, classify it as a fruit, because it contains seeds and its structure is definitely more like that of apples and pears than those of potatoes or spinach. This fact illustrates the important distinction between what psychologists term artificial (or logical) concepts and natural concepts. **Artificial concepts** can be clearly defined by a set of rules or properties. Thus, a tomato is a fruit because it possesses the properties established by botanists for this category. Similarly, as you learned in geometry, a figure can be considered to be a triangle only if it has three sides whose angles add to 180 degrees, and can be a square only if all four sides are of equal length and all four angles are 90 degrees. Such artificial concepts are very useful in many areas of mathematics and science.

In contrast, **natural concepts** have no fixed or readily specified set of defining features. They are fuzzy around the edges. Yet they more accurately reflect the state of the natural world, which rarely offers us the luxury of hard-and-fast, clearly defined concepts. For example, consider the following questions:

Is chess a sport?
Is a pickle a vegetable?
Is a psychologist a scientist?
Is someone who helps a terminally ill person commit suicide a murderer?

As you can readily see, these all relate to common concepts: sport, vegetable, science, crime. But what specific attributes are necessary for inclusion in each concept? If you find yourself puzzled, don't be surprised; the boundaries of natural concepts are somewhat indistinct.

Such natural concepts are often based on **prototypes**—the best or clearest examples (Rosch, 1975). Prototypes emerge from our experience with the external world, and new items that might potentially fit within the concept. For example, consider the following natural concepts: *clothing, art.* For clothing, most people think of items like shirts, pants, or shoes. They are far less likely to mention wet suits, mink coats, or coats of armor. Similarly, for art, most people think of paintings, drawings, and sculptures. Fewer think of artwork such as the light show at Disney World.

In determining whether a specific item fits within a natural concept, then, we seem to adopt a *probabilistic* strategy. The more similar an object or event is to others already in the category, especially to the prototype for the category, the more likely we are to include the new item within the concept. In everyday situations, therefore, concept membership is not an all-or-nothing decision; rather, it is graded, and items are recognized as fitting within a category to a greater or lesser degree (Medin & Ross, 1992).

Concepts: How They Are Represented That concepts exist is obvious. But how are they represented in consciousness? No firm answer to this question exists, but several possibilities have been suggested. First, concepts may be represented in terms of their features or attributes. As natural concepts are formed, the attributes associated with them may be stored in memory.

Why Annotate Your Text?

Annotating your text is an effective strategy for several reasons. Annotation helps you:

■ **Select Information.** By annotating your texts, you are selecting important information that you want to remember. Much of what is written in textbooks is filler, so your job is to whittle down the information to just the key information, details, and examples.

■ **Reduce Information.** You reduce the information you need to study into more manageable amounts.

■ **Organize Information.** Sometimes textbooks fail to do a good job of organizing information. Through annotation you can reorganize the material in a way that is meaningful for you, which makes it easier for you to remember what you have read and to prepare for exams.

■ **Identify Key Concepts.** Annotation also helps you differentiate between major concepts and supporting ideas. Although for most courses you will have to know something about both major concepts and supporting details, by determining what is really important you will know how to focus your studying. Annotation helps you study concepts rather than small bits of information.

■ **Monitor Your Learning.** Because you annotate in your own words, you can monitor your understanding of what you are reading. If you are unable to put the information in your own words, you are alerted to the fact that your comprehension is breaking down.

How Do You Annotate?

There are some basic guidelines to follow regardless of the type of text you are annotating. Although you might have to modify these guidelines slightly for special kinds of texts, they will work in a majority of instances.

■ **Read First, Then Annotate.** To help you decide what to annotate, read a section and then think about what would be important if you were going to teach the material to someone else. When students try to read and annotate at the same time, they end up writing either too much or too little. We generally suggest that if your text does not have clearly defined sections, read at least two or three paragraphs before stopping to annotate. Another alternative is to keep reading until the text seems to move to a new topic. When you first begin to annotate, it's okay to read just one paragraph and then write down the key information. However, as you become a seasoned annotator, you should be able to read more before you begin to make your annotations.

■ **Write Your Annotations in Your Own Words.** Don't copy directly from the book, unless you are annotating something that must be learned exactly as it is stated in the book—such as a chemistry or statistics formula. When you are annotating definitions, you will want to simply paraphrase the author's words so that you don't change the meaning of the definition. Otherwise, put all information into your own words. (See the following table for examples of the difference between paraphrasing and writing in your own words.) Keep in mind that stating things in your own words is a good way of monitoring what you understand. Don't skip over information you don't understand. Ask for help from another student or from your professor.

Difference Between Paraphrasing and Writing in Your Own Words

	Your text states...	Your annotations...
Paraphrasing	The term *intelligence* refers to individuals' abilities to understand complex ideas, to adapt effectively to the environment, to learn from experience, to engage in various forms of reasoning, to overcome obstacles by careful thought.	Intelligence = how one understands ideas, adapts, learns fr. experience, reasons, solves problems through thinking
Writing in Your Own Words	Johnson's vision of the Great Society extended to the broader quality of life in the United States. Health care was perhaps the most fundamental issue for citizens' sense of personal security. After 1965, the new Medicare system paid for the medical needs of Americans aged sixty-five and older, and Medicaid underwrote health care services for the indigent.	LBJ's Great Society—extended quality of life, esp. in health care EX. Medicare for seniors & Medicaid for the poor

■■■

GET GOING

Staying Motivated Through Previewing and Annotating

Sometimes just getting started is half the battle. Because previewing takes such a small amount of time and has such a big payoff, it may be the motivator you need to keep up with your reading assignments. Once you have spent ten minutes previewing, go into annotation mode. By previewing and annotating, you just might be able to stick with it a while longer to get some reading completed.

What Type of Information Should You Annotate?

Remember that the purpose of annotation is to isolate information that you will need to study and remember. Although disciplines are different in terms of the types of concepts you will need to focus on, you should look for the following types of information whenever you annotate. Specific recommendations for annotating in the humanities, social sciences, and hard sciences will be presented in later chapters.

- **Definitions,** especially content-specific terms and concepts. Content-specific terms are words you find in that particular subject. These terms are generally identified for you with bold or italicized print. Sometimes they are even pulled out in the margins or in a list at the end of the chapter.

- **Examples** are also important to annotate because they depict specific instances, theories, experiments, cases, and so forth. Examples mentioned in the text often show up on your tests, so it is crucial to note them. You also should include personal examples when you can, because relating the information to what you already know will help you better remember the information. If the text does not provide an example, but you can think of one that helps you, add that information to your annotations.

- **Predicted test questions** are also an important consideration. When you read, try to predict likely test questions about the material. Be sure to ask higher-level questions (those that begin with *how* or *why*) as well as questions that connect your reading to the class lecture. Higher-level questions require more than just memorization of facts; they require application of the concept. You can begin the prediction process when you preview and then hone those questions during annotation.

- **People, dates, places, and events** if they are important in your text. However, this should not be the only type of information you annotate. The types of questions you will usually be asked in college require you to think at a higher level about the significance of the names, dates, and events. The only reason you annotate this type of information is to get a chronology of events. Be sure to think about how the information fits into the larger context of the material.

- **Numbered lists or characteristics** contained in your text should also be annotated. If your text states that "there are three major causes of" or "reasons for" or "factors that contribute to" a certain idea, annotate them by numbering them in the margin. In this way, you are connecting and learning those ideas together. Reader-friendly texts generally cue you to how many reasons or characteristics you should annotate; but less friendly texts do not. Even though the text may not point out how many there are, you should be aware and number the lists.

■ **Relationships between concepts,** such as cause/effect or comparison/contrast, are important to note. When you read your text, look for relationships between concepts, even if the text doesn't explicitly point them out. They will help you reorganize the information in a meaningful way.

■ **Graphs, charts, diagrams,** and other visuals are important to annotate because they often contain information that is not anywhere else in the text. In addition, graphs and diagrams can provide good examples of the concepts presented.

TIMELY TIPS

Annotation Pays Off

One of the major complaints that students have when they first begin to annotate is that it takes too long. However, if you gear up first, stick with it, and try different approaches to annotation, there is a huge payoff in the end. And, in the long run, annotation actually ends up saving time since you are able to remember and understand much more of what you read and annotate as you prepare for exams.

Studying Your Annotations

If you have done a good job of annotating, studying your annotations is actually quite simple. To use your annotations to help you study, cover up the text with your hand or a piece of notebook paper. Read over your annotations a few times to be sure that you understand the concepts. When you feel comfortable with your understanding of the material and are confident that your annotations are complete, talk through the major points in your annotations without looking at the text. You should be able to talk about each topic that is annotated and you should be able to give examples and details as well. If you find that there is a section that you don't know, then reread your annotations. If you still don't understand, then reread that section in the text, ask a friend, look at your lecture notes, or ask your professor. Note that if you reread your text, you are only rereading paragraphs or sections that you don't understand, not the entire chapter.

When you talk through your annotations, be sure that you are precise and thorough in your explanations. Being precise means that what you are saying is accurate information, that the conclusions you are drawing are logical, and that you can see relationships between ideas. Being thorough means that you know all of the important information—not just the main point. It's also important to know examples, explanations, and, in many cases, details. For example, you should understand the *whys* and *hows* of a particular event— not just the chronology.

It's also a good idea to review your annotations a little bit each day so that when you are ready to study for an exam, you already know a lot of the material. These review sessions are a good time to link your lecture notes, secondary texts, and discussion group notes to your annotations. Pulling everything together as you go along makes studying from your annotations an active approach that is efficient and effective.

Another effective way to study your annotations is by asking yourself questions based on what you have written. Be careful not to simply ask *what* questions or questions that require one-word answers. You will want to be sure that some of your questions begin with *why, how,* and *explain.*

Some Common Concerns About Annotation

Annotation is a strategy that many students find is one of the best ways to help them focus on their reading. However, many students have concerns about their annotations.

■ **How Do You Know What Is Important to Mark?** Deciding what is important to annotate is sometimes tricky. Obviously, you want to note what the text emphasizes, but you also want to annotate information the professor stresses in class. You can often tell what is important by looking at the headings and subheadings in your book. Most students find that the more they annotate in a textbook, the more familiar they become with how the text is written and what the professor thinks is important. Therefore, even if you are having trouble organizing the information right now, eventually you should feel more confident about it.

■ **Doesn't This Take a Lot of Time?** Yes, in the beginning annotation does take more time than reading alone—maybe even twice as long. However, if you have annotated properly, you have already taken a big step in preparing for exams. When you annotate, you have pulled out all of the information you will need to study, so you shouldn't have to reread the material unless you need some clarification about a specific concept. In addition, because you have actively studied the text material from the start, you will be able to remember more. This will cut your study time prior to an exam. Most students say that they find that the extra time spent annotating is worth it when they go back to study because they are sure they understand the material.

■ **How Can You Be Sure That You Are Annotating the Information That Will Be on the Exam?** By listening to class lectures and discussions you should be able to determine most of the important information. However, the goal of annotation is to learn the concepts that are presented in the text, not to guess exactly what will be on the exam. If you understand all of the information in the text, you will be prepared for almost any exam question on that topic.

SUCCESS AT A GLANCE

Model Annotations

Model Annotations	Passage
Culture-fair tests = designed to help do away with cultural bias	In an effort to eliminate cultural bias from intelligence tests, psychologists have attempted to design *culture-fair* tests. Such tests attempt to include only items to which all groups, regardless of ethnic or racial background, have been exposed. Because many minority children are exposed to languages other than standard English, these tests tend to be nonverbal in nature. One of these, the *Raven Progressive Matrices* (Raven, 1977), is illustrated in Figure 7.22. This test consists of sixty matrices of varying difficulty, each containing a logical pattern or design with a missing part. Individuals select the item that completes the pattern from several different choices. Because the Raven test and ones like it focus primarily on *fluid intelligence*—our basic abilities to form concepts, reason, and identify similarities—these tests seem less likely to be subject to cultural bias than other kinds of intelligence tests. However, it is not clear that these tests, or any others, totally eliminate the problem of subtle built-in bias.
■ Include items that are nonverbal	
■ Useful with all races and ethnicities	
■ EX. Raven Progressive Matrices	
Has 60 matrices of varying diff. Ind. must choose which missing pieces complete matrix	
Focuses on fluid intell. Ability to form concepts, reason, and find similarities	
■ Probably doesn't totally do away with bias	

Real College

Hillary

DIRECTIONS: Read the following "Real College" scenario and respond to the questions based on what you learned in this chapter about gearing up and annotating.

Hillary is a returning student. After 20 years she has decided to quit her job and return to school full time. Because she wants to get off to a good start, she bought herself all the supplies she thought she would need—pencils, notebooks, pens, and especially highlighters. Hillary doesn't see how she could study without her highlighter. Her approach is to open her textbook to the assigned chapter and immediately jump right in, putting her highlighter into warp-speed. Her daughter jokes that most of the pages in her books are now bright yellow.

For Hillary's sociology class she must read her textbook and the local newspaper. When she reads the text, she tries to highlight everything that seems important. One problem is that it *all* seems important so she sometimes ends up highlighting whole pages. There are so many details in the textbook that she is not sure what the professor will focus on for the exam. She is especially careful to note every name and date discussed in the book, but she doesn't spend a lot of time reading the newspaper because the professor barely mentions the newspaper in class. Basically, she just skims the articles for the facts. Hillary did not do well on the first essay exam even though she studied for hours. The test seemed to focus on relating the sociology topics to the newspaper articles. She knows that she needs a new approach to studying her textbooks. When she studies, she finds that she rereads almost every chapter because all the text is highlighted. She hardly has time to read all of her text once, much less twice.

Using what you know about gearing up for reading and annotating texts, what advice would you give Hillary so that she can read and remember more effectively? What insight would you give Hillary about how she should approach her sociology readings?

ADD TO YOUR PORTFOLIO

1. Select one of the courses you are taking this semester and preview your next reading assignment. Preview a chapter and then answer the following questions: How did you preview the chapter? Did your previewing help motivate you to read the chapter? Did your previewing enable you to get a good grasp of the concepts presented in the chapter? How might you modify your previewing for different courses?

2. Annotate the text for one of your classes for one week. Remember to annotate in your own words and to mark all of the important information contained in the text. Turn in at least five (photocopied) pages of annotation.

3. Reflect on your learning of the material you previewed and annotated. Do you remember the concepts in the chapters you annotated better than the concepts in other chapters? How do you feel the strategy will benefit you when you begin to study for your exam?

Take Note! Lectures
A Different Kind of Text

READ THIS CHAPTER TO ANSWER THE FOLLOWING QUESTIONS:

- Why is it important to take good lecture notes?
- What should I do before, during, and after class to take good notes?
- How can I use my notes to self-test?

SELF-ASSESSMENT

DIRECTIONS: Examine your notes from one of your classes and evaluate them on a scale of 1 to 5, with 1 being "hardly ever" and 5 being "almost always."

	Hardly ever ←→ Almost always				
1. My notes are organized.	1	2	3	4	5
2. My notes distinguish main points from details.	1	2	3	4	5
3. My notes include examples.	1	2	3	4	5
4. I take notes over class discussions.	1	2	3	4	5
5. I test myself over my notes.	1	2	3	4	5
6. My notes accurately reflect the content of the lectures.	1	2	3	4	5
7. My notes contain abbreviations.	1	2	3	4	5
8. I review my notes as soon after class as possible.	1	2	3	4	5
9. My notes are complete.	1	2	3	4	5
10. I compare my notes to the text when I study.	1	2	3	4	5

The more 5s you marked, the better. Many students find that they need more efficient strategies for note taking. Read on to find out how to improve your note-taking skills.

The Importance and Characteristics of Good Lecture Notes

In college, a large percentage of information is conveyed to you through lecture. In the traditional lecture format, professors explain information that they believe is important for you to learn. Most professors expect you to take notes in an organized way so that you can study and review the notes throughout the course. Note taking isn't too difficult when you have a professor who speaks slowly and clearly and lectures in an organized fashion. But many professors

Example 1: Good Lecture Notes

	Intelligence	*Nov. 15*

○

What is the def. of intelligence?

Intelligence- differing views
Def.= -ability to understand complex ideas
        -adapt to environment
        -reason effectively
        -overcome problems through thought

What is intel. related to?

Related to mastering new ideas, school + job success, getting along w/ others; however other factors play a role in life outcomes.

Explain the dif. b/t unitary & multifaceted views.

Differing views
  1. <u>Unitary view</u>= single dimension (Spearman)-how one did on a cog. task depended on a <u>general</u> (g) factor; based on idea that subscores on IQ tests correlate highly ∴ IQ was related to 1 factor
  2. <u>Multifaceted view</u>= IQ consists of many unique abilites that operate independently; can be high on some + low on others (Thurstone said IQ was composed of 7 mental abilities
        EX. verbal, number, + space abilities)

○

How do the 2 views relate to the modern view?

Modern view is somewhere in between- could be a general factor <u>BUT</u> intelligence is expressed in diff. ways.

Explain Garner's Theory of X intell.

Garner's Theory of X intell.
-Theory= study persons at extremes of intell. rather than just who is in middle as has been done
-Believes there are several types of intell. impt. to understand all of them
        <u>Quest.</u> Does a talented gymnast have a certain kind of intell. that enables her to perform those moves?

Example 2: Weak Lecture Notes

Intelligence

Intelligence includes understanding ideas, reasoning + adapting.
Main views are unitary and multifaceted (Spearman and Thurstone).
Garner's is more like multifaceted; it has several levels of intelligence.

Example 3: Very Weak Notes

Intelligence
Understanding stuff blah, blah, blah
think about it differently
Spearman → -Spear man! ha! IQ I am smart!

Garner's theory   sooooo...boring!!!

Call Chris later   CHRIS

aren't the world's most top-notch, engaging lecturers. Therefore, students should be able to supply their own organization, get down the important points, and fill in the gaps when necessary.

It's important to be able to take good lecture notes for several reasons:

■ They serve as a record of what goes on in class each day. Without a complete record, it's difficult to have all the information you need to prepare for subsequent classes or exams.

■ When your notes are organized, they can help you identify patterns in your professor's lectures. Once you see patterns, you get a better idea of what your professor believes is important.

■ Your notes will help you spot overlap between your text and the professor's lecture. These overlaps are fertile ground for test questions.

Studying Smarter

Stay actively involved during lectures by writing for the full period. Then, review your notes as soon after class as possible.

What distinguishes good notes from poor notes? As you will see, good notes are more than just readable. As you read about the characteristics of good notes, look at the examples of good, weak, and very weak lecture notes related to a portion of the text titled "Cognition and Intelligence." We will refer to these examples throughout the chapter.

Characteristics of good notes include the following:

■ **Good Notes Are Organized.** When you look at the three examples of lecture notes, it is easy to see which one is best organized. The notes in the first example use organizational strategies such as underlining the main points, indenting details, noting examples, and numbering viewpoints. This differs dramatically from the notes in the second and third examples. In the second example, it's difficult to tell where one idea stops and another begins or what is a main point and what is a detail. Much of the information written in the notes in the second example is lost or difficult to link together. And what can we say about the notes in example three? Some students actually have notes that are this bad! Incomplete notes—those that are inadequate as well as imprecise—occur most frequently in courses that students find uninteresting or for students who have not yet mastered the art of active learning.

■ **Good Notes Distinguish Main Points from Details.** Every lecture has both main points and details. The main points might be reasons, characteristics, or theories. Details include information that supports or explains the main points. It's important to write your notes in such a way that the main points are distinguishable from the details. If the information runs together or if you have only written down the main points and excluded the details, your notes will be of less use for studying.

■ **Good Notes Include Examples.** Often when professors get to the point in the lecture at which they are giving examples, students are nodding off or thinking about what they plan to have for lunch. But examples often surface on exams, so it's crucial to write down every example of a particular main point that the professor provides. These examples should stand out in some way so that as you study, you know what they illustrate.

■ **Good Notes Clearly Indicate Lecture Patterns.** Most professors use the same pattern of speech in all of their lectures. The two most common are the *deductive* pattern and the *inductive* pattern. **Deductive lectures** begin with the generalization ("There are three main reasons for...") and then fill in the reasons, details, and examples. **Inductive lectures** do the opposite. They progress from the specific to the general. For example, an inductive lecturer would provide a series of reasons or characteristics and conclude with a statement such as, "So, all of this means...." This concluding statement is the generalization that helps make sense of the lecture. It is generally easier to follow lectures when they are presented in a deductive manner. The style your professor uses should become apparent to you after the first few class sessions, and your notes will need to reflect this lecture pattern. Moreover, different disciplines may lend themselves better to one type than the other. Chapters 12–14 provide examples of how to modify your notes depending on the course content.

■ **Good Notes Allow for Self-Testing.** Students don't usually think about how the way they take notes will influence the way they study. Most students merely read over their notes again and again. This approach often gives them a false sense of knowing the information when, in fact, they do not. Instead, try writing questions or key words in the margin of your notes to help you test yourself. Note the difference between the notes in the three earlier examples. The notes in the first example have questions in the margins that you can ask yourself, which will help you determine your knowledge of the material. (We will discuss self-questioning of lecture notes, or self-testing, in more detail later in the chapter.)

■ **Good Notes Stand the Test of Time.** Because your notes are a daily record of what is said in class each day, they should make sense to you long after class is over. You should be able to read through your notes two days, two weeks, two months, or even two years later and find they are still understandable. Because of the way memory works, you will be unable to remember everything your professor says in class every day. That's why you take notes to begin with. It's important, then, to be sure that your notes are organized in such a way that they will make sense down the line and that they include as much detail as you can reasonably get on paper.

■ **Good Notes Use Abbreviations.** Because most professors speak faster than you can write, it's important to use abbreviations that make sense to you. For example, if your professor were lecturing on the Industrial Revolution, it would be too time consuming to write both words out every time they were mentioned. Using *Ind. Rev.* or even *IR* saves a considerable amount of time. It is also a good idea to develop a series of abbreviations for common and high-use words. See the "Success at a Glance" box for some suggestions.

It is becoming more common for professors to put their notes on the Web or to have students purchase copies of their notes to follow during the lecture. These alternatives are useful as long as you continue to take a good set of notes yourself. We know that simply using someone else's notes, even if they are the professor's, rather than taking your own does not maximize your learning. Many students find that they tune out when they don't take their own notes—and often miss important points. The better approach is to take notes yourself and then compare them with the Web notes.

SUCCESS AT A GLANCE	
Abbreviation Examples	
&	and
b/c	because
b/4	before
/	the
=	means, definitions, is equal to
w/i	within
+	in addition to, positives
-	negatives
$	money, wealth
<	less than
>	greater than
↑	increased
↓	decreased
∴	therefore
*	very important

Taking Good Lecture Notes

Taking good notes involves active listening, attentiveness, concentration, and the ability to synthesize and condense a considerable amount of information on the spot. Effective note takers know that a lot of thinking goes on during note taking. Most students probably enter the lecture situation with every intention of staying alert, paying attention, and taking good notes. But for a variety of reasons, many students do not prevail.

From our observations, it seems that several factors enter into students' abilities to take good notes:

1. **Class Size.** The larger the class size, the easier it is to become unconnected with what the professor is saying. In addition, the further back or to the side that students sit in a classroom, the worse the problem tends to become. That's why it's important to stay in the professor's line of vision, sitting either close to the front or in the middle section of the room.

2. **Professor's Lecture Style.** When a professor speaks in a monotone, it is hard to stay focused and actively involved in listening. Students' minds sometimes wander during lectures by professors who are difficult to follow or who speak rapidly. But we have also found that students pay less attention when the professor has put notes on the Web or reads directly from PowerPoint slides.

3. **Time of Day.** Interestingly, students are most likely to fall asleep in an early morning class, presumably after they have had several hours of uninterrupted sleep. Granted, many students would consider themselves night people whose body clocks resist going to bed before the wee hours of the morning and also resist getting up prior to noon. If you count yourself in these numbers, try to avoid scheduling an early morning class. Some students also seem to have trouble paying attention right after lunch (because they are full and sluggish) or during the late afternoon hours (when they feel hungry and tired). If you have a class immediately after lunch, try to eat a light meal; if a late afternoon class is on your schedule, try eating a snack before class to keep up your energy.

4. **Health (Both Emotional and Physical).** Breaking up with your boyfriend or girlfriend, family problems, sick children, illness, or taking medications all can influence your attentiveness in class. Everyone experiences problems at one time or another, and no one can expect to be perfectly attentive all the time. But when emotional or physical problems become constant barriers to learning, it's time to think about a course of action to get back to health.

TIMELY TIPS

The Importance of Sleep

It is worth mentioning the importance of getting an adequate amount of sleep. Lack of sleep impairs concentration by making it difficult to focus and stay on task. If you go to bed at a decent hour, you should be able to get up at a decent hour to make the most of your day. Additionally, when you don't get enough sleep, you tend to get sick more often and nap too long, both of which can cause you to fall behind in your classes.

General Note-Taking Guidelines

Let's begin our discussion of how to take good lecture notes with some general guidelines. These guidelines tend to work for every type of lecture, regardless of class size:

■ **Sit Front and Center.** As we mentioned, students who sit in the front of the classroom or in the professor's line of vision tend to be more attentive and listen more actively than those who sit in the back. This holds true in both large and small classes. In small classes, students who sit in the front tend to ask more questions and get to know their professors better. Also, research indicates a significant relationship between students' grades and seat location. That is, the closer they sit to the front, the higher their grade tends to be.

■ **Adjust Your Note Taking to the Professor.** Every professor lectures a bit differently. Some are well organized, and taking notes from them is a breeze. Others are unorganized, provide few transitional cues, and get off the topic very easily. Whatever your professor's lecturing habits seem to be, you need to figure them out early in the term and make the appropriate adjustments in your note taking.

■ **Listen, Think, and Write.** Students who try to copy down everything the professor says tend to miss many key points because they can't keep up. Rather than trying to write down every word, listen first, think about what the professor is saying, and then write that thought, as much as possible, in your own words. Because professors tend to repeat information or say it a few different ways, it's important to listen and think before you write. Your intent should be to understand the concepts rather than get down every word.

■ **Be Prepared.** Students who prepare before they go to class by reading the book or reviewing class notes find that the lectures become more interesting and more organized. Preparing before class will help you figure out important points and will even help you stay focused during the lecture.

■ **Paraphrase.** Sometimes professors speak so quickly and try to cram so much material into a lecture that it is virtually impossible to get down all of the key points. If you find yourself getting more half thoughts than complete thoughts in your notes, or if you read over your notes and find that you can't piece together the important parts of the lecture, then you probably need to begin to do some serious paraphrasing. Paraphrasing, in this case, means getting down key concepts in your words and then filling in the details after class with information from the text.

Learning how to take good lecture notes is an integral part of being a successful college student and an active learner. Like approaching textbook reading, taking good notes and using them as a successful study aid involves preparing to take notes, being an active listener during the lecture, and then rehearsing and self-testing after the lecture.

Getting Ready to Take Notes

Doing some preparation before you begin to take notes can make the difference between being an active and a passive listener. In order to get ready to take notes, you should:

■ **Do the Assigned Reading.** Most professors expect you to read the appropriate text chapters before you come to class. Reading before the lecture gives you the advantage of making connections between the text and lecture. You will also be able to follow the "listen, think, write" rule better, because being familiar with the lecture topic will allow you to take down the key points in a more organized fashion. If you run out of time and can't read the text in its entirety, at least skim the chapter(s) using the techniques described in Chapter 9 to give you some idea of the key points that will be covered in the lecture.

■ **Review Your Notes from the Previous Lecture.** Spend five or ten minutes before class to read through your notes from the previous lecture. By reviewing, you are refreshing your memory and getting your mind ready to become actively involved in learning. In addition, when you review, you can be sure that you understand the information that has been presented. Because many professors begin each class by answering student questions, you can get unclear information explained.

■ **Have the Extra Edge.** Try to get to class with plenty of time to spare. Plan to use that time to review. Get out your notebook, get your paper ready (we'll talk more about this later), and—of course—sit in the front or in the professor's line of vision.

Staying Active During Note Taking

In this section we will discuss not only the format and organization of good notes but also the kinds of information that you should include in your notes. By following these suggestions, you will be able to remain alert and active throughout the class.

Format and Organization

If you were to examine the notes of five different college students, you would probably see five different kinds of formats. Perhaps none of the formats would match up with the method we recommend—the split-page method. We will concentrate on this particular method because it allows for self-testing, which we believe is crucial for active learning. Look again at the first note-taking example presented earlier in the chapter. You can see that there is a line down the left-hand side of the paper, creating a two- to three-inch margin. You take your notes on the wider right-hand side of the paper and then after class use the left-hand margin to pull out the key points. You should draw your lines, write the date, and number several pieces of paper before your professor begins to lecture.

As you take notes, use the following guidelines:

■ **Use a three-ring binder** rather than a spiral-bound notebook. A binder allows you to include class handouts and easily remove and insert notes. Although we think binders are the way to go, we have noticed that many students prefer notebooks. If you really dislike the binder idea, be sure to use a spiral-bound notebook with pockets for your syllabus and other course handouts.

■ **Take notes in simple paragraph or bulleted point form,** rather than as a tightly structured outline. Outlines cause many students to get hung up on the outline format rather than the content of the lecture.

■ **Leave spaces between ideas and underline key points** to enable you to see where one idea stops and another begins. This also helps to distinguish between the key points and the details.

■ **Try to make your notes inviting to review.** Neatness and organization count because you will not want to spend much time with your notes if they are difficult to read and review.

■ **Indent and mark details and examples.** Indenting helps you know what information is related. If your notes all run together, it's difficult to tell what is a key point and what is supporting information.

■ **Make numbered lists**—reasons, characteristics, types, and so forth. Numbered lists enable you to know at a glance how many factors on the list you need to remember.

■ **Use abbreviations whenever possible.** Abbreviating saves time and can distinguish certain kinds of information, such as indicating an example with "ex.," a definition with "def.," important information with an asterisk (*), and so forth.

Active Listening

It's not only important to know how you should take and organize your notes, but it is also important to be aware of the kinds of information you should include. Of course, the kinds of information you should put in your notes vary from class to class. For example, although you may include names, dates, and events in your history notes, your psychology notes will probably be more focused on research and theories than on key events. Listen for the following cues that your professor may give as a way of figuring out what is important to note:

■ **Lists.** Lists of things begin with cues such as, "There were three major reasons why President Johnson committed more troops to Vietnam." "Short-term memory has five characteristics." "Mitosis progresses through eight stages." Any time you hear a number followed by several factors, stages, or characteristics, make sure you write the number of things along with the explanation. In other words, don't just write the stages of mitosis in your notes. Write down what happens in each stage as well.

■ **Cause/Effect.** When you hear your professor discuss causes and effects, be sure to write them down. Cause/effect cues are common in history and political science. For example, there might be an event that caused a president to make a certain decision, and this decision, in turn, had numerous effects on other events and decisions. In science, cause/effect can deal with concepts such as diseases or the food chain.

■ **Definitions.** Perhaps the most frequent type of information your professor will give in a lecture will be definitions. Your professor might cue you by saying something as basic as, "*Intelligence* can be defined as...." It's a good idea to write definitions in your notes precisely. If you only get down a portion of a definition or aren't sure that you have it exactly right, check your text or with your professor as soon after class as possible.

■ **Examples.** Definitions are quite frequently followed by examples; yet, often students will see "example time" as an occasion to tune out. But examples discussed in class make for prime test questions. If you have to choose, we believe that it's more important to get examples than definitions in your notes (you can get the definitions from your textbook).

■ **Extended Comments.** When the professor spends a lot of time explaining something, you can be sure that it is important information. Try to stay connected with the lecturer during extended comments, and take down as much of the information as possible. Essay, short-answer, and higher-level multiple-choice items often come from these extended comments.

Studying Smarter

Some professors put their lecture notes on the Web daily. If any of your professors do this, check out their Web site. There are advantages and disadvantages to Web notes, however. Students who simply print out the notes and study them right before the exam tend to score lower than students who use the Web notes as a supplement to their own notes. If your professor supplies the notes for you, take them to class and follow along during the lecture. You'll be able to add more details during class.

■ **Superlatives.** Any time a professor uses words such as "most important," "best explanation," or "least influential," be sure to write it down. For example, there may be several explanations as to what constitutes intelligence, but your psychology professor might believe that one explanation is the best. These are the kinds of things professors love to ask about on exams.

■ **Voice or Volume Changes.** When professors think something is important or they want to stress it, they generally speak louder and slower. A change in voice can be a clear indication that something important is being said.

■ **Process Notes.** Process notes consist of information the professor gives about tests, how to study, when study or review sessions are held, how to think about the information, or how he wants an essay structured. They can also include clues about what information might be on the exam and other hints related to task that we discussed in detail in Chapter 4. Process notes often come right at the beginning of class, before some students are ready to take notes, or at the end of class, when some students are packed up and ready to leave. Sometimes professors will even comment after a particular lecture something to the effect, "Hmmm...Wouldn't this make an interesting essay question?" This is all vital information that you should write down in your notes.

Becoming an active listener takes time, especially for classes in which you have little interest. It's not too difficult to stay connected with the lecturer in classes that you like or in classes where you have a professor who is dynamic. It's much more difficult in those courses that are, in some way, less appealing. But try to think about the bigger picture. If you are an active listener and take organized notes for the entire class period, studying and learning the course material will be a much easier task.

Being Flexible: Four Methods of Note Taking

Many students have just one way that they take notes. But these students may run into trouble when they are in a course that would benefit from a different kind of note taking. In these cases, some students get frustrated and take no notes at all. To save you from this situation we discuss four methods of note taking that can be used in a variety of disciplines; then in Chapters 12–14 we will show you examples of how to use these methods.

Method 1: Split-Page (Cornell) Notes

Using split-page notes is an effective strategy that will be appropriate in most of your lecture courses. This is most likely the method you will use the majority of the time. In the split-page method you divide your page just like the example on the facing page. Draw a line down the left-hand side of the paper, creating a 2-inch margin. During class, take your notes on the wider right-hand side of the paper, and then after class use that margin to test yourself over the material. You should draw your lines, write the date, and number the pages before your professor begins to lecture. See page 188 for an example of using the split-page method in the sciences.

Format for Split-Page Notes

Date	Title	Page #
Use the margin after class to predict test questions or pull out key points	Use this side of the page to take notes during lecture. Remember: • Use bulleted points rather than formal outline format. • Skip spaces between ideas. • **Highlight** key concepts. • Include both content and process notes.	

Interacting with your notes after the lecture is perhaps the most important phase of note taking. As soon as possible after the lecture, it's important to read over your notes carefully to be sure that you understand all the major concepts presented. This is when you use the margin on the left-hand side of your paper. As shown in Example 1 at the beginning of the chapter, this margin can be used to write in the key points or pose questions. You can then use the key points or questions to self-test as you study the course material.

In the margin plan to do the following:

- Focus on the major points or broad topics.
- Get at higher-level thinking by asking "how," "why," or "for example," instead of "what" questions.
- Be brief.

Creating the self-testing component for your lecture notes as soon after the lecture as possible helps get the information into your memory and helps you keep it there. When you go through your notes, you can also determine if you have questions about what was presented in class. Writing questions or key points in the margin gives you immediate feedback about what you understand and what you need clarification about.

When it comes time to prepare for the exam, follow these steps to use your annotations or questions to self-test:

1. Read your notes, either silently or out loud, trying to get the information fixed in your memory.

2. Fold your paper back, exposing only what you have written in the left-hand column.

3. Ask yourself each question and explain each concept.

4. Flip your notes over to see how much of the material you have remembered.

5. If you are able to explain each item *accurately and precisely*, go on to the next concept. If you have problems, read your notes another time or two and try again.

6. As you master the concepts, check them off in the margin.

7. When you begin the next study session, review what you know, but concentrate your efforts on what you don't know.

Self-testing by using questions in the margin of your notes should give you confidence as you enter a testing situation. When you self-test, you monitor your understanding, and therefore you get a fairly accurate idea of the concepts you comprehend and those that may still be unclear.

ON YOUR OWN

Reflecting on What You Have Read

Using what you have learned in this chapter, think about your own learning situation and write a response to the following questions: What changes might you need to make to your current note-taking methods? What are the greatest challenges in terms of note taking in your current courses? What are the benefits and drawbacks of reviewing your notes each day? What are the benefits of testing yourself on your notes?

Method 2: Parallel Notes

Professors often use a range of technology—Web notes, PowerPoint presentations, graphs, and visual aids—in their classes. This can lead students to feel that their attention is divided, which makes it difficult to take notes. A strategy to help you concentrate in these classes is parallel notes. First, print out the notes the professor supplies before class and place them in a 3-ring binder. As the professor lectures, take your own notes on the blank facing page, following along with the notes the professor supplied and filling in any gaps or added information. After the lecture, create your self-testing questions as described in the split-page method. (See facing page for an example of how to set up parallel notes and page 161 for an example using parallel notes in social sciences courses.)

Format for Parallel Notes

This page contains the notes you take in class.

Date	Title	page #
Use this column after class to predict test questions or pull out key ideas.	Use this page to take your own notes during class. Remember: • Listen for material presented that is not contained in the notes supplied by the professor.	

This page contains the notes supplied by the professor.

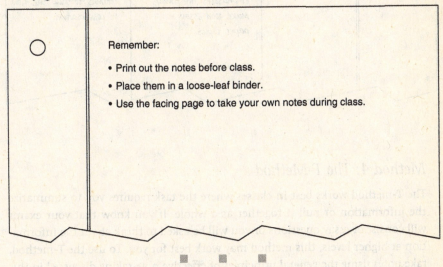

Remember:

• Print out the notes before class.

• Place them in a loose-leaf binder.

• Use the facing page to take your own notes during class.

Method 3: Discussion Columns

If your class is based on discussion instead of lecture, you will need to modify the note-taking process somewhat. Your job in class is to record the class conversation in as much detail as possible. Rather than dividing your paper into narrow and wide margins, divide it into three equal columns. In the first column, write the question that is being posed or the theory that is being debated. In the second column, take notes on what the professor has to say about the topic. In the last column, take notes on what your classmates say. Then, when you are studying, you can evaluate your classmate's comments, see which points the professor expanded on, and even figure out possible test or paper topics by seeing the flow of that day's discussion. The following example shows how to format your page for discussion columns.

Format for Discussion Notes

Date	Title	Page #
Question Posed	Professor's Comments	Student Comments
Use this column to write down the question posed for discussion.	Use this column to note professor comments. Remember to note topics that the professor emphasizes. They may make good essay or paper topics.	Use this column to track your classmates' comments. You can format the columns to show the flow of conversation.

Method 4: The T-Method

The T-method works best in classes where the task requires you to summarize the information or pull it together as a whole. If you know that your exams will consist of essay questions or you will be asked to think about the information at higher levels, this method may work best for you. To use the T-method, take notes using the general principles of effective note taking discussed in this chapter. Then, instead of using the margin of your paper do the following:

1. Draw a T on the bottom 1/4 of your last page of notes (you can use the back of the page if you need more room).
2. On the left side of the page, summarize the key points of the lecture.
3. On the right side of the page, create your self-testing component by predicting some test questions about the material.

The following example shows how to format your page for the T-method.

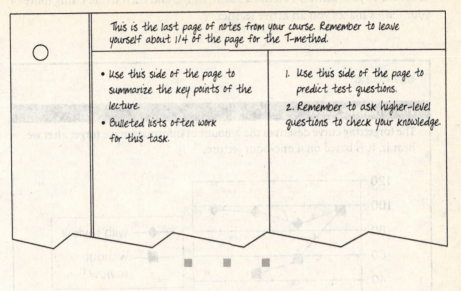

This is the last page of notes from your course. Remember to leave yourself about 1/4 of the page for the T-method.

- Use this side of the page to summarize the key points of the lecture.
- Bulleted lists often work for this task.

1. Use this side of the page to predict test questions.
2. Remember to ask higher-level questions to check your knowledge.

Note-Taking Myths

We end this chapter by discussing some myths—information that students tend to believe about note taking that isn't necessarily true.

■ **Myth 1: If I Can't Keep Up with the Professor, I Should Record the Lectures.** The truth is that when students tape lectures, they generally don't listen to the tapes. It's easy to understand why. If you are taking five classes, you hardly have time to do all your reading, studying, and other learning activities, let alone sit and listen to lectures for a second time. In addition, students who record lectures find it much easier to tune out what the professor is saying and will miss information written on the chalkboard or overhead. Our advice to you is to go to class, take the best notes you can, and supplement those notes with information from the text or by forming a study group that has as one of its goals to share notes with everyone. Unless you have a disability that necessitates recording class lectures, tape recording simply is not an efficient and active way to learn.

■ **Myth 2: Copying a Classmate's Notes Is Better Than Struggling with Them Myself.** Think back to your distant past when you actually may have copied someone's homework. How much did you learn from that experience? We would guess not much. You won't learn much from copying someone else's lecture notes either—even if they are better than yours. A better plan is to compare your lecture notes with a classmate's. This can be a very positive and active strategy, and you just might learn from your classmate some ways to take better notes. Also keep in mind that taking your own notes forces you to use more of your senses: You must listen, think, and then write. Using more of your senses makes you an active learner.

GET GOING

The Forgetting Curve

The forgetting curve describes the amount of information we forget after we hear it. It is based on a one-hour lecture.

Notice how without review you remember less than 20 percent after 30 days. But if you review your notes within one day of taking the notes and then spend some time with your notes each week, you can raise the curve to remembering almost 100 percent.

■ **Myth 3: If My Professor Provides Notes by Putting Them on the Web or Handing Them Out in Class, I Don't Have to Take Notes.** We have noticed that students tend to earn lower grades in classes where the notes are provided. This is probably because most students don't regularly review such notes and therefore don't learn the material until test time. If your professor provides the notes or has you purchase them as a package, we suggest that you take them to class each day. As you listen to the lecture, fill in gaps by adding details and providing examples. You can also stress the topics emphasized by the professor. Then, to be sure you understand the concepts in your notes, after each class use the T-method or parallel notes. If your professor puts her notes on the Web after class, attend class and take notes as you normally would. Then, when you get the professor's notes off the Web, you can compare the two sets and fill in any gaps.

Using Course Management Systems

Professors are using online course management systems for many course tasks. They may place their syllabi, quizzes, assignments, and other course information there. They may also post student grades or have virtual chats with the class. We know one professor who conducts exam reviews online and another who posts important class information and updates. If your professor uses these systems, plan to visit the site often.

■   **Myth 4: It's Impossible to Take Notes in a Class That Involves Discussion.** When we have observed students in classes that involve a lot of discussion, we see very little note taking. Students seem to think that only information presented by the professor has merit, and they fail to write down comments made by their peers. However, if you think about the purpose of classes that involve discussion, you'll realize that the professor's role is generally just to initiate the discussion. It's the students who actually generate the ideas, and those ideas often find their way to the exam. Using the discussion columns method should help you record the discussion and complete the course tasks more effectively.

Real College

Chad

DIRECTIONS: Read the following "Real College" scenario and respond to the question based on what you learned in this chapter.

"Why did I ever sign up for this eight o'clock class?" Chad wondered as he dragged himself out of bed around 7:30 A.M. Every day it was a real challenge—and he even liked Professor Wilson's anthropology class. He was, however, experiencing some trouble.

Chad never had problems taking notes in high school. His teachers wrote everything on the board and would repeat information when students asked. Plus, most of his high school teachers gave study guides to prepare for the tests, so all he had to do was look up the answers, which came mostly from the teacher's lectures. But Professor Wilson talked so fast and tried to get so much into one lecture that Chad usually only got a small portion of the key ideas that were presented. Then, because he was often late to class, he would walk in during the middle of a topic and would be unable to figure out what Professor Wilson was talking about. His notes were disorganized and full of doodles, and more than once he almost fell out of his seat when he nodded off. Chad tried two different solutions prior to the first exam. First, he gave up taking notes altogether and brought a tape recorder to class. Second, he borrowed a classmate's notes and copied them. He made a very low D.

After this poor performance, he decided that he really didn't know how to take notes from Professor Wilson. He wanted to put in a concerted effort to take notes once again, but he was unsure of what to do.

What advice would you give to Chad so that he can improve? (You are not allowed to advise him to drop the class or take it later in the day during the next term.)

ADD TO YOUR PORTFOLIO

1. Try taking notes in your classes using the four note-taking methods (the split-page method, discussion columns, parallel notes, and T-method) for one week. First, decide which one of the methods is the most appropriate for each course; then try it out. Be sure to write self-testing questions. Evaluate what you like and don't like about each method. How might you modify these methods to suit your own note-taking preferences?

2. For each of your current classes, try to determine how much overlap there is between the text and the lecture. Do your professors' test questions come primarily from the lectures or the text? How will this information affect your note taking?

Rehearsal and Review Strategies

READ THIS CHAPTER TO ANSWER THE FOLLOWING QUESTIONS:

- What are rehearsal strategies?
- Why is it important to know how to use a variety of rehearsal strategies?
- What are the differences between rehearsal and review strategies?
- How can reviewing improve memory?

SELF-ASSESSMENT

DIRECTIONS: Think about the types of rehearsal and review strategies you currently use. Answer *yes* or *no* for each of the following questions. Do you:

	Yes	No
1. Create note cards, concept maps, or charts to rehearse information?	_____	_____
2. Vary your studying techniques depending on the course?	_____	_____
3. Create a study plan before each exam?	_____	_____
4. Connect ideas together as you study?	_____	_____
5. Study with the intent to really learn the information?	_____	_____
6. Self-test as a way of monitoring what you know?	_____	_____
7. Review on a daily basis?	_____	_____
8. Review with classmates?	_____	_____
9. Review several days before an exam?	_____	_____

If you answered *yes* to most of these questions, you are on the right track and doing what you need to in order to complete the studying process. Read this chapter to discover additional rehearsal and review strategies you might use. If you answered *no* to several of these questions, rethink how you rehearse and review information as you read this chapter.

Rehearsing

Just as actors rehearse their lines to remember them, so students must rehearse what they want to learn. Rehearsal means engaging in activities, either written or spoken, that will help you learn information from a variety of sources. You might say the information out loud, write it down in an organized fashion, or discuss it with a classmate. We present many ways that you can go about rehearsing later in the chapter. What's important at this point is that you understand what rehearsal is and why it is important to your academic success.

Rehearsal strategies help you organize the concepts that your professor expects you to learn. In Chapter 9, we stressed the importance of engaging your mind before you begin to read by prereading. This warm-up activity, which gets the mind ready for mental exercise, enables you to actively read and annotate. You're putting the information in your own words and beginning to see how the concepts relate. If everything goes well, you understand what you have read. Well, sort of. You have comprehended it, but you just can't remember all of it. This is where the next step—rehearsal—enters the picture. Rehearsal helps you to actually learn and remember the material. You organize the information from your text and lectures, make it meaningful in some way, write it, and then say it to yourself. Rehearsal allows you to use more of your senses in learning, which will help you retrieve the information at exam time.

Why Is Rehearsal Important?

We already touched on why rehearsal is important, but let's think about this a little more by reviewing how memory works. In Chapter 3, we discussed two theories of memory—the parts theory and the levels of processing theory. It matters little which theory you believe more accurately reflects how memory actually works. What does matter, however, is that in order to get information into long-term memory (LTM) or to process it deeply, you must rehearse in some meaningful way. Just reading over the material is not enough. At the rehearsal stage of learning, it's time to further organize by pulling out key ideas and supporting concepts and to personalize or *elaborate* on the ideas to the point where you have not just memorized; you have conceptualized and truly understand.

In this chapter we will introduce the principles of rehearsal. Chapters 12–14 will give examples of how to use these strategies in the social sciences, humanities, science, and mathematics.

Written and Oral Rehearsal Strategies

Now that you have an idea of what rehearsal is and why it is important to use rehearsal strategies, let's think about two different types of rehearsal strategies: written strategies and oral strategies.

1. **Written Strategies.** When you use written strategies, you record the important information in an organized fashion. The way you organize depends on the task your professor expects from you, the texts you are using, and the particular way you learn best. In other words, because the tasks and materials vary from course to course, the written strategies that work well for you in biology will probably be very different from those that work for you in history. Likewise, what works well for you may not work for the person sitting next to you. Specific written strategies include: CARDS, concept maps, concept charts, questions and answers, and time lines.

2. **Oral Strategies.** Oral strategies are those rehearsal strategies that require talking rather than writing. They work well for students who are more auditory learners, meaning those who learn better through hearing rather than by reading or writing information. You say the information out loud and then check your accuracy. Like written strategies, the oral strategies you select depend on all the other factors that impact learning—your characteristics, the task, and the text—although we believe that talk-throughs benefit all students because saying the information out loud will help you recall the information come test time. The specific oral rehearsal strategies that will be presented are reciprocal questioning and talk-throughs.

It is important to understand that there is no single best strategy, either written or oral. The best rehearsal strategies are those that work for you in a particular situation. And the best students know, modify, and appropriately use a variety of strategies, both written and oral.

Components of Good Rehearsal Strategies

When you were in high school you may have used rehearsal strategies without even knowing it. Perhaps you made outlines after you read your text or put vocabulary words or foreign language terms on note cards. You may have had a family member or friend ask you questions before a test. Or you may have learned a more rigid study strategy such as SQ3R. All of these are examples of rehearsal strategies, some of which are better than others. It is our hope that you learn to distinguish good strategies from those that are less effective. Use the following guidelines to help make this distinction.

Good rehearsal strategies:

■ **Allow for Self-Testing.** When you self-test, you rehearse without actually looking at the answer. For example, if you need to learn the different theories on human intelligence for a psychology exam, you say the theories to yourself or out loud and then immediately check to see whether you were correct. This process differs greatly from looking over or reading though information and having no real idea of whether or not you know the material. Good rehearsal strategies allow you to monitor what you know and allow for the element of self-testing.

- **Are Flexible.** You may have learned strategies in the past that seemed like they required too much work for the task you needed to do. Good strategies are those that are flexible and can be modified to suit a variety of situations.

- **Include Complete and Precise Information.** Have you ever taken a test, particularly a multiple-choice test, where the information seemed familiar, yet you had a difficult time selecting the correct answer? If so, you probably didn't rehearse completely and precisely. Like good text annotations, good rehearsal strategies require you to say or write *all* the information related to a concept and to see relationships among ideas.

- **Are Organized.** Good strategies have some structure to select the important information in a way that makes sense and helps you remember it. Your brain files information very much like a computer does. That is, concepts are stored in a logical way. Likewise, your rehearsal strategies need to have a logical flow as well.

- **State the Ideas in Your Own Words.** Few professors test you over verbatim information from texts or lectures. Rather, they paraphrase and synthesize concepts; they put them in their own words. Thus, trying to memorize material straight from the text or lecture will cause problems at test time when the exam questions are written in another way. If you are confused by the text questions, or if after a test you find yourself thinking, "The professor never talked about the information that way in class," you probably need to put the information in your own words as you study.

Studying Smarter

Don't be a one-trick pony! Use different rehearsal strategies for different content areas.

- **Help you Monitor and Evaluate Your Learning.** Every strategy will create a way to check your knowledge so that by the time you finish studying you can feel confident that you know the information and are ready for whatever task you are asked to do.

Written Rehearsal Strategies

CARDS: Cognitive Aids for Rehearsing Difficult Subjects

Of all the rehearsal strategies we will present in this chapter, you are probably most familiar with CARDS: Cognitive Aids for Rehearsing Difficult Subjects. You may have used flash cards or note cards in high school, but there are a few key differences. Like flash cards, CARDS is a strategy in which you write a key concept on the front of index cards. But instead of having only one term on the front of the card, you will also write another word or phrase, called an organizing term, in the top right-hand corner. This is an important element of CARDS because it allows you to see how ideas are grouped by this organizing term, and it gives you a way to retrieve the information. You should also write the source of the information—the text page, date of the lecture, documentary notes, and so forth—on the front of the card.

On the back of the card you write all of the material you want to learn about this particular concept in an organized fashion *and* in your own words. Because most college professors expect you to go beyond memorization, you should include examples, links to other concepts, and a general synthesis of the key points you need to remember about the concept.

Format for CARDS

Front of CARDS

> *Organizing term*
>
> *Key term*
>
> *Page # or date of lecture*

Back of CARDS

> *Definition*
>
> *Examples*
>
> *Key points to remember*

Using CARDS has several major advantages.

■ **They Are Easy to Carry Around.** You can stick them in your back-pack or pocket, and then easily pull them out when you have a few minutes to rehearse, such as while you are standing in line at the bookstore or waiting for class to begin. When you rehearse 10 minutes here or 15 minutes there, the additional study time quickly adds up.

■ **They Are Versatile.** CARDS works well in classes that require you to learn numerous terms, and if composed correctly, they can help you to see connections among ideas. For example, suppose you were in a biology course and you were reading a chapter on meiosis. Many terms go with this overriding concept. Rather than making just one card with a weak definition of meiosis, you would use meiosis as the organizing term and write it in the upper right-hand corner of all the cards relating to meiosis. Then you would clip all of your meiosis cards together so that you could see how the different terms relating to meiosis connect. CARDS also works well for learning vocabulary, rules, conjugations, and so forth in foreign languages or in mathematics, statistics, or chemistry, where you have to learn and apply formulas.

■ **They Provide Multiple Ways to Recall the Information.** When you use traditional flash cards, you have only one path to the definition. Because you use the organizing term, examples, and links to other concepts in the CARDS system, you have several pieces of information that can help you learn the concept more fully.

How Do You Use CARDS to Study?

1. **Organize the CARDS.** Use the organizing term in the upper right-hand corner to group all like terms together.

2. **Start with One Organizing Term.** Read the key concept on the front of the first card, flip it over, and read the information through a couple of times. Flip the card back over to the front and see how much of the information you can say to yourself without actually looking at it. Turn the card to the back again, and see how much you remembered. Repeat with each concept. Then return to the organizing term. Think about how all of the concepts you just learned relate not only to the organizing term but also to each other. Try to group the CARDS by their organizing terms so that you can study the topic as a whole.

3. **Separate What You Have Learned.** Review your CARDS each day, using those small pockets of time. Separate the CARDS you have learned from those you need to spend more time on. Spend more time concentrating on the concepts that are giving you the most trouble.

4. **Review with a Classmate.** Once you feel that you know most of the material on your CARDS, have a classmate ask you the term and then check to see how much of the material you are able to say accurately and precisely. Then exchange roles. (See the section on reciprocal questioning later in the chapter for some tips on how to quiz each other effectively.) Be sure that you can clearly discuss how the smaller concepts relate to larger ones and how the larger concepts relate to each other.

Concept Maps

Concept maps are visual representations of information, so using this strategy is very useful for students who tend to learn visually. A concept map is organized in such a way that it is easy to see the major concept that is being mapped, related concepts, and how everything is related.

Concept mapping works well when it is important to see the relationship between complex concepts, and it works particularly well in courses where many ideas are related or interconnected. For example, mapping might work well to see the relationship between hormones of the endocrine system or the fallout from the Tet Offensive in Vietnam. Mapping is especially useful for students who like to personalize strategies because there is no right or wrong way to map. The important thing is that the way ideas are linked together be clearly shown in your concept map.

How Do You Use Maps to Study? When you study your map, you can begin by rehearsing one concept at a time. Then cover up everything except the main concept, and begin to talk the information through. Say the related material and then check your accuracy. Focus on how the concepts are related to each other because that is the major strength of mapping. Rather than viewing ideas one at a time, as you would with CARDS, mapping enables you to understand how these ideas fit together.

Format for a Concept Map

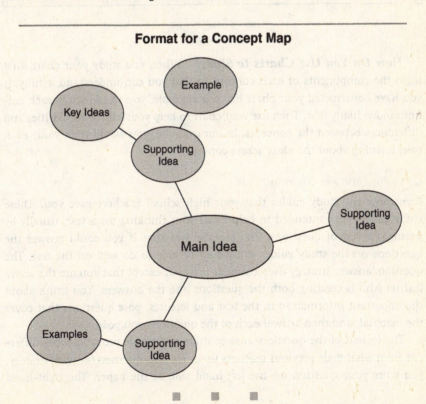

Charting is similar to mapping but is useful in different kinds of situations. Charting helps you synthesize information and is especially helpful when you are asked to compare and contrast ideas. To make a chart, start by looking at your annotations to see the types of materials you want to compare. This will help you come up with the categories you will use and will differ depending on the type of course and the way you will be tested over the material. In general, a chart will help you pull ideas together and will help you see the differences between ideas that may initially appear similar.

Format for Charting

	Concept 1	Concept 2	Concept 3
Key ideas/ definitions			
Supporting details			
Examples/ evidence			

■   ■   ■

How Do You Use Charts to Study? When you study your chart, first learn the components of each concept so that you can understand it fully. If you have constructed your chart like our example, you would study each column individually first. Then use your chart to help yourself see similarities and differences between the concepts. In our example, you would then study each row, learning about the ideas across concepts.

Question/Answer Strategy

Remember the study guides that your high school teachers gave you? These study guides were intended to help focus your thinking for a test, usually by posing a series of questions. The premise was that if you could answer the questions on the study guide, you would be able to do well on the test. The question/answer strategy uses a similar premise, except that you are the active learner who is creating both the questions and the answers. You think about the important information in the text and lectures, pose questions that cover the material, and then answer each of the questions you pose.

The format of the question/answer strategy example probably looks different from what your previous teachers used. For this question/answer strategy, you write your question on the left-hand side of the paper. The right-hand space is for answering the question and is wider than the left side. This format should give you a clue that the questions you pose should require more than a one-word answer.

When you are posing your questions, think about Bloom's Taxonomy (discussed in Chapter 4). Try to create questions that focus on higher-level thinking—questions that typically begin with *why, how, explain,* or *compare*. By higher level, we mean questions that encourage synthesis of the information to be learned. Try to ask questions that require you to understand the entire concept—not just the small pieces. Most importantly, the questions you write should reflect the kinds of information that your professor expects you to learn.

To answer the questions, you would read your text annotations and lecture notes. As with all of the strategies, your question/answer strategy will not be effective if you leave out important information or include information that is wrong or incomplete. Also, whenever possible, put the material in your own words to help you remember it better.

Format for Question/Answer Strategy

Question	Answer
How does the role of X impact Y?	X greatly impacts Y because . . .
Explain the key factors that led to the development of Z.	There were three main factors that led to Z's development. They were . . .

■   ■   ■

How Do You Use the Question/Answer Strategy to Study? When you study using the question/answer strategy, fold your paper so that just your questions are showing. Ask yourself or get someone else to ask you a question. Then answer it by saying the information out loud. Check to see how much of the material you remembered correctly. If your answer matches what you wrote, repeat the process with the next question. If your answer is incomplete or wrong, read the correct answer several times and try to say it again before moving on to the next question. In addition, because the questions on the exam will most certainly be in random order, don't always begin with your first question and work your way through to the end. Instead, vary the order; start with the last question, do every other question, or use some other pattern.

Unlike the other strategies we have discussed, time lines are appropriate only in specific situations. Basically, you can use time lines when it is important to know chronology—the order of something that happened over a period of time. For example, you might use time lines in a history course when it's important to know the chronology of the Vietnam conflict, in an art appreciation class when you need to be able to compare and contrast major artistic movements, or in a geology course when you're expected to trace the evolution of the earth's crust over millions of years. Hence, you can use time lines in many different disciplines, but they do have a very specific function.

In the majority of studying situations, time lines should be supplemented with other strategies such as CARDS, concept maps, or charts. This is because time lines only show the chronology—which events happened when. But that would be insufficient knowledge to have when preparing for an exam. You would also need to know *why* the event happened, *what* the impact of these acts were, and *what* the details of each act entailed. This information cannot be gleaned from the time line alone.

Format for a Time Line

Date 1	Description and explanation of significance 1
Date 2	Description and explanation of significance 2
Date 3	Description and explanation of significance 3
Date 4	Description and explanation of significance 4
Date 5	Description and explanation of significance 5

How Do You Use Time Lines To Study? When you study with time lines, use the dates only as the cue. Talk through the important events, laws, battles, and so forth that occurred on each date. At the same time, use your other strategies to talk through the nature of each of the events, thinking about cause and effect, or how one event influenced another, when appropriate. Use newspaper questions—who, what, where, when, why, and how—to be certain that you are fully describing each event. In addition, it's important to understand how events are related, so be sure that you see the big picture as well.

Oral Rehearsal Strategies

Oral rehearsal strategies are those that involve talk in some way—reviewing out loud by yourself, rehearsing silently by yourself, or practicing with a study partner. Although it may seem odd to talk to yourself as you study and learn, saying information out loud is a powerful tool because it is a form of active learning that keeps you connected with what you are learning. Talking and listening as you study also help you use more than one of your senses. Remember, the more senses you use when you study, the easier learning will be. We will discuss two different oral strategies: reciprocal questioning and talk-throughs. Each of these strategies is a form of verbal summarization and each is generally used along with written strategies.

Reciprocal Questioning

Reciprocal questioning involves two learners—one who takes the role of the teacher and the other who takes the role of the student. The "teacher" asks questions from the written strategies described earlier in the question/answer strategy, from text annotations, or from lecture notes. Most should be questions that elicit higher-level or critical thinking rather than those that require memorization or one-word answers. The "student" answers the question and the "teacher" checks his answer against the written strategy. If the student answers the question correctly, the teacher asks the next question. If the question is not answered adequately, the teacher gives some hints and tries to guide the student to the answer. The goal is to help the student learn the material rather than just provide the correct response. Repeat the questions that the student missed at the end of the study session.

After all of the questions have been asked and answered and, if necessary, reviewed, the "student" and the "teacher" trade roles. The new teacher should be sure that she asks the questions in a different order and adds new questions.

Reciprocal questioning can be a powerful strategy for several reasons:

■ **It Brings More Senses into Play.** You have read the information using the visual sense, you have written important concepts down in an organized fashion using the kinesthetic sense, and you are now hearing the information using the auditory sense. Using more than one sense helps you remember better because it makes you a more active learner.

■ **It Encourages Multiple Perspectives.** The old adage "two heads are better than one" is true in this situation. One person may be very strong in understanding concept A and the other very knowledgeable about concept B. Pulling the ideas of two people together generally makes for clearer, more precise learning for both.

■ **It Encourages You to Use Your Own Words.** Because professors rarely write questions that come exactly from the text, it's important to put information in your own words so that you will recognize it in a slightly different form on the test. When you have two people putting it in their own words, you begin to think outside of the textbook, and you get another perspective of how the information might be phrased.

SUCCESS AT A GLANCE

Summary of Rehearsal Strategies

Rehearsal Strategies	Courses	Types of Questions
CARDS	Hard sciences, foreign languages, mathematics, statistics, any course where you have to learn many new terms	Best with objective questions; can be modified for use with either memory-level or higher-level questions
Concept Maps and Charts	Hard sciences and social sciences, history; if you are a visual learner; when you need to see relationships	Can be used for both objective and essay questions; best for higher-level questions that require you to see the big picture
Questions/Answers	All courses	Best for objective test questions unless you plan to modify them to predict essay questions
Time Lines	History, art history, music history, anthropology, any course where you need to know chronology	Memory-level questions; can supplement this strategy with others such as concept maps, charts, or CARDS
Reciprocal Questioning	All courses	All types of questions, but works well when rehearsing answers to higher-level questions
Talk-Throughs	All courses	All types of questions; helps you concentrate on key concepts rather than small details

■ **It Helps You to Monitor Your Learning.** When you are asked a question and then provide the answer, you get immediate feedback about your knowledge on that particular topic. This helps you monitor what concepts you know and focus on the concepts that need more work.

Talk-Throughs

As the name of this strategy suggests, talk-throughs involve saying the information (talking it through) to yourself, either silently or out loud to monitor your learning. When you talk through the concepts you become both the student and the teacher because, rather than having someone ask you questions or ask you to explain concepts, you fill both roles. Start by making a talk-through list on an index card. A talk-through card simply lists, in an organized fashion, the major concepts you need to learn and remember. When you create your talk-through, indent the supporting ideas so it is easy to see how the ideas are connected. Although this is not always the case, examining headings and subheadings is a good way to start your talk-through card because they give you the overall big picture of the chapter.

After you make your talk-through card, begin rehearsal by saying what you know about the first major concept. Talk it through, looking back at your written strategies, if necessary, including text annotations and lecture notes. In fact, after you have said the information silently or out loud, it is a good idea to go back to your strategy and read over the information again to be sure your answer is complete and precise. As you learn each piece of information, also be sure that you can make connections between the major concepts and the supporting details. Explain to yourself how the pieces fit together.

Reviewing

Reviewing is the step you take after you rehearse. When you rehearse, you write, say, and listen to the information until you know it very well. You look for connections between ideas and understand how concepts are related. Reviewing, on the other hand, is a way of making sure you have learned important information in a way that it is complete, organized, and precise. Reviewing ensures that the information will stay fixed in your memory. By reviewing daily, you remember about three times more than if you had not reviewed. Thus, there is a tremendous payoff in review. You can use reviewing at various times during the studying process. For example, when you read Chapter 10, you learned about taking effective lecture notes. In that chapter we emphasized the importance of reviewing notes daily. Getting to class ten minutes early and using those ten minutes to read over your notes is a form of reviewing. This type of review refreshes your memory of what happened in the last class and prepares your mind to receive new information, making it easier to connect ideas. But the kind of reviewing that we focus on in this chapter is generally done as a final phase of studying and test preparation. You review by self-testing to monitor your learning and gain a better understanding of the information you know very well and the information that requires further study through additional rehearsal.

Making a Specific Study Plan

We have talked in other chapters about the importance of planning. Rather than having a random approach to test preparation, think about how much time you will spend studying and what you will do during those study sessions. It's particularly important to structure specific study and review sessions as the time for the exam draws closer. That's why we suggest that you develop a Specific Study Plan (SSP) for each exam you take. Although some students get to the point where they know what they are going to do in each study session just by writing a few notes, it has been our experience that most students benefit from creating a more structured plan. Therefore, we suggest that you write out a study plan and clip it in your daily planner.

Construct your study plan about a week before the exam. Think about your goals by asking yourself a series of questions about the task:

1. What grade do I want to earn on the exam? (Note: Do not automatically say an "A" in response to this question. Instead, think about how much time and effort you are willing to invest to earn the grade you desire.)
2. How much time do I need to invest in order to make this grade?
3. Where will I find the extra time? Will I have to give up other activities in order to carve out time to study?
4. What kind of exam is it? Multiple-choice? Essay? What kinds of problems do I usually have when I take tests of this nature?
5. Do I know the balance of items? Is this a memorization task, or will I be expected to answer higher-level questions? What proportion of questions will come from the text and the lectures?
6. What kinds of rehearsal strategies will I need to create that will work best for this exam?

After you have answered these questions, you are ready to construct your SSP. An SSP outlines what you will do in each particular study session. It shows which rehearsal or review strategies you will use, which concepts you will study, and approximately how long each study session will last. Also note that each study session begins with a review of information that was rehearsed in the previous session. Each session should end with a review of what was learned in the current session.

Session date and time:	What I'll do:	Strategies I'll use:	Reflection and evaluation:

When you complete each study session, check it off, evaluate how long it actually took to complete, and think about any changes you might need to make for your next session. Did you need more time? Were you studying at a time when you were most alert? Did you minimize your distractions? Reflecting on these questions will help you as you develop an SSP for the next exam in this course.

SSPs use several types of review at different times in the review process.

1. **Begin** each session with a review of what you learned previously. Using your talk-through card as a guide, say what you remember from the earlier study session. If there's material that is still giving you problems, begin the current study session with it.

2. **End** each session with a review of only those concepts you concentrated on in the current session. This type of review serves as a monitoring device to let you know what you actually remember from the session. If you start this review and find that you are having problems, you can return to those concepts immediately and rehearse some more. This is the monitoring part of your review when you discover whether you will need to devote more time to the study session than you originally planned.

3. **In the day or two before the test,** continue to monitor your understanding of all of the concepts you will be tested over. Concentrate the time you have left on the material that you understand least. Many students make the mistake of spending equal amounts of time on everything before an exam—even information that they know fairly well. Learn from their mistakes. The closer the exam, the more you want to concentrate on concepts you don't know well.

Studying Smarter

Say not, when I have leisure I will study; you may not have leisure.

—The Mishnah

Setting some goals for yourself and making an SSP for each exam helps you stay on track with both rehearsing and reviewing. Remember to focus on learning specific concepts, not on the amount of time you actually have allotted for studying. Students who plan around time rather than around mastery of the information can easily go into a testing situation unprepared.

Especially for Working Students

If you are holding down a job or returning to college after several years, you may find the SSP to be an invaluable strategy. When you are juggling work (even part time), family needs, and your other responsibilities, creating a studying plan that lets you know exactly how much time you will need to prepare can help you find balance in your busy life.

Forming Study Groups

One of the best ways to review is by forming study groups. Some students establish study groups that meet weekly to talk about and review what went on in class that week. Other students form study groups just before an exam to review and perhaps get a new or different perspective on what they have learned. Either way, study groups have big advantages if they are done right.

Perhaps the biggest advantage of being part of a study group is that it allows you to listen to information in another person's voice, which can provide insights that you may not have considered. In a traditional course, you listen to your professor's interpretation of the information during lectures, you read the text for another interpretation, and through these two sources, you come up with your own interpretation or meaning. You have listened to, read, and written down material, so you have used several of your senses. All of this interaction should help you gain a greater degree of understanding of the material. It stands to reason, then, that by listening to and talking with others who are also trying to understand the course information, you could gain a deeper understanding, be able to remember the concepts better, and subsequently do better on the exams.

It's important to think about the characteristics of *good* study groups. Just meeting with people in the same course does not necessarily make a study group. Productive study groups have the following characteristics:

■ **Everyone Comes Prepared.** Study groups do not replace studying on your own. Everyone should come to the group prepared to review the information, pose and answer possible test questions, and voice questions about material they don't understand. If the study group members have to spend all of their time trying to teach a large portion of the course material to someone who hasn't attempted to learn it on her own, most members will not benefit.

■ **Everyone Can Talk Through a Difficult Idea with the Group.** Divide the material among the group members. It helps if everyone selects something complex or confusing to discuss. During the study group, each member will lead the discussion on his topic. As you are reviewing your understanding of the concept, other members who may understand it better than you should be encouraged to offer additional explanations. Don't shy away from discussing information that you don't know very well; this defeats the purpose of the group.

■ **Members of the Study Group Should Be Classmates, but Not Necessarily Friends.** Everyone knows what can happen when friends get together to study: Everything goes fine for the first few minutes, but it's easy to get off track. It's much better to recruit serious students, who all have the goal of doing well, into your study group rather than just including friends. That's not to say that studying with friends will never work; it's simply harder to study with friends than it is with classmates working toward a common goal.

■ **Meet at a Place That Is Conducive to Studying.** Campus libraries often have study rooms set aside for just this purpose. If your library doesn't have study rooms, dorms often have common areas equipped with study rooms. Empty classrooms or a local coffee shop also can work well. If your only alternative is to study in someone's room or at someone's home or apartment, remind yourself that the purpose of the session is to review the course material for a test, not to socialize.

■ **Have Clear Goals and Structure.** When you initially form a study group, you should have a more specific goal than to get together and study. Most groups meet at regular times. We know of a study group in a statistics course that meets weekly to review the important ideas presented that week and then also meets a couple of times right before the exam to review what its members know and to predict and solve possible test questions. Groups that have a game plan before they come together are generally the most successful. Along those lines, if you're really serious about having a good study group, it doesn't hurt to set some ground rules right from the beginning to prevent difficulties later on. For example, what will happen if someone comes to the group without doing any preparation on his own?

Almost everyone can benefit from belonging to a study group at one time or another, but study groups work particularly well for students who learn through discussion and for students in courses they find problematic. We don't know of any student who is in a study group for *every* class, but if you are taking a particularly difficult course, it often helps to have the opinion and input of others.

ON YOUR OWN

Reflecting on What You Have Read

Write a paragraph about how you currently review. In a second paragraph respond to the following questions: What are the advantages of saying information out loud as you review? Think of your own experiences working in groups. What makes a study group successful? What makes it unsuccessful? In which of your courses this semester would study groups benefit you the most? Why?

Improving Your Memory Through Reviewing

Reviewing can help you remember almost three times more information than if you hadn't reviewed. You can maximize the amount you remember, thereby improving your memory, if you keep in mind five basic reviewing principles:

1. **Organize.** Research indicates that people tend to remember information the way that they have organized it. So, the first step you should take as you begin to rehearse and review course material is to be sure that it is organized, and therefore stored, in an easily retrievable way. Remember, you don't have to organize the material in the same way the text or your professor does. Create an organization that will work for you.

2. **Use Images and Other Mnemonics.** The word *mnemonics* comes from the Greek word for "mindful." Mnemonics are memory devices—little tricks you can use to help you remember specific kinds of information. As discussed in Chapter 3, one way you can use mnemonics is to learn a list by taking the first letters of the items you are trying to memorize and making them represent something memorable. Your mnemonic device doesn't have to make sense to anyone but you. In fact, the more outrageous the memory device, the easier it generally is to remember. For example, a mnemonic used by physics students to remember the Maxwell relations in thermodynamics is "*Good Physicists Have Studied Under Very Fine Teachers,*" which helps them remember the order of the variables in the square, in clockwise direction.

3. **Say It Rather Than Reread It.** We have stated more than once that rehearsal is a much more effective way to learn information than rereading. This is true for three reasons. First, few students have time to reread large portions of text. Second, when students reread, they pick up very little additional information. Third, students who only reread get overly dependent on the wording used in the text. If the professor asks questions in even a slightly different way, they often get confused because they have not thought through the items on their own. When you say the information, however, you tend to summarize the key points in your own words. This makes verbalization particularly effective for review. If you ask yourself questions (or get someone else to ask them) and then answer the questions, you will remember considerably more than if you simply tried to reread the material.

4. **Have Several Review Sessions.** Research indicates that students who read, rehearse, and review in a short time frame do not do as well as those who spread their study out over time, even when the amount of time engaged in learning is about the same. Therefore, we would expect the student who studied five hours spread out over a period of four days prior to the exam to do better than the student who spent five hours "studying" the night before an exam. Students who space their learning by using several study sessions

tend to get less tired and can concentrate better during studying, thus improving the amount they can recall on test day.

5. **Overlearn.** We add this suggestion to make you aware of the difference between "kinda" knowing something and learning it to the point at which it is almost automatic. When you overlearn something you know it so well that you don't even have to think about it. We have all overlearned things—the Pledge of Allegiance, "The Star Spangled Banner," nursery rhymes, the lyrics to popular music. If only you could remember the information for your biology or anthropology exam in the same way. The reason you can remember some information so easily is that you have been exposed to it over and over and over again. Contrast that with the feeling you have when you have studied but you know that you do not know the information very well. By reviewing course information repeatedly, you will become more familiar with it.

Reviewing is important as a final step in the active learning process. You can review alone or with a study group. No matter how you choose to review, remember that self-testing and monitoring your understanding is key.

Real College

Conrad

DIRECTIONS: Read the following "Real College" scenario and respond to the questions based on what you learned in this chapter.

Conrad is a first-year college student who is pretty nervous about doing well in his courses. He is particularly unhappy with his inability to see the big picture in some of his courses and is surprised that his classes seem to require him to study in different ways in order to do well. By his own admission, he is a slacker and prides himself on being a laid-back, low-stress guy.

In high school, Conrad simply skimmed the parts of his texts to answer questions on the study guides that most of his teachers provided. He would memorize this information and do well on almost every exam. But in college, three of his professors expect him to conceptualize information. That is, he has to understand scientific processes in biology, he is expected "to put information in a historical perspective" in history, and he has to think about how character development and use of language relate to the plot in short stories in literature class. He is worried that he might actually fail a course this term.

Conrad doesn't even know where to start studying for these courses. In high school, he used to put lots of information on note cards, and sometimes he would make complex outlines, but he doesn't know any other study strategies to consider.

What would your advice to Conrad be? What rehearsal and review strategies would you recommend for each of his courses and why?

ADD TO YOUR PORTFOLIO

1. Construct a set of ten questions/answers for a chapter from a textbook assigned for a course in which you are currently enrolled. Be sure to ask some higher-level questions that begin with the words *how* and *why*.

2. Construct one of the following strategies for a course in which you are currently enrolled. Be sure to consider the task before you select your strategy.

   ■ Twenty CARDS

   ■ One concept map

   ■ One chart

3. For the next exam in one of your classes, set goals by answering the following goal-related questions. Then construct an SSP. Remember to set aside time in your SSP for rehearsal and review. Also remember to begin and end each study session with review.

My goals and SSP for _____ test.

1. What grade do I want to earn on the exam?

2. How much time do I need to invest in order to make this grade?

3. Where will I find the extra time? Will I have to give up other activities in order to carve out time to study?

4. What kind of exam is it? Multiple-choice? Essay? What kinds of problems do I usually have when I take tests of this nature?

5. Do I know the balance of items? Are there more text or lecture questions? Is this a memorization task, or will I be expected to answer higher-level questions?

6. What kinds of rehearsal strategies will work best for this exam? Will I need to begin by reformatting or constructing any strategies that I have already made?

Session date and time:	What I'll do:	Strategies I'll use:	Reflection and evaluation:

Strategies for Social Science*

READ THIS CHAPTER TO FIND ANSWERS TO THE FOLLOWING
QUESTIONS:

■ How do I read strategically in social science courses?
■ What strategies should I use to be successful in social science courses?
■ How can I modify my strategies to suit different types of courses and texts?

SELF-ASSESSMENT

DIRECTIONS: Respond to the following statements for at least one social science course you are taking this term or that you have taken recently in college.

	Course 1	Course 2
(course name)	___	___
I read the text before class.	Yes/No	Yes/No
I read the text after class.	Yes/No	Yes/No
My class lecture follows the text.	Yes/No	Yes/No
I am responsible for reading multiple texts for this course.	Yes/No	Yes/No
I try to study in the same way for each course.	Yes/No	Yes/No
I understand the professor's expectations for this course.	Yes/No	Yes/No

The way you have responded to these questions gives a good indication of how you approach reading and studying in your social science classes. Keep these answers in mind as you read the rest of the chapter.

---

*As you read this chapter, you may want to refer to Chapters 4, 9, 10, and 11 to refresh your memory about general guidelines for strategy use.

Characteristics of Social Science Courses

Social science courses are concerned with what happens in a society. The social sciences involve the study of people in terms of political, economic, social, interpersonal, and cultural aspects of society. Such courses would include sociology, psychology, economics, anthropology, and political science. Professors who teach these courses assume that you have some knowledge of human behavior. Social science courses generally are lecture oriented; therefore the ability to take good notes is important. In addition, there is a considerable focus on comparing and contrasting theories. Finally, as a student in a social science course, you may be required to participate in experiments (psychology) or work on long-term projects.

Studying Smarter

Although most social science professors will expect you to read your text before you come to class, it's always good to check the syllabus or ask the professor for guidance. Sometimes the material is easier to understand if you listen to the lecture and take good notes before you read the text.

Figuring Out the Task

There is a wide range of tasks possible in social science courses. In fact, many professors will ask objective questions (for example, multiple choice, true/false, matching) and also include some essay, short answer, or identification items. Although it's important to know what percentages of the exam will be objective and essay, it is equally important to know the level of thinking your professor requires. If she wants you to memorize, many of the items will begin with "what"; if she expects you to think on higher levels, she will ask you *how* or *why* questions and will ask you to recognize or generate examples. Look at the following two questions. Which one is a higher-level question? Why?

1. *Crystallized intelligence* refers to:
   a. information that we store and apply
   b. a specific aspect of intelligence
   c. inherited abilities to think and reason
   d. all of the above

2. Which of the following is an example of crystallized intelligence?
   a. how many vocabulary words you can use
   b. applying what you learned in algebra to everyday life
   c. making connections between historical events
   d. all of the above

Social science courses also tend to be what are often termed "heavy lecture courses." That is, you will need to use active listening strategies, be able to take good notes, and synthesize your notes and lectures. Your professor's lectures should place considerable emphasis on what she considers important for you to know, thus helping you greatly in determining the course tasks. For these reasons, it's important to get down as much information as you can during lectures and then go back and reduce the information.

TIMELY TIPS

Figure Out the Task Early

The earlier in the term you can figure out the task, the more successful you will be. In the social sciences, use your syllabus and the way your professor lectures to help you determine what she expects you to do and how she expects you to think. Compare what is covered in your text with what is covered in lectures to figure out how much overlap there is between text and lecture. Remember, the greater the overlap, the easier it should be to come up with a plan for test preparation.

Reading Social Science Textbooks

Social science texts are usually arranged topically, but most of the topics can stand on their own. This means that your professors can teach the material in any order they choose and not follow the order in which the book has been written because, unlike math or science, the information in later chapters is not dependent on your understanding of earlier chapters. The texts usually present ideas in topical or chronological form. For example, a psychology text often presents ideas by topic, but an anthropology textbook usually discusses events in the order they occurred in time (chronologically).

Social science texts are often filled with terms that may seem familiar but have a specialized meaning. For example, the word *class* has a very different meaning in a sociology course than it has in an education course. The word *performance* has a different meaning in psychology than it does in the arts.

Social science texts, especially psychology books, tend to be reader friendly, providing an abundance of background information. They also tend to be well organized. Terms are often defined for you, there are questions to guide your reading and understanding, and introductions and conclusions are commonplace. All of these aids can help you if you use them properly.

Sections of social science texts are often highlighted in text boxes or in some other manner. In high school, you probably skipped these text boxes. However, in college, text boxes often contain important information that does not appear elsewhere in the text. Sometimes they contain supporting articles, examples of a principle outlined in the text, or copies of original documents discussed in the chapter. Many of your exam questions may come from text box information. Professors are aware that students tend to skip text boxes and they want to make sure students pay attention to the important information contained in the boxes, so they base test items on them. Our advice is to follow this general rule: *Read the text boxes.*

Gearing Up for Reading

When gearing up for reading social science texts, it's important to first activate your prior knowledge by reading the chapter title and then asking yourself, "What do I already know about this topic?" You can answer the question by making either a mental or written jot list. As you continue your preview, pay particular attention to the chapter organization because this will help you identify key ideas and help you begin to make connections between the ideas presented. Read over the text supports—terms that are defined for you in the margins and text inserts—and read the captions to the visual aids as you look over the visual. Finally, if there is an introduction and conclusion to the chapter, read these as well. If each section has an introduction and conclusion, you might read each of them—particularly if you have little background knowledge on the topics being presented.

ON YOUR OWN

Reflecting on What You Have Read

Turn to the psychology excerpt on page 228 in Appendix A and respond to the following questions: What information would you want to include in your preview? Which strategies would make the most sense to use to study for a multiple-choice exam over this material? Why? Which strategies would be best to prepare for an essay question? Why?

SUCCESS AT A GLANCE

Features in Social Science Courses

Most social science courses have at least some of the following features. Check your social science books to see how many features are present.

Chapter introductions	Section introductions
New terms highlighted	New terms defined in margins
Questions to guide reading	Headings/subheadings
Visual aids	Sidebars containing
End-of-chapter questions	supporting information
End-of-chapter glossary	

What and How to Annotate During Reading

It's probably a good idea to read your social science textbook before you attend class so that you are ready for a class discussion or lecture. As you read, annotate the text and any diagrams or other typographical aids. Identify comparisons and contrasts between ideas because they often make their way into social science exams. In addition, note possible test questions.

If it has been a while since you read Chapter 9, you might want to go back and review the general strategies for annotating texts. These suggestions cut across all disciplines and texts. What follows here provides you with more specific detail in annotating social science materials. Examples from psychology, which is representative of the social sciences, are also included to help you get a better "feel" for what your annotations might look like.

One of the most important things to remember when you annotate social science or any other texts is that your annotations should match your professor's expectations. In other words, effective annotators understand the course tasks. The most common types of information that you annotate in social science texts are:

- Tenets of major theories
- Characteristics, stages
- Experiments, particularly the results and implications, in the case of psychology
- Ideas that are compared and contrasted
- Examples
- Lists

In social science texts, use cue words, especially list and example cues as a guide for annotation. These cues include the following words and phrases:

- **Example cues**—for example, suppose, in one study, one situation, an illustration of
- **"Rest of the story" cues**—in addition to, moreover, furthermore, however, but, may, if…then, also, because
- **Summary cues**—hence, thus, therefore, in sum, the moral of the story
- **List cues**—first, (1), second, (2),…etc., next, finally, similarly, last
- **Hedging cues**—maybe, may be, perhaps, probably, generally, occasionally, sometimes, suggested
- **Superlative cues**—best, most, least, major, worst, particularly important, key (meaning major, as in "key finding")

As you annotate, be sure to think about how the terms fit together. In other words, you look for the big picture and then annotate the supporting information so that you have a precise and concise record of all of the key information. Now look at the sample psychology annotations on pages 158 and 159 and note not only what is annotated but also how the information is organized. These annotations begin with a definition of *hypnosis*, but they don't stop there. They also pull out other information that would be important to know about this topic. For example, they highlight who can be hypnotized and what some of the criticisms of hypnosis are. In addition, the three theories that account for hypnotic behaviors are numbered, annotated, and explained. Note also that these annotations go considerably beyond the two questions that are posed in the margin: *What is hypnosis, and when is it most useful?* and *What are the three main theories that have been proposed to explain hypnosis?* Although these two questions are a good beginning point, you would need to elaborate on these points in order for your annotations to be effective.

Example of Annotations in a Psychology Textbook

Brain-imaging studies show that blood flow increases in the cerebral cortex during meditation, indicating that it is a complex cognitive task (Newberg et al., 2001). Moreover, prayer can induce psychological and physiological states very much like those associated with meditation (Bernardi et al., 2001).

Herbert Benson (1975) suggests the contemplation of any word or sound can be used for meditation, although some would disagree with him. Moreover, he claims that the beneficial effects of meditation can be achieved through simple relaxtion techniques. Do *Try It! 4.2* to experience Benson's relaxation response.

Hypnosis

Hypnosis may be defined as a procedure through which one person, the hypnotist, uses the power of suggestion to induce changes in thoughts, feelings, sensations, perceptions, or behavior of another person, the subject. Under hypnosis, people suspend their usual rational and logical ways of thinking and perceiving and allow themselves to experience distortions in perceptions, memories, and thinking. They may experience positive hallucinations, in which they see, hear, touch, smell, or taste things that are not present in the environment. Or they may have negative hallucinations in which they fail to perceive things that are actually present.

About 80–95% of people are hypnotizable to some degree, but only 5% can reach the deepest levels of the hypnotic state (Nash & Baker, 1984). The ability to become completely absorbed in imaginative activities is characteristic of highly hypnotizable people (Nandon et al., 1991). Silva and Kirsch (1992) found that proneness to fantasizing and the expectation that one will respond to hypnotic suggestions were predictors of individuals' hypnotizability.

Despite what many people believe, and what is often portrayed in the media, people who are hypnotized retain the ability to refuse to comply with the hypnotist's suggestions, and they will not do anything that is contrary to their moral beliefs. Moreover, although it is true that hypnotized subjects supply more information and are more confident of their recollections, the information is often inaccurate (Dywan & Bowers, 1983; Kihlstrom & Barnhardt, 1993; Nogrady et al., 1985; Weekes et al., 1992). In fact, in the process of trying to help people recall certain events, hypnotists may instead create in them false memories, or *pseudomemories* (Lynn & Nash, 1994; Yapko, 1994).

Handwritten annotation (left margin):

Hypnosis

(def) - procedure where power of suggest. used to create change in thought or beh.
- may exp. + or - hallucinations
- 80-95% can be hypno'ed...BUT only 5% to deep level
- Will NOT do anything under hypno. that is against morals
- Sometimes info recalled not accurate
(def) - pseudo memories = false memories

What is hypnosis, and when is it most useful? ▶

hypnosis
A procedure through which one person, the hypnotist, uses the power of suggestion to induce changes in thoughts, feelings, sensations, perceptions, or behavior of another person, the subject.

Thus, hypnosis is not like a truth serum; people can keep secrets or lie under hypnosis.

Still, hypnosis is recognized as a viable technique for use in medicine, dentistry, and psychotherapy (Lynn et al., 2000). For example, experimental studies have shown that patients who are hypnotized and exposed to suggestions designed to induce relaxation prior to surgery experience less postsurgical pain than do nonhypnotized controls (Montgomery et al., 2002). Hypnosis has also been used successfully to treat posttraumatic stress disorder (Cardena, 2000). However, hypnosis has been only moderately effective in weight control and virtually useless in overcoming drug and alcohol abuse or nicotine addiction (Abbot et al., 2000; Green & Lynn, 2000; Orne, 1983).

What accounts for people's behavior under hypnosis? According to the *sociocognitive theory of hypnosis*, the behavior of a hypnotized person is a function of that person's expectations about how subjects behave under hypnosis. People are motivated to be good subjects, to follow the suggestions of the hypnotist, and to fulfill the social role of the hypnotized person as they perceive it (Spanos, 1986, 1991, 1994).

However, Ernest Hilgard (1986, 1992) has proposed a *neodissociation theory of hypnosis*, suggesting that hypnosis induces a split, or dissociation, between two aspects of the control of consciousness that are ordinarily linked—the planning and the monitoring functions. During hypnosis, it is the planning function that carries out the suggestions of the hypnotist and remains a part of the subject's conscious awareness. The monitoring function monitors or observes everything that happens to the subject, but without his or her conscious awareness. Hilgard called the monitoring function, when separated from conscious awareness, "the hidden observer."

Bowers and his colleagues (Bowers, 1992; Woody & Bowers, 1994) have proposed an explanation called the *theory of dissociated control*, maintaining that hypnosis weakens the control of the executive function over other parts (subsystems) of consciousness. In their view, the hypnotist's suggestions not only affect the executive function, but influence the other subsystems directly. Bowers further believes that the hypnotized person's responses are automatic and involuntary, not mediated by normal cognitive functions (Kirsch & Lynn, 1995). And, indeed, some research supports this belief (Bowers & Woody, 1996; Hargadon et al., 1995).

> • can lie under hypno.
> • Used in medical, psych. & dentistry
> Experiment found those hypno'ed during sugery exp. less pain after
>   HOWEVER...
> only moderate effects for weight loss, drug, alcohol, and smoking.
> 3 theories to acc'nt for behavior
> ① sociocognitive-Spano → you know how you are supposed to behave so you do
> ② neodissociation-Hilgard → hypno. causes a split b/t planning & monitoring funct.
> ③ dissociated control-Bowers et. al → hypno. weakens control of exec. func. & infl. other subsystems.

◄ What are the three main theories that have been proposed to explain hypnosis?

GET GOING

Uncertainty Is Okay…Sometimes

Social science texts tend to contain lots of uncertainties. By this we mean that in the social sciences much of what you read will be theory that is not proven. Texts will often provide several theories for a particular concept, which may initially seem strange to you. In fact, it is part of the discipline to think about a variety of ways to explain the same phenomena. For example, there are several theories of intelligence and learning. What this means is that sometimes you have to learn to live with this uncertainty, which in the long run can help you have a broader understanding of the field.

Taking Notes in Social Science Courses

As we previously mentioned, social science courses tend to be lecture courses. The professor usually lectures for the entire period, focusing on information that he feels is important for you to learn. Some of what your professor lectures on will be in your text, but most teachers supplement it with new material. That's why you need to find a method of note taking that works for you. The T-method combined with the split-page method discussed in Chapter 10 tends to work for social science courses. Using this method is similar to using the question/answer strategy in that you are posing and answering questions that pull out the key points discussed in each day's lecture. Then, as you are preparing for an exam, you can concentrate on the information in your T-notes.

T-notes for a psychology lecture on memory might look something like this:

Example of the T-Method

Summary	Questions
Memory consists of 3 systems 1. encoding, 2. storage, 3. retrieval—information first goes to short-term memory through rehearsal (maintenance or elaborative) where it is either encoded or forgotten quickly (less than 30 sec.) Information that is encoded goes into long-term memory	1. What are the three memory systems? Define and describe characteristics. 2. Compare and contrast maintenance and elaborative rehearsal. 3. How does information move from STM to LTM?

When your professor is lecturing, you need to listen for the same kinds of material you annotate in your social science texts—definitions, theories, lists, characteristics, examples, and the like. Listen for cue words and be sure you number lists. For example, in psychology, there might be three theories of intelligence discussed, and it would be important to get those three theories down. But maybe your professor thinks one theory is the "best" or "most plausible." These types of cues can be very helpful in identifying information that your professor might ask you on an exam.

Example of Parallel Notes

Your Notes	Self-Testing
Much $ spent on getting out the vote.	
Over several decades, turnout has declined.	Decline in voting— reasons
Presidential elections have fallen from nearly 65% in the 1960s to just over 50% in the 1990s.	
Efforts are often only in the states and congressional districts where elections are expected to be close, and are often partisan.	Partisan vs. non-partisan effort
But there are also less partisan efforts designed to boost turnout overall.	
—Voter participation in the United States is lower than most other well-established democracies.	
Questions to think about 1. Why is turnout lower in the United States than in other advanced democracies?	Would make good essay question!
2. How have turnout rates been changing for the electorate as a whole and for specific social groups? What are the implications of those trends for the two major political parties?	

Professor's Notes

Impact of Voter Mobilization

- Mobilization matters.

- What the parties and the campaigns do has an impact on who and how many people turn out to vote.

- But you can only mobilize when there is a chance that you can win.

- Turnout is generally low in one-party dominant areas where the general election is noncompetitive.

Online Notes in the Social Sciences

We have found that it is very common for professors in the social sciences to put their notes online. Perhaps that's because they rely so heavily on lecture. If your professor puts her notes online, use the parallel method of note taking. The figures on page 161 shows an example of parallel notes taken from a political science course. Using this method, the professor's notes serve as a guide, but you should continue to take a good set of notes on your own. In addition, when you download your professor's notes, read them carefully to see how they are organized and how much information she is putting in the notes. Some professors provide a fairly basic outline and expect you to fill in the gaps. Others will provide a full set of notes, perhaps filled with material that is not very important. So use your professor's notes, but remember that they supplement and don't take the place of taking notes on your own.

Studying in Social Science Courses

Because you will be asked to read and understand many new concepts in social science courses, you will need strategies to help you organize large amounts of information. Students sometimes experience difficulty in social science courses because they try to memorize facts, forgetting that because the social sciences predominantly are based on theories, there are few "facts." Also, some social science texts deal with large time spans, making it hard to simply memorize facts. An anthropology class, for instance, could cover thousands of years in one semester.

If your professor gives objective tests, the best strategies to use would be CARDS and the question/answer technique, especially in courses like psychology. Charts and maps would also be appropriate for comparing and contrasting theories and for organizing difficult information in order to see how concepts are related.

CARDS

For the psychology chapter, using CARDS is appropriate because there are many new terms. Look at the concept card on page 164 for the term *heritability*, taken from the "Cognition and Intelligence" excerpt in Appendix A.

In the social sciences, it is particularly important to use appropriate organizing terms and to be sure that you go beyond definitions. In the example, the organizing term is *Heredity and intelligence*, which indicates that this card will be grouped with others relating to it. This suggests that *heritability* is only one of the ideas related to heredity and intelligence and that it is linked to other ideas. Without the organizing term, it would be easy to simply memorize a definition for *heritability*.

Now look at the back of the card. The definition appears here, but there is also supporting information that would be important to know. An example, which cites research on the IQ of twins and includes a statement about which theory this supports, is also written on the card. Using this information to study from would help you answer several different types of questions and certainly goes beyond simply memorizing a definition for *heritability*.

Once you have a good set of CARDS, you can study them front to back and back to front. You can also lay them out on the floor or on your desk to form a concept map when you are dealing with information for which it is important to see relationships.

Question/Answer Strategy

The question/answer technique can help you study for both objective and short-answer questions. The key is asking the "right" questions. In the social sciences, it's common for students to pose questions beginning with *what* because there tend to be lots of definitions. In the earlier CARDS example for *heritability* taken from the psychology excerpt, we discussed the importance of adding information that goes beyond the definition of the term. The same holds true for the question/answer strategy. Look at the following three examples of the question/answer strategy. These three questions begin with the words *explain* or *how*. Note that each of these good questions is followed by a *what* question that would only help you answer a memorization-level item on an exam. For example, rather than posing the question, "What is processing speed?" the instruction, "Explain how processing speed is related to measuring intelligence," forces you to think beyond definitional information and prepares you for almost any question that can be asked on that topic.

Although CARDS and questions/answers are probably the best strategies to use in preparing for objective social science exams, students who are strong visual learners and need to "see" how concepts fit together could certainly map the material. Because maps show how an individual conceptualizes the relationships between ideas, no two maps on a topic will ever look exactly the same.

Example of CARDS for Psychology

Heredity and intelligence

Heritability

Chapter 7 p. 277

Front of CARDS

Def. The proportion of variance in intelligence that can be linked to genetic factors.

Seems to increase with age (ex. 35% in childhood to 75% in adulthood)

ex. IQs of twins raised together or apart are nearly identical. This supports theory of heritability of intelligence

Back of CARDS

Example of the Question/Answer Strategy

Questions	Answers
1. Explain how processing speed is related to measuring intelligence. (What is processing speed?)	1. _____ _____
2. How does one's environment affect intelligence? (What is environmental deprivation?)	2. _____ _____
3. How does heredity affect one's intelligence? (What is heritability?)	3. _____ _____

Real College

Frank

DIRECTIONS: Read the following "Real College" scenario and respond to the question based on what you learned in this chapter.

Frank is a first-year student who is pretty sure he wants to major in psychology. He likes his psych course this term, but his "the quickest way is the best way" of doing things doesn't seem to be working for him as it has in the past. Although this may be a good motto to follow in some things—Frank can always find the quickest way to work, the fastest Internet connection, the shortest line at the grocery store—when it comes to studying and learning psychology, the quickest way often doesn't pan out.

Frank was a fairly conscientious student in high school. He did what he needed to do to make good grades, and he was able to do it at warp speed. He really never had to read his high school textbooks because his teachers gave him study guides and other studying supports that didn't make reading necessary. But things have changed now that Frank is in college. He is excellent at finding the quickest route to his classes, but his quickness isn't paying off when it comes to reading his textbooks and preparing for exams. Because he never had to read much in high school, he thinks that if he just sits down and plows through the assigned psychology reading he will get it done. "Read it fast and move on." The same goes for studying for his tests: "Look over the notes quickly and ace the exam." However, he has found out that his approach isn't going to work. He has been getting through the reading and studying fast, but it has been wasted time. He can't remember anything that he's read or studied and has a difficult time making connections between ideas presented in the chapters.

What advice would you give Frank about what he can do in psychology that might be effective as well as efficient?

ADD TO YOUR PORTFOLIO

If you are taking a social science course this semester, answer the following questions, providing samples of your work when appropriate.

1. What course(s) are you taking?
2. How is the course structured (topically, sequentially, chronologically, etc.)?
3. What are the tasks for the course? Write a paragraph describing the course tasks.
4. What kind of information should you annotate? Provide a five-page example of your annotations.
5. Which strategies work best for this course? Why? Provide an example of one of the strategies you are using.
6. How will you prepare for your next exam? Why do you think your preparation strategies are appropriate? Write a paragraph discussing these questions.

Strategies for the Humanities*

> **READ THIS CHAPTER TO FIND ANSWERS TO THE FOLLOWING QUESTIONS:**
>
> - How do I read strategically in humanities courses?
> - What strategies should I use to be successful in humanities courses?
> - How can I modify my strategies to suit different types of humanities courses and texts?

--- **SELF-ASSESSMENT** ---

DIRECTIONS: Answer *yes* or *no* to each of the following statements for each humanities course you are taking this term. Think about how you prepare for each class.

(course name)	Course 1	Course 2
I read the text before class.	Yes/No	Yes/No
I read the text after class.	Yes/No	Yes/No
My class lecture follows the text.	Yes/No	Yes/No
I am responsible for reading multiple texts for this course.	Yes/No	Yes/No
I try to study in the same way for each course.	Yes/No	Yes/No
I understand the professor's expectations for this course.	Yes/No	Yes/No

The way you have responded to these questions gives a good indication of how you approach reading and studying in your humanities classes. Keep these answers in mind as you read the rest of the chapter.

---

*As you read this chapter, you may want to refer to Chapters 4, 9, 10, and 11 to refresh your memory about general guidelines for strategy use.

Characteristics of Humanities Courses

Humanities courses focus on all areas of human endeavor—invention, relationships, and creation. Just about any area you can think of is represented in the humanities. In this respect, the humanities include courses as broad and diverse as literature, philosophy, and fine arts (including music, art, and theater), foreign languages, and history. With so many different areas, it is difficult to generalize about humanities characteristics.

As with social sciences, there is generally a lot of lecture combined with discussion in humanities courses. Specifically in history, there is also a considerable amount of reading to go along with the lecture and discussion. Lectures supplement the text and attempt to help you put events into a historical perspective, synthesize information, and view history as an interpretation of events rather than encourage you to memorize events, names, and dates. Professors expect you to know more than the facts. In other words, humanities courses ask you to think on higher levels and to analyze the material.

Studying Smarter

Because the humanities cover vast and varied courses, it's important to be flexible when selecting strategies for studying in these classes. Clearly think through the task first; then select the strategies appropriate for the particular task.

Figuring Out the Task

Although in high school you may have had lots of experience with fact-based multiple-choice tests, in college you will find that recall tests—short answer, essay, identification—are much more common. Even if you have multiple-choice exams in your college humanities courses, you will be required to think at higher levels, synthesize information, and react critically to the information. It's sometimes difficult to figure out the task in courses like history, where you may have had a steady diet of fact questions throughout your schooling. In addition, even if your professor is very explicit about the task and states clearly that you are expected to think about history differently, it's very difficult for some students to change. A situation that we have encountered over and over again serves as a good example.

Most history professors on our campuses expect students to begin to think about history a bit differently than they have in the past, and the professors' task demands clearly indicate this. Students are still asked to respond to identification items, but in addition to explaining them they must also discuss their significance. For example, on one test, students were given the term *Statue of Liberty* to define and provide the significance of. Few students had any trouble defining the term, but when it came to writing about the significance, most students fell short. Some even ignored the significance portion of the identification altogether and therefore received only partial credit for this item and others. The message here is clear. Listen to the hints your professor gives you about how she expects you to think. Think about how the course lectures are arranged and the information your professor stresses in class. How does your professor tie information together? How does he go beyond what is in your text(s)?

For literature-based courses, the task generally involves writing about more abstract ideas—mood, character development, themes, and the like. This is why it is imperative to devise a method of reading and studying that will be effective in tying such information together at exam time. As with history, most literature professors will expect you to think about critical issues, provide support and examples for your stance, synthesize information, and then write a cogent essay. As such, you will encounter few literature-based courses that ask factual, recognition items.

Reading Humanities Textbooks

Initially, many students think that humanities texts are easier to read than the texts in more fact-based courses like math or science, but humanities courses can be challenging because they require students to interpret, analyze, and evaluate the text. In general, humanities textbooks do not introduce much new content vocabulary, but you may encounter unfamiliar use of words or dialects. Topics in humanities textbooks are often presented chronologically, as in a history textbook that is arranged by years, decades, or even centuries. Literature texts are often arranged by when each story, poem, and play was written or according to genre—poetry, short stories, epic, tragedy, and comedy, for example. However, sometimes they are organized topically, as in a philosophy textbook organized by themes. In history texts, concepts do not really build on one another as they do in the sciences, but chronologically arranged texts are usually read in the order they are presented. In other words, you will probably read about World War I before you read about the Vietnam conflict.

Humanities texts, especially history books, tend to have lots of photographs, maps, and text boxes that can provide helpful background information. There are few new terms, but there are lots of people, events, and chronologies to learn, many of which you have probably already been exposed to prior to college. Because history texts often read like a story, it's sometimes more difficult to pick out the important information.

For humanities courses that are discussion-based and literature-based, for example, it is important to read the text before attending class. As you read, you should focus on analyzing and interpreting the information. Ask yourself questions such as:

- What is the significance of what I am reading?
- Why did the author write this?
- What themes or metaphors are being used?
- How does this piece compare to other readings in this course?

GET GOING

A Heavy Load

Because the reading load tends to be quite heavy in humanities courses—it's common to read 150-200 pages per week—it's important not to get behind. Try to read and annotate your text every day and think about how your reading relates to what the professor deems important in lecture. If you approach humanities in this manner, it will be much easier to prepare for your exams.

Gearing Up for Reading

Because the humanities include such varied content areas, we will focus the examples in this chapter on history to avoid confusion. Preparing to read history textbooks requires a little different approach than the social sciences or sciences. Chapter titles tend to be very broad (for example, The Vietnam Conflict) and headings and subheadings very brief. Such text aids provide little information that helps you organize what you read and may only give you an extremely global picture of what the chapter is about. In addition, many of the typographical aids, especially photographs of people, are there to provide interest more than anything. Therefore, you will need to preview your text a bit differently by focusing on other features. First, look for introductions, summaries, and conclusions. If they are present, read them to fill in some of the gaps that the headings and subheadings leave out. Then, ask yourself some questions, particularly those that begin with *how* or *why*. For example, in previewing the "The Nation Divides: The Vietnam War and Social Conflict, 1964-1971," in Appendix B, which includes an excerpt on the Great Society, you might ask yourself these questions: What was Johnson's vision of the Great Society? What was the purpose of the program? How was it carried out? How did the Great Society improve the quality of people's lives? Finally, look over maps, charts, and tables so that they will be familiar to you when you begin reading the entire chapter.

You probably have already been introduced to a lot of the information presented in your history book, so use your experiences to help you activate your prior knowledge during the preview. By taking time to think about what you already know, you will be able to annotate more efficiently and effectively.

When you gear up for reading literature, your approach will also be a bit different from the ones you use in science or the other humanities courses. Usually there is an introduction with some background about the author (for example, Byron, Keats, or Shelly), the period (the Romantics), and his country of origin (Great Britain). It's important to read this as part of your preview to get your mind thinking about what you should be looking for. Likewise, following a group of poems, a short story, or a play, there are usually discussion questions that will help you focus on key elements. It's best to read these questions before you begin reading and then return to them after reading and class discussion.

NETWORKING

A Virtual Museum

If you are in an art history course, try going online to view collections at various museums. Most major museums now have at least part of their collections online. You can download photographs of different pieces, paste them on note cards, and then make additional notes about each piece of art and artist. You can also find out additional information, often right at the museum site, about the pieces and the artists.

What and How to Annotate During Reading

There tend to be three major problems students experience when they are learning to annotate, and these problems tend to surface most commonly in history courses. In order to help you avoid these pitfalls and to assess your own annotations, we will outline these pitfalls here and offer some suggestions for overcoming them.

1. **"Medieval Monk" Syndrome.** This happens when a student annotates by copying the text almost word for word. Sometimes students fall into this trap because they are trying to memorize information instead of really learning it. Students who write too much in the margins may be afraid that they will leave out something important if they try to paraphrase. However, with practice, you should be able to tell the difference between key ideas and details. If you find yourself experiencing the medieval monk syndrome, be sure to do a thorough job of previewing the text before you read so that you

are somewhat familiar with the chapter contents. Read longer sections at a time before marking. After reading each section, think about what would be important information to tell someone about the material you just read and write it in your own words.

2. **"Nothin' Here" Syndrome.** Students who use this approach do not annotate very much at all. They may have random words annotated, or they may just copy the heading or bold-faced words in the margin. This is a problem because if there is not enough information annotated in the margins, there is little content to study. It leads students to believe that they have learned all the important material when, in fact, they have not. Sometimes students don't annotate enough because they feel that the strategy takes too much time. If this is a concern you have, try annotation with one course this term. You will probably find that it actually *saves* you time when you go to study because you have already thought about the information and organized it in some way. Occasionally, students do not annotate enough because the margins in the text are very small. If this is a problem, write annotations on sticky notes and stick them in the margins.

3. **"Rest of the Story" Syndrome.** Students who demonstrate this pitfall may identify the key topics but do not annotate complete ideas. Sometimes students only partially mark ideas to save time, but because they do not pull out entire ideas, they will have trouble using their annotations to help them study. This is especially a problem in courses that give cumulative finals. If you did not annotate in enough detail, you may have to resort to rereading just to make sense of the information. Sometimes, students try to annotate only the information they don't know. In other words, when they come across a topic that they know a little bit about, which is very common in history, they will only annotate the new information. However, one of the benefits of annotation is that it helps you connect new ideas with prior knowledge, which helps you remember the new information. A student who doesn't link the information together will be less likely to remember it on an exam. To overcome this pitfall, write everything you think you will need to remember, even if the information seems like common sense now. Read over your annotations to be sure they are complete and they make sense. One way to know whether they are complete is to ask yourself—and be honest about this—if you were allowed to use only your annotations to prepare for an exam over the material, would you be able to do well based on what you have selected to annotate?

Now that you understand some of the pitfalls of annotating history texts, let's turn to what your history annotations should look like. There are several things to keep in mind. First, as with any discipline, it's important

SUCCESS AT A GLANCE

Annotation Pitfalls and Models

Medieval Monk	Nothin' Here Syndrome	Rest of the Story
By 1966 the civil rights movement split apart because it realized it hadn't been very successful. Society still not colorblind.	1966—Civil rights movement was divided	1966-Civil rights movement had limited success
White conservatives still very prejudiced and white liberals from Johnson and Kennedy administration not very trustworthy.		Liberals not trustworthy
Civil rights workers were very unhappy with white liberals because they felt betrayed		

to match your annotations to course expectations. For example, if you have exams that simply ask you to memorize people, events, dates, etc., it's fairly straightforward what you will annotate. However, if—as is the case for most history courses—your professor expects you to think on higher levels, you will annotate to reflect this. Second, it's important to concentrate on cause and effect and sequences of events. Pay attention to words such as *causes, results, consequences,* and *reasons why.* In addition, you shouldn't ignore people, events, laws, acts, policy decisions, and so forth, but your annotations should reflect how these facts relate to causes, results, consequences, etc. You should also reflect on the questions you posed when you were gearing up.

Look at the model history annotations on page 174, taken from the text excerpt in Appendix B. These annotations should give you a good idea about how your annotations might look. Note several features:

1. The text is condensed and well organized.
2. Lists (for example, *Measures to combat poverty*) are numbered, making it easy to study.

Model Annotations	Passage
By 1966—CR movement realized it had only limited success	By 1966 the civil rights movement fractured as it confronted the limits of its success. It had achieved the goals of ending legal discrimination and putting southern African Americans in the voting booth, but it had not brought about a colorblind society. Racial prejudice among white conservatives remained virulent, and white liberals, such as those in the Kennedy and Johnson administrations, revealed themselves as not always trustworthy allies. Expecting only hostility from conservatives, civil rights workers were more disillusioned with what they saw as liberal betrayals.
■ Southern blacks could vote BUT color was still a big issue	
■ Conservatives—still very prejudice	
■ Liberals—not very trustworthy B/C they didn't expect much from conservatives, CR workers were more disillusioned with liberals.	

3. Reasons why are clearly annotated (for example, why LBJ changed his position on race issues).

4. Annotations are abbreviated and information is paraphrased, not copied straight from the text.

As previously indicated, literature requires a different approach to annotating. It's particularly important to know the task; in other words, what does your professor want you to know about the pieces of literature you are reading? At the very least, you will need to think about things such as character development, themes that run through the piece, and literary devices. You can annotate such information in the margins, tab it with sticky notes, and, if you like, color code it by highlighting your annotations. For example, once you have read and annotated a short story, you can go back and highlight all of the characteristics of John Jones in blue and all of the characteristics of Mary Smith in yellow. This way you will be able to not only know these characteristics, but you will also be able to give examples of where they occurred in the story. And, here's a chance for you to use all of those highlighters you bought.

"Great society" = War on
poverty. + lived ↓ pov.
line 5

Measures to combat pov.
1. ↑ $ + food stamps
through welfare
pgrms.

2. raised social
security
3. Improved
educational opp.
-Head Start
-Elem. + Sec. Ed.
Act
-expanded student
loans
-Job Corps. for
employee training
-VISTA

Race Issues— LBJ
changes position on race
due to
1. ≠ weakened US
competition w/
China + USSR
2. AA struggle in
South had reached
a very hostile stage

The Great Society: Fighting Poverty and Discrimination

In pursuit of what he called the Great Society, Johnson first declared a "War on Poverty." No citizen in the richest nation on earth should live in squalor, he believed. More than one out of five Americans still lived below the conservatively estimated official poverty line ($3,022 for a nonfarm family of four in 1960), and 70 percent of these were white.

The president and a large congressional majority passed several measures to alleviate poverty. They sharply increased the availability of money and food stamps through the Aid to Families with Dependent Children ("welfare") program, and they raised Social Security payments to older Americans. Several programs focused on improving educational opportunities as an avenue out of poverty: Head Start offered preschool education and meals for youngsters, the Elementary and Secondary Education Act sent federal funds to the least affluent school districts, and an expanded system of student loans facilitated access to college. The Job Corps provided employment training, and Volunteers in Service to America (VISTA) served as a domestic Peace Corps, funneling people with education and skills into poor communities to serve as teachers and providers of other social services.

No barrier to opportunity in the early 1960s was higher than the color bar. Both opportunist and idealist, Johnson as president shed his segregationist voting record (necessary for election in Texas before 1960) and became the most vocal proponent of racial equality ever to occupy the Oval Office. Two factors facilitated his change in position. Blatant inequalities for American citizens weakened the United States in its competition with the Soviets and Chinese for the loyalty of the nonwhite Third World majority. Moreover, the African American freedom struggle in the South had reached a boiling point. Black frustration was mounting over white brutality and the seeming indifference or even hostility of the national government.

■ ■ ■

Taking Notes in Humanities Courses

Because many history professors tend to lecture by presenting history in a storytelling mode, it is easy to get wrapped up in the story and not take very good notes. It is also difficult to determine what is important. In addition, as we have mentioned, students tend to believe that they have quite a bit of background

TIMELY TIPS

Choosing Paper Topics

In many humanities courses, the professor outlines assignments for papers early in the semester. In this kind of situation, choose your topic early and keep it in mind each time you read for the class. Then you can pull out key quotes, major arguments, and other information that you will be able to use in your paper. You will find that choosing your topic early can be a huge timesaver.

ON YOUR OWN

Reflecting on What You Have Read

Annotate a section (at least five to eight pages) from the textbook for one of your humanities courses. Once you have completed the annotations, it is time to evaluate them critically. Write a paragraph that evaluates your annotation. Think about the following: Did you find that you have fallen into the Medieval Monk, Nothin' Here, or Rest of the Story pitfalls—or a combination of them? Then outline three changes you can make to your annotations to make them better and a more valuable study tool, and try these out with the next humanities chapter you are assigned.

information in history because they have been hearing about many of the same people, struggles, and wars throughout their schooling. This factor can cause students to tune out and not write down everything they should. Keep in mind that you need to stay focused and take notes for the full period. Even if you think "I already know this," take notes anyway. You can always go back later and pare them down.

One of the most important factors to consider when you take notes in history is whether your professor lectures in an inductive or deductive method. Figuring out the lecture style can also help you determine the task. If your professor lectures inductively, she provides lots of facts and information and then concludes with a generalization that pulls everything together (specific to general). If your professor lectures deductively, he provides the generalization first, and then fills in the support (general to specific). As a rule, inductive lectures are harder to follow for most students because it's more difficult to figure out where the lecture is going and to separate unimportant from important information.

Because there is usually so much information being thrown at you in history courses, it becomes particularly important to follow the "listen, think, and then write" rule. That is, listen first, think about what is important, and then write that down in your own words. If you try to write down everything your history professor says, you will end up getting "half thoughts," and there's a good chance you will fail to include some important information. Look at the example of a professor's notes and the student's paraphrased notes below.

Example of a Professor's Notes and a Student's Paraphrased Notes

Professor's Lecture Notes

In 1964, President Lyndon Johnson took several steps to show the United States' commitment to defend South Vietnam. In February, Johnson ordered the Pentagon to prepare for airstrikes against the North. In May, his advisers drafted a resolution that authorized the military to escalate action. In June, General Maxwell Taylor, who was a strong proponent of more U.S. involvement in the war, was appointed ambassador to Saigon. And, in early August, patrol boats from the North supposedly clashed with two U.S. destroyers in the Gulf of Tonkin. Evidence of a real attack was skimpy at best. Johnson stated, "For all I know, our navy was shooting at whales out there." Nonetheless, Johnson announced on national television that Americans had been victims of "open aggression on the high seas." Withholding the fact that the U.S. ships had been assisting the South Vietnamese commando raids against two North Vietnamese islands in a secret operation planned by American advisers, the president condemned the attacks as unprovoked. He ordered retaliatory air strikes against the North for the first time and called on Congress to pass the previously drafted resolution giving him the authority to "take all necessary measures to repel any armed attack against the forces of the United States and to prevent further aggression." Assured

Student's Paraphrased Notes

Tonkin Gulf Incident: Steps leading to:
- Feb. 1964—LBJ ordered Pentagon to prepare for airstrikes against N. VN
- May 1964—LBJ's advisers draft resolution to increase military action
- June 1964—Taylor a strong supporter of ↑ involvement in VN becomes ambassador to Saigon
- Aug.—Tonkin Gulf incident occurs—"assault" on U.S. ships in Gulf; little evidence that it happened; LBJ says U.S. was a victim of aggressive acts that were unprovoked.

(continued)

by the president that this meant "no extension of the present conflict," the Senate passed the so-called Gulf of Tonkin Resolution 88 to 2; the House vote was 416 to 0. Johnson had not only signaled America's determination to stand by its allies, but also stymied Goldwater's effort to make Vietnam a campaign issue. He also now had a resolution that he likened to "grandma's nightshirt—it covered everything." His attorney general would soon describe the resolution as "the functional equivalent of a declaration of war" and the president would consider it a mandate to commit U.S. forces to Vietnam as he saw fit.

Steps taken by us:
1. Retaliatory air strikes against N. VN
2. Congress passes the Tonkin Gulf Resolution=give LBJ authority to use "all necessary measures to prevent further aggressions"; passed Senate 88–2 and House 416–0
3. Stymied Goldwater's attempt to make VN a campaign issue.
4. LBJ could, in effect, do anything he wanted to escalate U.S. involvement

One of the big mistakes students make in courses where there is a considerable amount of discussion is that they don't take notes. They sit and listen, thinking that they will remember ideas brought up by classmates. However, in literature-based classes where the professor expects input from the class, it is usually important to take notes about what your classmates are discussing because professors often create exam questions based on the class discussion. Using the three-column method of note taking shown in the example below will be helpful in these courses.

Example of Discussion Notes

Question Posed	Professor's Comments	Student Comments
Must creativity result in a product?	So which is more important, process or product?	Depends on how you look @ it—whose perspective?
Possible TQ? Process is more important than product. Defend or refute this statement.	Does an idea count as a product?	Artist—process public—product

Studying in Humanities Courses

Once you have annotated your text and have taken good lecture notes, you will need to use strategies to pull the key information from those sources together. Time lines, questions/answers, and compare/contrast charting are three good strategies to use in humanities courses.

Time Lines

As the name suggests, time lines help you sequence information by arranging it chronologically—in the order in which it happened. Time lines can cover a long period of time, such as decades or centuries, or a relatively brief period of time, such as a specific war or presidency. They are easy to construct and you can supplement them with your CARDS or simply by putting enough information into your time line to make it an effective study aid on its own. The time line example below shows many of the different bills and acts that were part of LBJ's Great Society. Although this example indicates the order in which events occurred, it would be insufficient to study from. You would need to supplement your time line with further explanation of each event that occurred. For example, you would need to know *why* Johnson felt the need for the Great Society, *what* the impact of these acts were, and *what* the details of each act entailed. This information cannot be gleaned from the time line alone.

Example of a Time Line

LBJ's GREAT SOCIETY

1964	■ Clean Air Act
	■ War on Poverty
	■ Food stamps
	■ Civil Rights Act
	■ Head Start
	■ National Endowment for Arts and Humanities
	■ Job Corps
1965	■ Voting Rights Act
	■ Medicare signed into law
	■ PBS TV began
	■ Cigarette Labeling Act
	■ Housing and Urban Development Act
1966	■ Clean Water Act
	■ Child Nutrition Act
	■ Fair Packaging and Labeling Act
1968	■ Wild and Scenic Rivers Act
	■ Open Housing Act

Question/Answer Strategy

We have discussed the question/answer strategy in Chapter 12, Strategies for Social Science, but it deserves mention as a useful strategy for the humanities as well. Because most humanities professors give exams in which you are expected to answer essay, short answer, or identification items, creating your own higher-level questions and then answering them can help prepare you for this task. When you are using this strategy to prepare for writing tasks, it's important to think about writing questions where you will have to synthesize and think critically about information. Therefore, few of your questions should begin with *what*. You will need to pose questions that match the task. For example, if your professor tells you to pay attention to cause and effect, your questions should reflect this. Or if you know that you will be expected to explain the significance of a particular event, bill, battle, and so forth, your answers need to reflect this type of information.

The following questions about the Johnson administration give you an idea of the difference between good and poor questions. Notice that most of the questions in the "Poor" column require only a one-word answer or simple memorization. The questions in the "Good" column are questions that require critical thinking, synthesis, and analysis and begin with the words *how*, *discuss*, and *why*. Remember when you construct your questions/answers to write the question in the left-hand column and the answer in the right-hand column.

Good Questions	Poor Questions
How did the Great Society aim to fight poverty?	What is the Great Society?
Discuss the impact of the Supreme Court's decisions under Justice Warren.	Name three decisions made by the Supreme Court in the 1960s.
Why did the Tet Offensive play such a pivotal role in the conflict in Vietnam?	What was the Tet Offensive?

Compare/Contrast Charting

Charting is useful in humanities courses in which you need to be able to compare and contrast ideas—perhaps two or more presidents, art movements, or philosophies. The important thing to remember about making your chart is that you should compare apples with apples and oranges with oranges. Therefore, you should choose your categories with care. Let's say you want to construct a chart that will enable you to see the similarities and differences between the Kennedy, Johnson, and Nixon administrations. Your categories might look something like this example.

Example of a Chart

President	Domestic Policies	Foreign Policies	Political Beliefs	Major Accomplishments
Kennedy				
Johnson				
Nixon				

■   ■   ■

Your categories at the top of each column should reflect the important information you should know about each president. You would complete the chart by filling in key material for each of the categories. You can study your chart two ways. First you should learn about each president independent of the others, so you are able to recite Kennedy's domestic and foreign policies, his political beliefs, and his major accomplishments. Then move on to Johnson and Nixon. Once you have learned the information horizontally across each row, examine each column to compare and contrast Kennedy's, Johnson's, and Nixon's domestic policies, foreign policies, and so forth.

In literature courses, in addition to reading before class and taking good notes during class, you should connect the reading to the class discussion during your review after class. This review may entail annotating your text about themes, metaphors, symbolism, or issues discussed in class, marking important passages or quotations, or connecting themes across readings. Because humanities courses often involve writing papers and taking essay exams, it is always a good idea to keep track of ideas for possible paper topics as you are reading and to try to predict essay questions after listening to the class discussion.

Real College

Harry

DIRECTIONS: Read the following "Real College" scenario and respond to the question based on what you have learned in this chapter.

Poor Harry. It's week four of the semester and too late to change his schedule or drop any of his courses without losing his financial aid. What was he thinking, deciding it was a good idea to take two humanities courses in the same semester? He has an introductory history survey course plus a world literature class. Although both are considered humanities courses, at least he has concluded that he can't approach them in the same manner. But that's about it; he really doesn't have a clue about what he should be doing in either course.

In history, his professor talks so fast that Harry's notes resemble a bunch of scribbles that he can't make much sense of once he leaves class. The textbook is easy to read, but it's hard to pick out the important information. His professor was very clear that students would be expected to go beyond the "facts" and put what the class is studying in a "historical perspective," whatever that means. To make matters worse, all of his tests in this course require written responses, unlike his history courses in high school where he was mostly required to memorize names, dates, battles, and events. He doesn't think he's a very good writer and has trouble putting his thoughts on paper in a way that makes sense to anyone else but him.

Then there's the world literature class—another torturous humanities course, at least from Harry's perspective. In this class, he reads these "works" (that's what his professor calls them) by mostly dead writers from all over the world. And he has to think about them in context of what was going on in the world at that particular time. He keeps up with the reading in this class because if you get behind, you're really sunk; but he really doesn't know how to organize the information or what strategies to use to think about it.

Using what you have learned about studying in the humanities, what advice can you give Harry about being successful in these two courses?

ADD TO YOUR PORTFOLIO

If you are taking a humanities course this semester, answer the following questions, providing samples of your work when appropriate.

1. What course(s) are you taking?

2. How is the course structured (topically, sequentially, chronologically, etc.)?

3. What are the tasks for the course? Write a paragraph describing the course tasks.

4. What kinds of information should you annotate? Provide a five-page example of your annotations.

5. Which strategies work best for this course? Why? Provide an example of one of the strategies you are using.

6. How will you prepare for your next humanities exam? Why do you think your preparation strategies are appropriate? Write a paragraph discussing these questions.

Strategies for Science and Mathematics*

READ THIS CHAPTER TO FIND ANSWERS TO THE FOLLOWING
QUESTIONS:

- How do I read strategically in science and mathematics courses?
- What strategies should I use to be successful in science and mathematics courses?
- How can I modify my strategies to suit different types of science and mathematics courses and texts?

SELF-ASSESSMENT

DIRECTIONS: Complete the following chart for each science and mathematics course you are taking this term. Think about how you prepare for each class.

	Course 1	Course 2
(course name)	————	————
I read the text before class.	Yes/No	Yes/No
I read the text after class.	Yes/No	Yes/No
My class lecture follows the text.	Yes/No	Yes/No
I am responsible for reading multiple texts for this course.	Yes/No	Yes/No
I try to study in the same way for each course.	Yes/No	Yes/No
I understand the professor's expectations for this course.	Yes/No	Yes/No

---

*As you read this chapter, you may want to refer to Chapters 4, 9, 10, and 11 to refresh your memory about general guidelines for strategy use.

The way you have responded to these questions gives a good indication of how you approach reading and studying in your science and math classes. Keep these answers in mind as you read the rest of the chapter.

Science Courses

Characteristics of Science Courses

Science courses can be divided into two categories—math-based science courses (also called problem-based) and text-based science courses. Each category has vastly different texts. Textbooks for math-based science courses, such as chemistry or physics, contain formulas similar to mathematics texts, but they also contain important diagrams explaining scientific processes.

Text-based science courses, such as biology, agriculture, forestry, botany, astronomy, and geology, are often more similar to social science courses than mathematics courses in text structure and strategies for learning. There is little mathematics involved; instead, you will be required to read, understand, and apply scientific processes discussed in the text. These courses often include a lab in which you experience hands-on application of scientific principles.

Figuring Out the Task

In science textbooks you will find many new terms and definitions. Often, the terms introduced in early chapters will be used later in the text to define other terms. So you need to be sure you understand the new terms as they appear to avoid trouble understanding future reading. Science textbooks also discuss proven principles and theories in terms of their relationship to each other. Therefore, it is important to be aware of the theories and understand how they connect and how they explain the science concepts you are learning.

NETWORKING

Visualizing Science Processes

Most scientists are able to picture science processes in their heads. They do this so regularly that they cannot imagine that anyone would try to learn science without visualizing it. However, because picturing science processes does not come naturally to many science students, you can go online to see video depictions to help you. There are many reputable science sites, teacher sites, or even sites such as Wikipedia with animated depictions of the information you will need.

For the most part, science courses rely heavily on lecture material, so it is important that you take excellent notes. In fact, some science professors expect students to use their notes as the primary source of material and the textbook as a supplement. However, because you may only have two or three exams, you cannot wait until after the first test to figure out your professor's expectations.

Science exams usually consist of multiple-choice questions, but the level of thinking required can vary. Some professors will ask mainly higher-level questions; others will focus on memorization of ideas. Most professors will ask a combination of both memory and higher-level items because, although they want you to pull the ideas together and think at higher levels, they recognize that there are a lot of new terms that you must commit to memory in order to understand the larger concepts. In addition, many of your test questions will require you to apply science concepts to new situations. To answer these questions you must understand and be able to describe each concept.

Reading Science Textbooks

Concepts in science textbooks are usually presented sequentially, which means the concepts build on each other. Your best plan is to test yourself as you read to make sure you fully understand each concept. It is also helpful to create reading goals to monitor what you are learning. This means that rather than focusing on getting through a chapter, focus on learning concepts every time you read. Adopt a scientific approach and ask yourself questions such as:

- What data support this concept or theory?
- What other theories is this concept related to?
- How does this phenomenon work? What is the scientific process involved?
- Why does this phenomenon occur?
- What does it show us?

It is also important to pay attention to the diagrams in each chapter. They are there to help you picture the science process so that you can see what is happening. Understanding diagrams is crucial to doing well in most science courses.

Gearing Up for Reading

Professors expect that you have some basic knowledge before you attend the lecture, so it is important that you read the text before class. To gear up for reading, start by reading the chapter title and thinking about what you already know about that concept. Focus on primary and secondary headings to understand how the chapter is organized and how the ideas are related together. If your text has an outline of topics at the beginning of each chapter, use it to help you think about the key points. If not, skim through the chapter for key terms and think about how they are related to the appropriate heading or subheading. Pay special attention to diagrams and figures, and think about how they relate to the overall focus of the chapter. Finally, read the chapter objectives and guiding questions if your textbook has these features.

What and How to Annotate During Reading

Because of the large amount of new terminology involved in learning science, it is important for you to read your science textbooks before class. In this way, you will be familiar with the terms and concepts discussed in the text and you will be able to build your understanding of the concepts as you listen in class. It is also a good idea to connect the concepts discussed in class with the concepts described in your text by comparing your lecture notes to your text annotations each time you read. This will help you follow the flow of the concepts and will help you understand how the ideas are connected.

When you annotate your science text, you need to match your annotations to the course expectations. For example, if you are expected to think at higher levels, be sure your annotations include more than just the bold-faced terms. If you are expected to be able to explain science processes, be sure your annotations help you learn to do just that.

In general, it is a good idea to limit the amount of material you annotate. Annotate big concepts and save the details for your rehearsal strategies. A big mistake that students make when annotating science textbooks is that they tend to have the Medieval Monk Syndrome (discussed in Chapter 13), and they wind up annotating everything. It is also essential to focus on putting the ideas into your own words. This will help you monitor your understanding of what you have read and will keep you from copying exactly from the text. In addition, look for experiments and results or conclusions drawn from scientific theories, and seek to make connections between the experiments and the concepts they generate.

Science texts often contain diagrams or charts to explain concepts. Because science exams usually contain questions about the concepts described in diagrams or charts, you must be able to read and understand each one. As you read your text, annotate the diagrams and take the time to reflect on what they are depicting. A good self-testing strategy to make sure you fully understand the concept is to cover up the words in the diagram and try to talk through the information. If you can explain how the concept works, you've shown that you understand it. If you find that you cannot explain it, reread your annotations or the diagram text to be sure you understand the key points.

In the following example, notice how the annotations focus on explaining the concepts rather than on just memorizing the terms.

Example of Annotations in a Science Textbook

Bile
Liver
Stomach
Gallbladder
Bile
Acid chyme
Pancreatic juice
Duodenum of small intestine
Pancreas

Figure 22.12
The duodenum.
Acid chyme squirted from the stomach into the duodenum (the beginning of the small intestine) is mixed with pancreatic juice, bile from the liver and gallbladder, and intestinal juice produced by the duodenal lining itself. As peristalsis propels the mix along the small intestine, hydrolases break food molecules down to their monomers.

The duodenum receives digestive juices from the pancreas, liver, and gallbladder (**Figure 22.12**). The **pancreas** is a large gland that secretes pancreatic juice into the duodenum via a duct. Pancreatic juice neutralizes the stomach acids that enter the duodenum and contains hydrolases that participate in the chemical digestion of carbohydrates, fats, proteins, and nucleic acids.

Bile is a juice produced by the **liver**, stored in the **gallbladder**, and secreted through a duct into the duodenum. Bile contains no digestive enzymes but does have substances called bile salts that make fats more accessible to lipase. Fats, including those from the cheese of the pizza we're following, are a special problem for the digestive system because they do not dissolve in water. The fats in chyme start out as relatively large globules. Only those molecules on the surface of the globules are in contact with the lipase dissolved in the surrounding solution. Agitation from the rhythmic contraction of muscles in the intestinal wall breaks the fat globules into small droplets, but without the help of bile salts, those droplets would quickly fuse again into larger globules that would be difficult to digest. Through a process called emulsification, bile salts essentially coat the tiny fat droplets and prevent them from fusing. Similarly, emulsification by a chemical additive helps keep oil permanently mixed with vinegar in some commercial salad dressings.

The intestinal lining itself also aids in enzymatic digestion by producing a variety of hydrolases. The cumulative activities of all these hydrolytic enzymes break the different classes of food molecules completely down into monomers, which are now ready for absorption into the body.

Absorption of Nutrients Wait a minute! The previous sentence said that nutrients "are now ready for absorption by the body." Aren't these nutrients already in the body? Not really. The alimentary canal is a tunnel running through the body, and its cavity is continuous with the great outdoors. The doughnut analogy in **Figure 22.13** should convince you that this is so. Until nutrients actually cross the tissue lining of the alimentary canal to enter the bloodstream, they are still outside the body. If it were not for nutrient absorption, we could eat and digest huge meals but still starve to death, in a sense.

Most digestion is complete by the time our pizza meal reaches the end of the duodenum. The next several meters of small intestine (called the jejunum and the ileum) are specialized for nutrient absorption. The structure of the intestinal lining, or epithelium, fits this function (**Figure 22.14**). The surface area of this epithelium is huge—roughly 300m², equal to the floor space of a one bedroom apartment. The intestinal lining not only has large folds, like the stomach, but also fingerlike outgrowths called villi, which makes the epithelium something like the absorptive surface of a fluffy bath towel. Each cell of the epithelium adds even more surface by having microscopic projections called microvilli. Across this expansive surface of intestinal epithelium, nutrients are transported into the network of small blood vessels and lymphatic vessels in the core of each villus.

Digestion Sm Intestine
- when food reaches sm int. it has been thru mech. and chem. digestion
- hydrolisis is initiated

Duodenum
1st ft. of sm int.
- where food is broken into monomers
- gets digest. juice from pancreas (pancreatic juice via duct—neutralizes stomach acid & contains hydrolases for chem digest), liver (bile), gallbladder (where bile is stored and via duct)
- Bile salts—make fats accessible to lipase thru emulsification—bile salts coat fat droplets to keep them separated (like oil and water in dressing) Int. lining produces hydrolases to get food ready for absorption

Absorption
Nutrients don't really 'enter' body until entering bloodstream. Nut abs occurs in jejunum and ileum (next parts of sm int.) Epithelium—int. lining (huge—300m², folded, and has villi. Very abosorptive. Each cell has microvilli—all help transport nutrients

SUCCESS AT A GLANCE

Features to Annotate in Science

Figuring out how to annotate a science text can be a challenge. Use this feature as a guide to help you focus as you read. As you annotate, pay careful attention to:

- Key terms and definitions
- Diagrams and figures
- Cause/effect relationships
- Scientific arguments
- Comparison/contrast relationships
- Experiments and results of experiments
- Differences between hypotheses and theories
- Events that occur during different science processes or phases of the processes
- Differences among similar ideas, processes, features (for example, How can you tell one leaf type from another? What is the difference between meiosis and mitosis?)

Taking Notes in Science Courses

Because many professors view the textbook as a supplement and class lecture to be the most important, up-to-date material, it is crucial that you go to class every day and take excellent notes. Your notes are the only record of what was said in class. Even if your professor provides notes or slides online, you need to be actively engaged in writing as your professor lectures.

If your professor uses diagrams, figures, or illustrations, it is important to put the visuals in your notes. In the example on the following page, the student writes the figure number so he can refer to it in the text later on. This is an excellent idea because he can review more easily after class. It is also important to write down any formulas, equations, charts, or graphs accurately and completely. Although we have discussed paraphrasing the professor's ideas and putting them into your own words as much as possible, in science there are some technical ideas that have specific meanings and should be written exactly as the professor specifies. In addition, use scientific notation and abbreviations as much as possible as you take notes so that you are comfortable with their meaning come exam time.

The following example uses the split-page method for a lecture on nutrition and digestion. This method works well in science courses because it helps you organize ideas and monitor your understanding. If your professor provides notes online, the parallel notes method would be the most appropriate one to use.

Example of Science Split-Page Notes

	Nutrition & Digestion	Nov. 10

Explain the 3 types of animal diets-give ex.	**Animal Nutrition**
	Animal Diets
	• Herbivores-eat plants, algae
	    • Ex. cattle, gorillas, sea urchins
	• Carnivores-eat animals (that ate plants)
	    • Ex. lions, snakes, frogs
	• Omnivores-eat both plants and animals
	    • Ex. humans, crows, cockroaches

How does food move through the 4 stages of processing?	**4 Stages of Food Processing** 1. Ingestion-eating (ex. chewing pizza) 2. Digestion-breakdown of food to simple sugars and amino acids • Mechanical digestion-physical process such as chewing. Exposes more food molecules
Why must chemical digestion occur?	• Chemical digestion-chem. breakdown of food to smaller molecules Why? 2 reasons 1. polymers must be broken into monomers b/4 cells can absorb
Fig. 22.3	2. most food polymers are diff. than animal polymers so must break down and use amino acids to build new proteins. (*see figure 22.3 in text) 3. Absorption-uptake of small molecules into cells lining digestive tract 4. Elimination-disposal of undigested materials

ON YOUR OWN

Reflecting on What you Have Read

Think about a science course you are currently taking (or one you have taken recently). Write a response to the following questions: How do the professor's lectures differ from the material presented in the textbook? What information does the professor expect you to know before you attend the lecture? Which note-taking method will work best with this professor? Your responses to these questions should help you better prepare for taking notes in class.

Strategies for Science Courses

For the majority of science courses you will need to go beyond memorizing bold-faced terms. To do this you will need strategies that will help you pull ideas together.

Concept Maps

Many students find that making a concept map of key terms and theories to see how the ideas relate is an effective strategy. When you preview each chapter, begin a concept map for the ideas contained in the chapter. As you read, fill in your concept map with the important scientific processes.

Look at the example below on the human nervous system. Notice how the map allows you to see the differences between the central and peripheral nervous systems.

Example of a Science Map

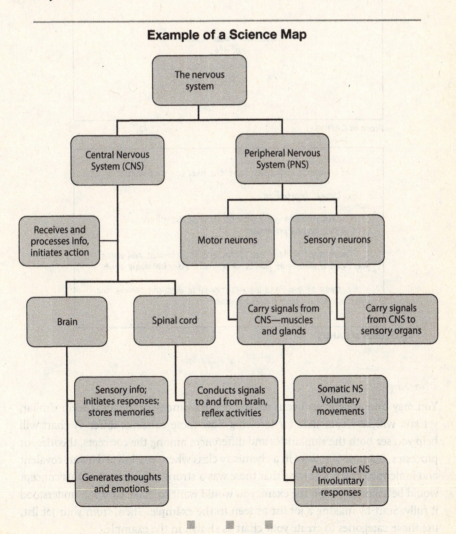

CARDS

To learn the new vocabulary and terminology, try using CARDS. Remember from what you learned in Chapter 11 that in order to be effective, of course, your CARDS must do more than just help you memorize the terms. Organize your CARDS by including a larger concept, which will often be a science process. Spread out your CARDS to show the hierarchy of terms or the order of the scientific process. This way you will be connecting the ideas together.

Example of Science CARDS

Essential Nutrients
1 of 4

Essential Amino Acids
p. 496

Front of CARDS

Def. —eight amino acids that the body can't synthesize

Ex. Lysine, tryptophan

—animal products are "complete" because they have all 8 in the needed proportions

—most plant proteins are "incomplete"; vegetarians and vegans must eat a variety of plants to get all 8 essential amino acids

Ex. combo of grain and legumes (beans) in diet can achieve the right balance of essential amino acids

Back of CARDS

■   ■   ■

Charting

You may find as your read your science text that many of the ideas seem similar, yet you will be responsible for knowing how these concepts differ. A chart will help you see both the similarities and differences among the concepts, theories, or processes. Suppose you were in a chemistry class where you learned about covalent and ionic molecules. Knowing that there was a strong possibility that this concept would be asked about on the exam, you would want to make sure you understood it fully. Start by making a jot list as seen in the example. Then, from your jot list, use those categories to create your chart as shown in the example.

Example of a Science Jot List
Molecular Bonds

Covalent

Molecules share electrons

Solids, liquids, or gases (water, ice, vapor)
Small electronegativity differences
Lower melting and boiling points

Ionic

Positive and negative ions
Ions held together by
electrostatic attraction
Crystalline solids (salt)
High electronegativity differences
High melting and boiling points

■   ■   ■

Example of a Science Chart

Molecular Bonds		
	Covalent	**Ionic**
Composition	Discrete particles—molecules. Molecules made up of atoms held together by covalent bonds (shared electrons)	Pos (+) and neg (–) ions. Ions held together by electrostatic attraction—ionic bond (opposites attract)
Forms	Can exist as liquid, solid, or gas	Exists as crystalline solids
Example	H_2O, water (can be ice, water, or vapor)	NaCl, salt
Properties	Lower melting and boiling points; small electronegativity differences	Higher melting and boiling points; high electronegativity differences

■   ■   ■

Studying Smarter

In your science courses, be sure that you can explain important diagrams in your text. Try to look only at the diagram (not the description in the text) and talk through the important information. This will help you prepare for almost any question the professor can ask on that topic.

You can study your chart by the categories either horizontally (across rows) or vertically (down columns). In fact, it is best to study charts both ways. Using the chart example, you would talk through the characteristics of covalent bonds, thinking about composition, forms, examples, and properties. Then you would talk through ionic bonds in the same fashion. Next, you would study your chart horizontally by comparing and contrasting the properties of covalent and ionic bonds across the different categories.

Mathematics Courses

Mathematics Textbooks

Reading a mathematics textbook is not like reading a novel or another textbook. Mathematics textbooks tend to use few words in order to keep ideas clearly outlined, so you must understand almost every sentence. You will be expected to comprehend abstract relationships and theories as you read about them. Mathematics texts tend to present new concepts, formulas, diagrams, and practice problems sequentially, which means that they build on one another. So mathematics learning is cumulative, which means that the concepts you are learning this week are based on the concepts you have already mastered.

You will find that mathematics textbooks are not very repetitive, making every concept count. With little chance of picking up missed information later in the text, you must be sure you have mastered each concept before moving on to a new one.

Study Strategies for Mathematics Courses

In general, college mathematics courses are based on problem solving. In addition to what we generally think of as mathematics courses (algebra, pre-calc, trig), computer science, engineering, statistics, chemistry, and physics are also math-based courses. Whether you are in a class of 10 students or 300 students, you will be asked to apply math principles and formulas in a variety of situations. Sometimes mathematics courses are discussion based, but usually they are lecture based, with the instructor explaining new concepts and the students, taking copious notes. Many times mathematics instructors focus lectures on working out problems in class.

It is a good idea to preview mathematics texts before class. If you find that you can read and understand the chapter before the lecture, that is even better; but many students find that they comprehend mathematics texts better after listening to the lecture and seeing some problems worked as examples in class. When you preview the text, note the concepts and formulas that are covered as well as any new terminology so that you will have some background information before listening in class. When you are in class, take good notes and ask questions. The more information and examples you have in your notes, the better it will be as you read the text.

GET GOING

Music and Math

Many students like to listen to music when they study because they find it motivating. Although music might prove distracting when reading history or literature, it may actually help you focus on learning in mathematics. Researchers have found that students listening to classical music in the background scored higher on math tests than students who were not listening to any music.

After class, read the text. It is best to read the chapter as soon after class as possible so that you will remember all of the key points and ideas discussed in class. Take your time as you read. Be sure that you understand each concept before moving forward. Annotate key words, formulas, definitions, and symbols in the margins to help you remember them. Note the symbols used in your text because they have very specific meanings and must be used correctly when working math problems. For example, to understand ab::cd, you must first understand that :: is the symbol for "is proportional to."

Because the information in math and math-based courses is cumulative, you cannot neglect math work. Plan to spend some time each night reading and working problems. As you read, work out the problems in your text. After reading examples, cover up the answer to the sample problem to work it out. It is also important to write down questions about concepts you need to have clarified so you can ask them during the next class period, before the class moves on to a new concept. Try to create your own problems and solve them for additional practice. If you find that you are experiencing difficulty understanding your textbook, you may find it helpful to use another math book (you can probably find one in the library) as a reference book to help clarify confusing points. In addition, try verbalizing the problems. Talking the information through by putting symbols into words, for example, can let you know where your understanding is breaking down.

TIMELY TIPS

No Procrastination Zone

You cannot procrastinate on math work. If you want to do well, plan to spend a little time each day learning formulas, solving problems, and understanding concepts. When you break up the work, it will not seem as overwhelming. If you find you need help, you can get it right away.

After you work the problems in each section of the chapter, it is essential in most mathematics courses to be able to pull the concepts together. Most professors will expect you to be able to respond to problems that combine several concepts—*even if they do not explicitly go over it that way in class*. Thus, it is a good idea to try to create and solve problems that require you to use several concepts presented in your chapters. It is also a good idea to belong to a math study group.

Real College

Stacy

DIRECTIONS: Read the following "Real College" scenario and respond to the question based on what you have learned in this chapter.

Stacy thinks she is in big trouble in her biology course. The class is supposed to be for nonscience majors, but she feels that the professor lectures as if everyone in the class is pre-med. Not only do they need to know all of the bold-faced terms (and there are loads of them), but they also need to be able to explain what is going on at particular points in a science process. Stacy was floored on the first exam when the professor put a diagram of cell division on the test and asked the students to write about what science process was occurring. Although Stacy was fully prepared to label that diagram, she did not even know where to start with explaining what it meant. Her next exam is in two weeks and she doesn't know what to do differently this time. For her last exam she read her book, looked over her class notes, and memorized all of the key terms.

Using what you know about learning in the sciences, what would you suggest Stacy do to prepare for her next exam in a way that will help her understand the science processes?

ADD TO YOUR PORTFOLIO

If you are taking a science or math course this semester, answer the following questions, providing samples of your work when appropriate.

1. What course(s) are you taking?
2. How is the course structured (topically, sequentially, chronologically, etc.)?
3. What are the tasks for the course? Write a paragraph describing the course tasks.
4. What kind of information should you annotate? Provide a five-page example of your annotations.
5. Which strategies work best for this course? Why? Provide an example of one of the strategies you are using.
6. How will you prepare for your next exam? Why do you think your preparation strategies are appropriate? Write a paragraph discussing these questions.

Using Technology to Learn

READ THIS CHAPTER TO ANSWER THE FOLLOWING QUESTIONS:

- How can technology be used in college classes?
- What are the benefits and drawbacks to online learning?
- How can technology be used in reading and studying?

SELF-ASSESSMENT

DIRECTIONS: On a scale of 1 to 5 with 1 being "rarely," 3 being "sometimes," and 5 being "most of the time," respond to each of the statements below.

1. I can use a computer to check and send   1 2 3 4 5
   e-mail.

2. I can use a word processing system well   1 2 3 4 5
   enough to type my papers.

3. I know how to send file attachments.   1 2 3 4 5

4. I can find information easily on the   1 2 3 4 5
   Internet.

5. I seek out my professors' Web pages   1 2 3 4 5
   when available.

6. I have taken or am considering taking   1 2 3 4 5
   an online course.

7. I feel comfortable using a computer.   1 2 3 4 5

8. I use my computer when I study.   1 2 3 4 5

The more 5s you have marked, the more at ease you are with the technology that will play a major role in your college life. Read on for some tips about the use of technology in college learning.

Computers are a necessity on most college campuses today. In fact, a good number of colleges are now requiring freshmen to purchase or lease a computer before they begin their first semester. Chances are you have been interacting with computers most of your life, but you might not have the skills needed for academic computing. This chapter will discuss ways that technology is currently being used in college classes and how you can use technology to aid your learning.

Technology in College Classes

Most of your college professors will incorporate technology (specifically computers and the Internet) into their classes. But expect to find a wide range in the level of integration. Some professors will be old-school, low-tech holdouts who won't even have an e-mail account. Other professors will use high-tech multimedia presentations during every class. Most professors fall somewhere in the middle and use technology where they find it to be most beneficial for explaining course content and supporting classroom instruction. You can expect to see some or all of the following uses of technology as part of your college courses:

- **Computerized Class Presentations (Such as PowerPoint).** Many professors use computer slides to outline their lectures. They may use overheads of diagrams or show video clips to emphasize points. They may also display Web pages or other Internet sources of information during class.
- **Computerized Notes.** It is becoming more common for professors to post their notes on the Web. We strongly believe that Web notes are best used as a supplement or guide for taking your own notes in class. You may also find yourself in a classroom equipped with computers or computer hookups that allow you to take notes on a laptop.
- **Computer Modules or Supplements.** Some professors place sample questions or problems on the Web so that students can evaluate their understanding of the course material as they prepare for exams. Other professors (especially in the sciences) provide supplementary material online. Generally this material consists of information that cannot be depicted in a text format, such as a video of a chemical reaction, but enhances the information discussed in a lecture or in the text.
- **Course Management Systems (Such as Blackboard).** Professors using these course management systems find many creative uses for them. They may place their syllabi, quizzes, assignments, and other course information there. They may also post student grades or have virtual chats with the class. We even know a professor who conducts exam reviews online. If your professor uses these systems, plan to visit the site often to keep up on new assignments or important information.
- **Course Exams.** Some courses will require you to take exams on a computer. Many mathematics courses are moving toward computerized exams,

and many English courses require students to write in-class essays on computers. An exam on a computer is a bit different from the old paper and pencil type. But don't abandon your old test-taking strategies. Continue to read each question carefully and answer the items you know first. However, you should find out whether you can return to a question or if you must answer each item before moving on to the next one. Taking exams on computers might take some getting used to, but once you have some experience, it is just like taking any other test.

- **Readings.** Your professors may assign readings that can only be found online. They may be from e-books, Web-based journals, the textbook publishers' Web sites, popular media, or any number of other sources. If you find you have trouble reading online, as many people do, you can print them out in advance.
- **Group Presentations.** At some point in your college career, you will probably find yourself in a course that requires a group presentation that has a technology component. Some professors require a Web-based presentation or a presentation that utilizes several types of media. We suggest that you meet with your group early and often and try out the technology several times before presenting it in class to work out any problems.
- **Discussion Groups and Listservs.** These supports are used to generate discussion outside the class. Some professors even require each student to post a certain number of messages each week to ensure that the listserv is used. You can ask questions or see what other people are thinking to gain multiple perspectives on the course information.

Studying Smarter

If you don't know, ask. Sometimes students don't use all the technology resources available because they don't know how to access them. Don't miss out; ask your professor if you are not sure.

Because advances in technology seem to happen overnight, you will probably find several other ways that professors incorporate its use into their courses as new tools become available.

Online Courses

Most college campuses offer some form of online learning. Online learning was started because colleges wanted to find a way to serve a greater population of people who, for a variety of reasons, could not attend courses on campus. Currently, many full-time students are taking online courses as well because they find them a convenient way to round out their schedule.

There are three main types of online-learning courses:

1. **Asynchronous Course.** This is the most common type. In an asynchronous course, classes do not meet at any particular time and you can learn at your own pace. When you have questions, you usually ask them online. You

take tests online and turn assignments in online as well. These courses are especially good for students who need the flexibility to do the course work at any time of day.

2. **Synchronous Course.** In this type of course, the students and professor meet online at a specified time. Such courses more closely follow the traditional classroom format. In fact, your professor may even use a computer interface that shows a row of desks and a teacher in the front of the room. Synchronous courses allow for more interaction between professors and students and questions can be asked as needed. Assignments and exams will usually occur online asynchronously.

3. **Hybrid or Blended Course.** Hybrid courses include more than one type of course format. The majority combine face-to-face classes with online (either synchronous or asynchronous) formats. Hybrid courses are gaining popularity on most campuses because they are more flexible to suit the needs of all types of learners.

SUCCESS AT A GLANCE

Benefits and Drawbacks to Online Learning

Benefits	Drawbacks
■ Can complete course work anywhere and at any time	■ Less (or no) face-to-face contact with professor and other students
■ Fosters independent work	
■ Provides greater access to college courses	■ Students need to be self-motivated, be good time managers, and have the ability to learn on their own
■ Good for students with work and family obligations	
■ Allows students to set their own learning pace	■ Can run into technology problems that interfere with the ability to get course information
	■ The technology can distract from the content
	■ Often, there is no one available to respond to questions quickly

To figure out if an online course might be right for you, think about the benefits and drawbacks listed above. Do you need the flexibility that an online course can provide? Will you be able to manage your self and your time so that you complete course requirements with very little guidance?

TIMELY TIPS

Online Safety

Using a safe password is essential in today's world. We suggest using letters, numbers, and characters to represent a phrase. For example, "I hate when I have no cash for fun" would become ih8wihn$4f. We have a few phrases like this that we have committed to memory.

Using Technology to Study

Some students have found that using technology can greatly aid in learning and studying for courses. Here are some of the ways that students are using technology in learning:

- **Organizing Lecture Notes.** Some students like to type their lecture notes because they find it helps them organize the information. We know of one student in an art history course who cut and pasted slides of paintings from her professor's Web site (and some from museum Web sites) right into her own notes. That way she could see the art as she studied her notes about it.
- **Creating Maps and Charts.** There are several software programs that can help you create wonderful concept maps and charts in a snap. These maps and charts help you organize and synthesize ideas (as discussed in Chapter 11).
- **Meeting with Virtual Study Groups.** Students can set up online study groups to meet at designated times before exams. This is a great way to study with others because the group tends to stay more on task than in a face-to-face study group.
- **Researching Information for Papers and Presentations.** The Internet can be a wonderful source of information when researching information for class presentations or papers. Of course, you need to be careful about the quality of the information you get (see the next section for strategies for evaluating Internet information). You also need to be careful that you do not plagiarize information from the Web.

This list is certainly not exhaustive. And with new technologies coming out every day, we are sure you will find other ways to incorporate technology into your learning and studying.

ON YOUR OWN

Reflecting on What You Have Read

Think about the courses you are taking this term. Write about the technology that is being used. Are some courses more technology based than others? To what do you attribute the differences you find?

How can you use technology to help you learn and study in each of your courses? Are there some courses that lend themselves better to the use of technology than others? If so, why?

Reading on a Computer

In addition to reading a traditional textbook, many professors will require you to read material online. Reading on a computer is different from reading from a book. In fact, research has indicated that people tend to read more slowly and with less accuracy when reading online. However, there are some great advantages to reading information on your computer. First, you have access to enormous stores of information on the Internet. Second, hyperlinks and other features allow you to quickly gain access to extended information. Third, reading online is convenient for most students because it can be done anywhere they have access to a computer and an Internet connection.

If your class has a lot of online reading, there are some things you should keep in mind. Reading on the screen requires a little more effort and for that reason can be more tiring. Some research has indicated that reading comprehension can suffer when reading online. Making sure you have a good monitor and that your monitor is at the optimal settings for picture quality and color can help counteract this. You also get better with practice. So if you find reading online a challenge for you, keep practicing.

Sometimes concentrating while reading online is challenging because of the many hyperlinks and other peripheral information on the screen. Hyperlinks can be useful when they contain information about word definitions or links to related material, but they can be a distraction as well when they hinder your concentration.

The more practice you have reading on a screen, the easier it will become for you. E-readers have made reading on the screen a more natural experience and some predict that e-books may soon take the place of traditional books.

GET GOING

Reducing Online Distractions

Many students find themselves losing time online. If you get sidetracked from schoolwork every time you go online, you need to rethink your approach. Instead of surfing first to "warm yourself up," use surfing as a reward. The next time you go online, set a timer for 20 minutes. When the timer goes off, if you have been on track the entire time, reward yourself with a few minutes of surfing (remember to set the timer again so you get back to work).

Note Taking on a Computer

Some students love using their laptops for note taking and others find it challenging. One of the greatest challenges is resisting the temptations of the Internet while trying to take notes and listen to the lecture. If you find you have trouble concentrating on what the professor is saying, we suggest you turn off your wireless network unless you need to go online for a specific (class-related) reason.

If you can curb your need to surf the Web, you might find taking notes on your laptop very helpful. After you take notes during class, you can easily reorganize them. You can use your notes to create study guides for your exams. You can easily compare notes with a classmate to make sure yours are complete.

If your professor posts class notes online, use them in a way that will help, not hinder, your learning. For example, we do not suggest skipping class and relying on the notes the professor supplied. Nor do we suggest downloading the notes and ignoring them until right before the test. Rather, we suggest you download the notes, bring them to class, and then use the parallel notes strategy discussed in Chapter 10. This is where you take your own notes to expand what the professor has supplied and can be an excellent method of note taking.

If you have not used your laptop for note taking, give it a try. You might find that you like it.

Real College

Leah

DIRECTIONS: Read the following "Real College" scenario and respond to the questions based on what you learned in this chapter.

Leah's parents bought her a state-of-the-art notebook computer as a high school graduation gift. She has had a great time using it to chat with her old high school friends and surf the Internet. Her father asked her how the computer was helping her in her studies and she just stared at him speechless. It hadn't even occurred to her to use her computer to study.

Leah decided that she would like to use her computer to study (she says that she'll take all the help she can get). This semester she is taking a history course that requires her to read a textbook, read a daily newspaper, and watch two movies about the Vietnam conflict. She will have to take several essay exams and write a paper connecting current events to the movies she has chosen to view.

She is also enrolled in an accounting course, which has turned out to be tougher than she expected. She is starting to get to know some of her classmates and hopes to form a study group before the next exam so that they can review problems together.

Leah is enjoying her biology class, but realized after speaking with her father that she has not even visited the professor's course Web page, which contains examples, diagrams, and sample problems.

Leah is not sure where to begin. She knows that she can use her laptop in all of these courses but does not know what to do. Based on what you have learned in this chapter, give advice to Leah. How can technology help her in each of these different situations?

ADD TO YOUR PORTFOLIO

Use one of the following methods in one of your classes for one week. Write up your reaction to the strategy.

1. a. If your professor provides online notes, print them out and use the parallel notes method. What do you like about this strategy? What challenges did you find?

    b. If your professor does not provide the notes, bring a laptop to class to take notes. What do you like about this strategy? What challenges did you find?

2. Reflect on how you currently use technology in your studying. What are you doing that is effective? What more might you need to add? What are you doing that is not effective? What might you need to change?

Preparing for Objective Exams

READ THIS CHAPTER TO ANSWER THE FOLLOWING QUESTIONS:

- What exam preparation strategies work in almost all situations?
- How should I prepare for objective exams?

SELF-ASSESSMENT

DIRECTIONS: Think about the following questions, and answer them honestly. Once you have finished reading this chapter, think about how you can change how you currently prepare for objective exams.

1. Taking a multiple-choice test is easy because all I have to do is recognize the correct answer.	T	F
2. To study for an objective test, I just memorize all the key terms.	T	F
3. It is best to spread out studying time over several days.	T	F
4. When I study, I choose one strategy that works and stick with it.	T	F
5. Cramming works because I can only get motivated under pressure.	T	F
6. Multiple-choice tests can ask application and synthesis questions.	T	F
7. To study for exams, I reread the text chapters.	T	F
8. When I study, I start with the first concept and work through all of the assigned reading in order.	T	F

You are on the right track in preparing for objective exams if you answered "false" to items 1, 2, 4, 5, 7, and 8 and "true" for items 3 and 6. Read the rest of the chapter to find the most efficient and effective ways to prepare for exams.

General Test-Preparation Strategies

Because we believe that preparing to take an exam begins on the day you begin to read about and listen to topics on which you will be tested, we feel almost as though having a special chapter on exam preparation goes against the philoso-phy of this book. That is, active learners are in a constant state of getting ready to take an exam—they don't distinguish when prereading, reading, and taking lecture notes turns into the re-hearsal and review that goes into test preparation. That said, we also know that many activities that occur as test time gets closer might be more appropriately labeled as test-preparation strategies.

Studying Smarter

Don't run out of time before you run out of test. When you go into a testing situation, have a plan to complete all of the items in the allotted time.

This chapter focuses on specific strategies that you can use to prepare for objective exams, and Chapter 17 covers essay and specialty exams. Still, there are some general test-preparation guidelines that apply to almost any type of exam. We address these general strategies first because they are "quick starters" that can get you moving in the right direction.

In general, you should:

▪ **Start Early.** Be sure that you have completed your assigned reading at least several days before the test. Remember that reading and studying are not the same thing. All of your reading should be completed *before* you begin studying.

▪ **Get Organized.** Organize all of your studying tools and strategies—notes, annotations, study strategies—so that you can dig right in.

▪ **Distribute Your Time.** Rather than trying to cram all of your studying into one or two days, distribute your time over several days. Spending a total of six hours studying spread over four days is much more effective than spending six hours studying the day before, or even three hours a day for two days before the test.

▪ **Break Up the Work.** If you begin studying several days in advance, you will be able to break up the information you have to study into chunks of major concepts. In other words, don't sit down to study with the idea that you will study every chapter and every page of notes. Study groups of information that seem to fit together, or at least identify which concepts you want to learn in a particular study session. This helps you stay more focused on the task at hand.

▪ **Stay Healthy.** Eat properly and get enough sleep. Try to remain in a studying routine rather than staying up all night cramming. Eat regular meals and exercise if that is part of your normal routine. Adequate sleep is crucial to being at the top of your game, especially on days that you take exams. It's also important to monitor your emotional health by evaluating your stress level. Too much stress influences other aspects of your performance and becomes a vicious cycle.

■ **Self-Test.** It's important to have a firm understanding of what you know and what you don't know. Remember that self-testing involves asking yourself questions about the material, saying the information to yourself or to someone else, and then checking to see whether you are correct.

NETWORKING

Online Exams

Many professors now have sample exams online. Check out your professor's Web page or the department Web page to see what is available. In addition, visit the Web site of your textbook publisher. There are often quizzes, sample exams, links to additional information, and chat rooms where you can discuss the text with other students nationwide.

■ **Study with a Classmate.** Studying with another serious-minded student has great benefits regardless of what kind of test you will take. One of the most successful models for studying with another student is for both individuals to study on their own and then to get together to ask each other questions a day or two before the exam. (See reciprocal questioning in Chapter 11.) Both parties can then find out which concepts they know very well and which ones they need to spend more time on.

Studying Smarter

Many campuses have test banks, which are places on campus where professors can put copies of retired tests on file for students to examine. If your campus has a test bank, use it to find out the types of questions your professor asks. As long as the professor knows that his test is part of a legitimate test bank, it is not academically dishonest to use these old tests.

■ **Look at Old Exams.** Talk to others who have previously taken the class. Finding out as much information about the test as possible, whether it's from looking at old exams or by talking to others, is simply a smart thing to do. It's not cheating; it's being an informed consumer, so to speak. If professors permit students to keep their exams, you can be fairly certain that they will not be giving that same test again. But it's probably also a safe bet that the kinds of questions asked will be similar. When talking with students who have already taken the class with the professor, it's a good rule to find out specifics about the level of questions and grading.

Many of these general tips are common sense. But they are tips that students often overlook as they get caught up in exam preparation. In the next section we will focus more specifically on preparation for and taking objective exams.

Objective Exams

Preparing for Objective Exams

Objective exams can consist of several different kinds of questions. The most common types are multiple-choice and true/false questions, but matching and fill-in-the-blank questions are also objective. Another name for these types of questions is *recognition items* because all of the information is there; your task is to recognize it. For example, for a multiple-choice question, you have to recognize which answer out of the four or five choices is correct. For a true/false question, you have to recognize whether the statement is true or false. These items are considered objective because there is (or should be) only one correct answer, if the test is well written. In other words, in a multiple-choice question, only one of the answers should be correct. Moreover, if you studied and really know the information, the correct answer should be obvious to you.

SUCCESS AT A GLANCE

Studying for Objective Tests

- Make a jot list of key points.
- Organize this information around broad concepts.
- Begin each study session with a review.
- Rehearse and self-test.
- Concentrate on areas of weakness.

Because of the precise knowledge required to answer objective items, it is extremely important that two key factors guide your preparation: (1) organization of information; and (2) thinking about the information the way in which your professor expects.

Organization

Let's start with an example. Suppose you are in an introductory psychology course and every two to three weeks you have a 50-item objective test—always multiple-choice items. In any given testing period, you have about 30 pages of lecture notes and three or four chapters of information to study. Where do you begin? We have found that the best place to start when you know you will have an objective test is to make a jot list of all of the key concepts from the text and lectures. The accompanying example shows what a jot list might look like for the history chapter, "The Nation Divides: The Vietnam War and Social Conflict, 1964–1971," which is located in Appendix B and begins on page 251. Notice that the jot list is not particularly formal. Rather, it simply forces you to think about the concepts before you begin to study. One way to come up with your jot list is to use the chapter headings and subheadings as a guide. Unless you make a conscious effort to jot down these concepts, you may leave out important information or simply gloss over concepts that you should spend a significant amount of time on.

Example of a Jot List

Chapter 26, "The Nation Divides"

LBJ presidency
   Great Society
   Liberal Supreme Court
War in Vietnam
   U.S. involvement
   Importance of 1968
Civil rights/Black power movement
New left (SDS movement)
Rebellion
   Women's lib
   Other rebellions
Conservative response
Nixon presidency
   Vietnam under Nixon

■ ■ ■

TIMELY TIPS

Organizing Information

In order to use your time effectively and efficiently when you are preparing for an objective test, organize the information as you go along. As you are annotating and creating your rehearsal strategies, keep an organized jot list of the key concepts that you will have to learn for the test. Then when it comes time to create a talk-through card, you will already have the information on hand.

Once you have made your jot list, you can organize the information to study. You will need to:

1. **Group together your rehearsal strategies** that relate to the overriding concept. (Let's use the history topic of "the LBJ presidency" as an example.) You should also know which sections of lecture notes go with this concept.

2. **Look for overlap** between the text and lecture and focus your studying on the big picture of the Johnson years rather than just concentrating on the text information one time and the lecture notes another time.

3. **Focus each study session** around a couple of broad concepts, such as "progression of the civil rights movement" or "the presidency of LBJ" rather than simply trying to read through everything you have to learn for the entire test. In other words, one night you might study all the material related to the LBJ presidency, the next night you could concentrate on Nixon, and the third night you would review issues concerning civil rights or the Cold War—concepts that spanned both the Johnson and Nixon presidencies. Following this procedure encourages you to think actively and critically. Use your jot list as a guide. Then rehearse and self-test the material from the next broad concept. Your study schedule might look something like the example study schedule shown below. Note that each study session begins with a review; after you have covered all the material, you end with a self-testing session when you identify specific areas of weakness.

4. **Concentrate on any weakness** as you and your study partner question each other in one final study session before the exam.

5. **Talk through** the couple of ideas that were still giving you difficulty on the morning of the exam.

GET GOING

Maintaining Motivation During Studying

Staying motivated when you are preparing for a big test can sometimes be difficult because it is easy to feel overwhelmed. Studying specific concepts at planned times rather than trying to study everything in one session is one way to help you maintain motivation. When you end your study session by self-testing and realize how much you have learned, you will feel motivated to continue the process until you have covered all the concepts.

Example of a Study Schedule

Session 1—Monday

Focus: 1964–1971 presidencies of Johnson and Nixon

4:30–5:00	Organize all information
5:00–6:00	Study: LBJ—Great Society, liberalism, early Vietnam (to 1968)
6:00–6:45	Eat dinner
7:00–8:00	Review: Great Society, liberalism, and early Vietnam
	Study: Vietnam after 1968, civil rights/black power, liberal movements, early Nixon years
8:30–9:00	Self-test

Session 2—Tuesday

Focus: Later Nixon years

10:00–10:30	Review 1964–1971: All concepts from LBJ and early Nixon years
10:30–11:30	Study: Later Nixon years
11:30–12:00	Lunch
12:30–1:50	Class
2:00–3:00	Continue study of later Nixon years
3:00–3:30	Self-test

Thinking

Organizing, both in terms of how you will group the concepts to be learned and how you will structure your study sessions, is crucial to performing well on objective tests. However, organizing won't help you much if you aren't sure about the level of thinking required. On essay tests, you can pretty much count on having to think critically and to analyze and synthesize information. But on objective exams, many students make the mistake of believing that the test questions are designed solely to see if they have memorized the material. That is, they think the questions don't go beyond asking for facts. Students who fall into this trap can experience grave difficulty and often don't do well. That's why it's important to know the kind of thinking that your professor expects. If she expects you to memorize the facts and most of the questions are factual in nature, you would study one way. If, however, she asks for application, synthesis, examples, and other types of higher-level thinking, you would study another way.

To clarify this point, let's look at several questions. Each of these questions is based on either the history or psychology chapters included in the appendixes of this book. The first example in each set of questions is a memory-level task. The second is a higher-level question. (The asterisk [*] indicates the correct answer.)

Set A (based on the psychology chapter)

1. (memory-level) The Raven Progressive Matrices intelligence test would be considered
   a. a culture-fair test. *
   b. an environmental deprivation test.
   c. a multiple intelligences test.
   d. all of the above.
2. (higher-level) According to the influence of heredity theory, which relationship would have the lowest correlation with intelligence?
   a. brother/sister
   b. identical twins regardless of gender
   c. cousins from the same side of the family*
   d. father/daughter

Set B (based on the history chapter)

1. (memory-level) The Civil Rights Act of 1964
   a. gave blacks the right to vote.
   b. outlawed discrimination in public facilities.*
   c. provided employment training for minorities.
   d. described the War on Poverty.
2. (higher-level) Overall, the goal of the Great Society programs was to
   a. assist blacks in breaking free of poverty.
   b. expand individual rights.
   c. institute and regulate the Medicare system.
   d. improve the quality of life for all Americans.*

It is fairly easy to see the differences in these questions. The first question in each set is very straightforward and requires little interpretation or thinking beyond the memory level. Studying for an objective test that asks this type of question would be a relatively easy task: You would simply identify the key terms and ideas and memorize definitions, component parts, or the like. But think about the problem you might have if you simply memorized information and then had an exam that asked questions like the second one in each set. You would have a much more difficult time because you would have thought about the information in an incorrect way. Even if you studied quite a bit, if you only memorized when the task was to go beyond memorization, taking the test would be a struggle.

The point is that you need to be clear about the professor's expectations and the way he tests, what we have called "task" throughout this book. As mentioned earlier, look at old exams, talk to students who have taken a class with the professor, or ask the professor. Whatever you do, have an accurate picture of the kind of test you will have. Then, as you are doing your rehearsal, review, and self-testing, you can frame your studying accordingly.

ON YOUR OWN

Reflecting on What You Have Read

In a paragraph, write down the differences between lower-level and higher-level questions, and look once again at the examples given earlier for the two text excerpts from the appendix. Now select a course in which you have objective exams. Write four lower-level, multiple-choice questions and four higher-level multiple-choice questions. How can you tell the difference between the two types?

Taking Objective Exams

You have studied, you feel good about what you know, and you are absolutely ready to take your exam. Well, you're almost ready. The next (or final) thing you need to think about is a game plan. A sports analogy fits here: The basketball team has studied the playbook, looked at films of itself and the opponent, and is mentally ready to play the game. The players are pumped and psyched. But if they don't have a game plan, all their work may not result in a win. Any athletic team going into a game needs a game plan to follow—some sort of strategy for winning the game.

A testing situation for you is just like game day for the basketball team. You have prepared, you are mentally ready to take the test, and you want to do well. Now you have to follow through with your game plan for taking the test. To plan your strategy, it helps to ask yourself some questions before you get into the testing situation:

■ How will I work through the test? Will I simply start with the first item and answer the questions in consecutive order?

■ What will I do when I come across an item I'm not sure of? Will I skip it and come back to it later, or will I mark something before going on to the next item?

■ How will I choose an answer when I can't even make an educated guess?

■ How will I approach answering true/false questions?

■ What will I do if I am running out of time and still have several questions to answer?

It's important to think about how you will approach an exam before you are actually in a testing situation. We suggest the following guidelines.

■ **Get to Class on Time.** Leave home early enough so that you don't have to rush. When you rush, you tend to get anxious, especially on an exam day. Once you get to class, get out your pen and anything else you might need. Relax and take a couple of deep breaths. Give yourself some positive reinforcement by saying such things as "I studied," "I know this stuff," and "I know I should do well on this exam."

■ **When You Get Your Exam, Take a Minute or Two to Look Through It.** See how many items there are so that you know how to divide up your time. Also, remember to do something that is very important and often overlooked: *Read the directions* so you know what you are required to do.

■ **Read the First Item.** If you don't know the answer, leave it blank and go to the next item. Do this with each item until you find one of which you are certain. We believe it is a good idea to do the items you know first and then come back and spend more time on those of which you are unsure. The only problem this seems to create is that students sometimes make mistakes by putting an answer in the wrong place on their answer sheet.

Therefore, if you are going to skip around on the test, you need to make sure that your answer goes in the corresponding place on your answer sheet.

■ **Eliminate Answers Whenever Possible.** On a multiple-choice question, you might be able to eliminate two answer choices immediately, but the other two alternatives might both be plausible. If this occurs, you at least have a 50-50 chance of choosing correctly.

■ **Use Information from Other Items on the Exam to Help You with Items You Don't Know.** Once you have gone through the entire test, you can often pick up information from one question that will help you answer another. That's why it's a good idea to go through and answer the items you know first.

■ **Use All of the Allotted Time.** Many students fail to use all of the class period to take their exam and then end up making careless mistakes such as leaving items blank when they could have at least guessed. Even when you have answered every question, it's best to go through the test one more time just to be sure. Remember, it's easy to mark a wrong answer when you actually know the correct answer.

■ **When Faced with a Situation in Which You Have to Guess, Make a Selection and Move On.** Go with your gut selection, and don't change your mind unless you have found information later in the test that helps you re-member an idea related to the question. On a multiple-choice exam, for exam-ple, some students will select the same answer choice for every question they don't know. For true/false questions you might answer all true or all false for items on which you guess. Whatever you do, never leave objective test items blank unless you are penalized for guessing.

■ **If There Are Questions That Involve Diagrams, Be Sure You Understand Them Before Answering the Questions.** Diagrams are especially prevalent on science exams, and sometimes you will have several questions on one diagram. Look at the diagram and talk it through in your head. Then read each question pertaining to the diagram, referring to it before answering the question.

Taking exams does not have to be extremely stressful. If you have studied well and have a game plan for taking exams, you'll probably be relaxed and do well.

Real College

Teddy

DIRECTIONS: Read the following "Real College" scenario and respond to the questions based on what you learned in this chapter.

In high school, Teddy was always a model student. He wasn't one of those kids who waited until the morning of a test to try to cram as much information as possible into his brain. Teddy usually started a day or two before his scheduled exams and reviewed the study guides that most of his teachers gave him. An hour or so of reading over this information typically resulted in a good test grade for him.

Now, early in his first semester of college, Teddy finds that these tactics aren't working so well for him. He earned a D on his first anthropology exam, and things don't look all that promising for the multiple-choice test that he has in a few days in psychology. It's not that he doesn't have the time; he just doesn't know what to do.

His professors don't seem to be of much help at all. Gone are the study guides that once made studying easy. Gone are the kind of tests he had in high school that simply asked him to memorize facts from class lectures. And gone are the frequent tests that he benefited from in high school. In anthropology he only has two more tests and a short paper. Teddy knows that he has to do something to get back on track.

For the impending psychology test, at least he has kept up with his reading—well, almost. And he does know what the task is: He is responsible for five text chapters, all of his lecture notes, and two outside readings that focus on psychological research. The test will contain 50 multiple-choice questions, most of which the professor said would be example and application questions. There are another 10 matching items where he will have to match researchers with important research they carried out.

What advice would you give Teddy about how he should get back on track? What general advice would you give Teddy for studying for objective exams? How might he have to change his studying from anthropology to psychology?

ADD TO YOUR PORTFOLIO

1. Create a study plan for your next objective test. What concepts will you concentrate on for each study session? How will you know when you understand and can remember all the information? How will you review?

2. Create a game plan for taking the exam.

Preparing for and Taking Essay and Specialty Exams

READ THIS CHAPTER TO ANSWER THE FOLLOWING QUESTIONS:

- How should you prepare for essay exams?
- What kind of a study plan should you have for preparing for essay exams?
- How should you study for special types of exams such as take-home and open-book exams?

———————————— **SELF-ASSESSMENT** ————————————

DIRECTIONS: The following questions are predictions for essay exams in a history course. For each of the questions, decide whether the question is too broad (B), too narrow (N), or would make a good (G) essay question.

1. _____ From 1914 through the 1990s there have been obvious demographic shifts. Discuss the factors contributing to these shifts and the effects the shifts have had technologically.

2. _____ How has life changed as a result of twentieth-century technology?

3. _____ Compare and contrast the weapons used in World War I with those used in World War II.

4. _____ What effect did the Great Depression during the 1930s have on politics?

5. _____ What influences did technological advances have on the progression and expansion of World War II?

Of course, your ability to respond to these essay questions depends on the content covered in class. Nonetheless, 1 and 5 would be considered good essay questions, 2 and 4 would be too broad, and 3 would be too narrow. Strive to predict good essay questions when you study for your own classes.

214

Essay Exams

Preparing for essay exams involves different strategies than preparing for objective exams. This often comes as a shock, especially to first-year college students who may have had little experience with essay exams in high school or, if they have had essay exams, may have prepared for them in the same way they prepared for objective exams. As a general rule, essay preparation requires a different type of approach, a different way of thinking, and a different way of organizing.

Studying Smarter

Prepare for essay exams by predicting questions and then practicing your answers.

When we use the term *essay exam*, we are referring to any type of question that requires you to write an extended response. In this instance, essay tests would include:

- Traditional multiparagraph responses to questions

- Short-answer questions that require you to write a paragraph or two in response to a more narrowly focused question

- Identification items, which require you to define a term, explain the significance of something, or write several sentences describing a person, a place, an event, and so forth

Sometimes these types of exams are referred to as *recall* tests because you are asked to recall all of the pertinent information from your memory. Unlike recognition questions (e.g., multiple-choice, true/false) that ask you to recognize the correct information, recall questions require you to remember the information on your own.

PORPE

PORPE, is an acronym for *Predict, Organize, Rehearse, Practice,* and *Evaluate,* a structured, organized strategy specifically designed to help you prepare for essay or short-answer exams.* You begin the PORPE studying process after you have completed your reading, constructed useful study strategies, and organized your lecture notes. As we explain the steps of PORPE, we have included examples based on a predicted essay question from the psychology chapter excerpt located in Appendix A.

   Step 1: Predict.   (Predict several days before the test.) The first thing you need to do is to predict broad questions that your professor might include on

---

*M. L. Simpson. (1986). PORPE: A writing strategy for studying and learning in the content areas. *Journal of Reading, 29,* 404–414.

SUCCESS AT A GLANCE

PORPE Time Line

P	O	R	P	E
Predict →	Organize →	Rehearse →	Practice →	Evaluate
Several days before	3–4 days before	3–4 days before	2 days before	After practicing

---

the exam. Simply put, the better predictor you are, the better you will do on the exam. But predicting questions can be a tricky business. It has been our experience that when students begin to use this strategy, they predict questions that are either far too broad or way too narrow. For example, predicting an essay question such as "Discuss the presidency of Lyndon Baines Johnson" would be too broad; a question such as "Why was the Head Start program started?" would be too specific. Generally, the fewer the number of questions you are required to answer on an exam, the broader your prediction questions should be.

Keep in mind when predicting that rarely will your specific question be precisely what the professor asks. But once you become a good predictor, there will be considerable overlap between what you predict and the actual questions on the test. The following is an example of a good essay prediction for a psychology course in which you were studying "Cognition and Intelligence," found in Appendix A.

***Step 1: Predict:* Predict a question that you think might be asked on the exam.**

Question: For decades there has been a controversy over the reasons for individuals' differing levels of intelligence. Discuss the two factors that contribute to this controversy. Then discuss the research that exists about the relative contribution made by each factor.

Step 2: Organize. (Organize three or four days before the test.) After you have predicted several questions, you need to organize the information. Most students like to use an outline to organize so that they can see the key points they want to make and the support they want to provide for each key point. Other organizing strategies, such as concept maps or charts, also work well (see Chapter 11). When you organize the material, think about both key generalizations and information to support those generalizations. Spend some time organizing your thoughts so that you will study worthwhile material.

As you become more focused and predict specific questions, your outline should be more comprehensive and detailed. To fill in your outline, use the pertinent information that you included in your text annotations (Chapter 9), what you gathered using rehearsal strategies (Chapter 11), and what you have annotated in your lecture notes (Chapter 10). Be sure that you draw from both the text and the lectures, as well as any other sources for which you are responsible. And be sure to write a detailed outline for each of the questions you predict. The following example shows what an outline would look like for the essay question we predicted in Step 1 of PORPE.

Step 2: *Organize:* In an organized fashion, write down the ideas you want to include in your essay.

Two explanations for differing levels of intelligence

1. Heredity
   a. Family relationships & IQ—the closer the family rel. the stronger the relationship (twins > brother/sister > cousins)
   b. Studies involving adopted children—adopt. children's IQs more closely related to biological than adoptive parents
   c. Quantitative trait loci—certain genes associated with high IQ
   d. Research on identical twins separated as infants

Conclusions:

Heritability of IQ = ~ 35% in childhood to 75% in adulthood

Increases in age shaped by environmental factors

Genetic factors play a role

2. Environment
   a. Flynn Effect—IQ has increased worldwide (~ 3 pts. but more in some areas) b/c of environmental factors, which include
      - Nutrition
      - Urbanization
      - TV
      - More and better education
      - Computers

Still lack of sufficient evidence

   b. Studies of environmental deprivation/enrichment
      - IQ reduced by lack of environmental stimulation
      - Ramey & Ramey study—conditions for increase in IQ include: early intervention, broad in scope, intensive, good schools, and so forth
   c. Biological factors encountered by children
      - E.g., malnutrition, pollution, drug and alcohol

Summary: Both factors play a role but there is some disagreement about the contribution of each.

■   ■   ■

Step 3: Rehearse. (Rehearse several times for each question, beginning three or four days before the test.) This is the time to commit the information in your outline to memory. Read one of the questions you predicted. Then read through your outline slowly and deliberately. "Listen" to what you are saying. Does it make sense? Do you have enough support? Do the ideas flow? After you have read through the outline several times, ask yourself the question again. This time, try answering it without looking at the outline. Be sure that you are rehearsing the concepts accurately. If you are not sure of something, immediately return to your outline and read that part through again, or if you are really experiencing problems, check your text or lecture notes to clarify or add support. Then try to restate the answer to that portion of the question. Always keep in mind that when you rehearse, it's important to also engage in self-testing.

Step 4: Practice. (Practice two days before the test.) This is the time to practice writing out answers to some of your questions. Write under the same conditions that you will have in class. For example, if you will be required to answer two essay questions in a 50-minute class period, take only 20 minutes to practice one of your questions. That would leave 20 minutes to practice on a second question and 10 minutes to go back and proof your work.

You should also construct each answer so that it is organized the same way that you will organize it in class. Write in complete sentences, include appropriate examples, and be sure to have an introduction and a conclusion. The following practice essay example shows an answer for the question we predicted in Step 1 concerning reasons for individuals' differing levels of intelligence (page 216).

Example of a Practice Essay

Question: For decades there has been a controversy over the reasons for individuals' differing levels of intelligence. Discuss the two factors that contribute to this controversy. Then discuss the research that exists about the relative contribution made by each factor.

There are two theories that attempt to explain why individuals have differing levels of intelligence. The first theory focuses on the role that heredity or genetics play in intelligence and the second focuses on the role that environment plays. Although neither theory totally explains intelligence, evidence exists that each makes contributions and that the two factors are linked.

There are four lines of research that support the influence of heredity. First, if heredity plays a role, the closer the family members, the larger the correlation will be between the family members. This prediction has been confirmed. Twins' intelligence is correlated at around .90, siblings' at .50, and cousins' at .15. Second, studies of adopted children show that their IQs are more closely related to their biological parents than their adoptive parents. Third, research in genetics has shown evidence that certain genes are associated with high intelligence. Finally, research on identical twins separated at birth and raised in different homes indicates that their IQs correlate almost as highly as those twins who are raised together.

But there is also evidence that environment plays a role in intelligence. First there is the Flynn Effect, which finds that in recent decades IQs have risen worldwide and at every age level. It seems unlikely that heredity could explain this rise. Rather, environmental factors such as nutrition, education, computers, and even television have been suggested as likely factors. In addition, studies of both environmental deprivation and environmental enrichment suggest that lack of stimulation early in life can lead to lower IQs. Moreover, if children are moved from nonstimulating environments (such as orphanages, for example) their IQs increase, sometimes dramatically. For these interventions to be successful, however, they must be early, intense, and broad in scope. Finally, there is considerable evidence that environmental factors such as malnutrition, pollution, and drugs and alcohol can affect intelligence.

Most psychologists would agree that both heredity and environment influence an individual's intelligence. What they do not always agree upon is the contribution of each. What we do know is that IQ is not related 100 percent to either factor.

■　　■　　■

Step 5: Evaluate. (Evaluate immediately after practicing.) Now comes the most difficult part—evaluating your own writing. After you have finished practicing, read what you have written. When you finish reading, get out your outline and any other study strategy materials you have been using and check for accuracy and completeness. Ask yourself the following questions:

- Is my introduction clear and focused?
- Are my generalizations complete and precise?
- Are my examples and supporting information accurate and complete?
- Do I have a conclusion that relates back to my introduction and overall thesis?

Once you have honestly answered these questions you can go back and do some rethinking and reorganizing, if necessary. You may even want to show your essay to your professor so that he can provide you with feedback. Or if your campus has a writing center, you may be able to get help with organizing your response.

NETWORKING

Critiquing Essays over E-mail

If you have been working with a classmate in a course that requires you to write essay exams, you might try sending your study partner a copy of a practice essay over e-mail. Have your study partner critique your essay by evaluating its strengths and weaknesses. You can do the same for your study partner.

> **TIMELY TIPS**
>
> **Writing Done Right**
>
> We believe that one of the most useful skills you can learn in college is the ability to write. Using components of the PORPE strategy can help you prepare for essays, but it can also help you to organize a paper, a group project, or just about any other writing task you may encounter in college or beyond. Most careers require you to be able to express yourself clearly in writing, and you just might find yourself using some of the elements of PORPE every time you write.

Taking Essay Exams

When you are in the actual test-taking situation, remember these three important factors: (1) the amount of time you have to write each answer; (2) how you will structure each answer; and (3) the guidelines your professor provides about how she will evaluate or grade your essay. Each of these factors has a bearing on how you will spend your in-class, essay-writing time.

Time Allotted for Writing

Time is usually your biggest enemy when answering essay or short-answer questions. When you are deciding on your approach for taking the exam, think carefully about how you will divide up your time. For example, if you have one essay question and five fairly comprehensive identification items to answer, would it be best to spend half of your time on the essay and the other half on the identification? Or would it be better to spend more time on the essay and less time on the identification items? It's all give-and-take, but a good rule of thumb is to begin with what you know best and feel most comfortable with. If you know the answers to all the identification questions and feel a bit shaky on how best to approach the essay, start with the IDs and then use the remaining time to do the best job you can on the essay. In addition, consider the point value of each question. If the essay is worth 40 points and each ID is worth 3 points, you should spend more time on the essay.

Structuring Your Essay

Few professors provide students with guidance on how they want essay or short-answer questions structured. As a result, many students will write a paragraph to answer an essay question and a sentence or two to answer a short-answer item. Usually when professors ask you to write an essay, they want extended comment; that is, they want you to write considerably more than a paragraph. For an essay, you should plan on writing at least an introductory paragraph, several paragraphs that discuss specific points you think are important to answering the question, and a concluding paragraph. Short-answer questions, as a general rule, are a paragraph or two long and tend to be somewhat less structured than an essay.

If your professor tells you exactly how she wants you to structure your essay, *follow exactly what she says.* However, if your professor does not provide any guidance, the following structure is generally accepted in most disciplines. We recommend that as you read each of the suggestions below you refer to the example of the practice essay provided earlier in this chapter (page 218).

■ Write an introductory paragraph that outlines your thesis and indicates that you understand what the question is asking. By thesis, we mean the overall focus of your essay or the argument you will be making. If the question has multiple parts, be sure that your introduction pulls in all of the parts. The first paragraph should not be long and involved, but it should be clear and concise and give the reader a picture of your overall points.

■ Each of your next several paragraphs should begin with a generalization about one of the key points you want to make. Don't worry about following the five-paragraph essay format you learned in high school. Instead, use as many paragraphs as necessary to answer the question fully. For example, if your question in political science asks you to discuss political, economic, international policy, and social issues, you would write four paragraphs, one dealing with each of the four issues. For each generalization, you should provide support in the form of events, names, dates, people, examples, and so forth—specific information that supports your point. Each paragraph should deal with only one key idea. Be careful about including several broad generalizations in the same paragraph. However, also be careful about writing a litany of facts without tying them together with generalizations. Whenever possible, have smooth transitions from one idea to the next by using words such as *first, second, third; furthermore; in addition to; moreover;* and so forth.

■ Unlike objective tests where we encourage you to guess if you have to, for essay exams follow the "when in doubt, leave it out" plan. If you are not completely sure of something, do not put it in your essay. If you have included wrong information in your essay, your professor has no alternative but to take points off. But if your essay is sound and you have made numerous good points, you might get few or no points taken off if you leave out a bit of information.

■ End your essay with a concluding paragraph that joins

Studying Smarter

Remember that a human being will be reading your essay. Although professors rarely take off points for neatness, your grade will suffer if they can't read what you have written. Try to make their job easier by writing as neatly as you can. It is also a good idea to underline key words or phrases that you want to be sure that your professor reads.

together the points you wanted to make. The conclusion doesn't have to be lengthy, but it should return to your thesis and pull together the most important ideas related to that thesis.

Few professors would oppose this structure; if your professor does not provide guidance about format, this one will rarely, if ever, get you into trouble. But, if your professor spends a lot of class time explaining the essay format he expects, be sure to get down as much information as you can about what he wants, and then use his model when you practice your essay.

Evaluation Guidelines

It's a tall order to write essays within the allotted time, have an acceptable structure, and manage to keep the mechanics and grammar errors down to a minimum. That's why it is important to know your professor's expectations before you go into the exam situation. For example, how strict will your professor be concerning mechanics, grammar, and usage? If your professor doesn't say anything in class about his expectations, be sure to ask. Most professors do not expect perfection, but they will probably deduct points on an essay that has so many errors that it is difficult to read and understand. The bottom line is to know what your professor expects and then do your best to balance time, structure/content, and grammar/spelling issues.

A Word About Identification Items

Identification items ask you to write what you know about specific events, people, laws, dates, and so forth. They differ from essay/short-answer questions in that they are more focused and usually require only a few sentences of explanation. Sometimes you can even write in phrases rather than in full sentences when answering identification questions. There are two ideas to keep in mind when preparing for identification items:

1. There are usually many options for the professor to choose from. In history, for example, where identification questions are common, every chapter and lecture is filled with material that could be included on a test. So how do you decide which terms are the most important to study? A good place to begin is with your text. If your text provides a listing of key terms or if there is a chapter summary, making sure that you can identify what is in either of those sources usually is your best starting point. Match up those terms with what your professor has spent time on during lectures. Look for overlap, because identification items usually focus on material that has been addressed in a lecture or has been pointed out in the text.

2. You have to know the kind of information your professor expects you to include. Most of the time, professors will want you to include more than just definitional information. They may want you to discuss the significance, provide an example, or explain how the item relates to some other issue or idea. Whatever the expectations, be sure that you know what they are. Many students receive only partial credit on short-answer items simply because they failed to include all the information requested by their professor.

GET GOING

Preparing to Answer Identification Items

When responding to identification items, few professors want you to just define the term. Rather, you also will be expected to give an example or explain the item's significance. This expectation should encourage you to think about and note examples or significant points in your annotations and your rehearsal strategies. If you do this as you go along rather than waiting until right before the exam, you will be much further ahead.

Specialized Exams

We conclude this chapter by briefly discussing how to prepare for specialized exams. Specialized exams may not be given frequently in your college career, but you need to know how to prepare for them when they do come along. We discuss three types of specialized exams: (1) problem-solving exams, the most common of the specialized exams; (2) open-book exams; and (3) take-home exams.

Problem-Solving Exams

Several types of courses, including mathematics, science, engineering, and business courses, require you to solve problems. Many students attempt to study for exams of this nature by doing the same problems over and over again, but we think it is important to use some additional strategies for studying for these types of exams.

Working the problems as a way of studying for this type of test is certainly a good idea and should be part of your studying routine. Note that we said "part of," because if all you do is work the same set of problems over and over again, you probably will not do very well. The important thing to remember is that you have to think about and conceptualize what you are doing. You won't get those exact same problems on the exam, so you have to think about the concepts underlying the problems. That's why we suggest that you talk through your problems. Put words to them. As you do a problem, think about and verbalize what you are doing. Annotate formulas into words that indicate you understand the problem. If you can't talk through problems as you solve them, you probably don't understand the concept.

Let's look at an example and talk through some of the thinking that would make it easier to solve this problem. Thinking about math problems in this manner, especially word problems, also lets you know if you understand the reasoning behind your method of solving the problem.

The Problem: Susan begins a 20-mile race at 7:00 A.M., running at an average speed of 10 miles per hour. One hour later, her brother leaves the starting line on a motorbike and follows her route at the rate of 40 miles per hour. At what time does he catch up to her?

The Question: What is the problem asking for? You are supposed to solve this problem to find out what time he catches up with her, so you will need to make sure that the answer you come up with is reflected as time.

The Solution:

1. **Visualize the Problem.** This diagram shows that when Susan's brother overtakes her, they have both traveled the same distance.

   Susan >>>>>>>>>>>>>>>>>>>>>

   Her brother >>>>>>>>>>>

2. **What Is the Basic Idea Behind the Problem?** Both are traveling at a constant rate of speed, so we would think about the basic equation as:

$$\text{Distance} = (\text{Rate})(\text{Time})$$
$$d = rt$$

3. **Explain the Variables.**

   Let t = # of hours Susan runs until her brother catches her.

   Then $t - 1$ = # of hours Susan's brother rides until he catches up (he leaves 1 hour later so he travels 1 hour less).

4. **Write and Solve the Equation.**

$$10t = 40(t - 1)$$
$$10t = 40t - 40$$
$$-30t = -40$$
$$t = \frac{-40}{30} = \frac{4}{3} = 1\text{-}1/3 \text{ hours} = 1 \text{ hour and } 20 \text{ minutes}$$

5. **The Solution.** Remember that the question asked for time. Susan's brother caught her 1 hour and 20 minutes after she began the race at 7 A.M. Therefore, he would catch up with her at 8:20 A.M. If you wrote 1 hour and 20 minutes as your answer, you would not receive credit because you did not answer the question that was asked.

The following will help you prepare for problem-solving exams.

■ **Make Up a Test for Yourself with the Types of Problems You Will Be Tested On.** Put some problems on note cards and then use them as a way of seeing whether you understand the concepts. After you have worked through the problems, shuffle the note cards and work on them again in a different order, concentrating on those that gave you problems.

■ **Get Help Early.** Courses such as mathematics, physics, and chemistry tend to be arranged sequentially. That is, the ideas build on one another. If you miss or don't understand something presented in week two of the term, chances are you are going to have trouble with what is presented after that. If you think you are "mathematically challenged," you should arrange to be part of a study group, get a tutor, or make regular appointments to meet with your professor right at the beginning of the term.

■ **Know the Processes.** In sciences you are often asked to label diagrams or point to a particular process from a figure. If this is a requirement for your course, be sure to practice by talking through the process or figure as you study.

Open-Book Exams

Open-book exams allow you access to your text, and sometimes even your notes, during the examination period. Open-book exams are generally given in the usual class period, which means you take them under timed conditions. This type of exam is often given in literature courses so that students can have access to specific pieces of text that they have been asked to read.

When students are told that they will have an open-book exam, they often breathe a sigh of relief. We have even heard students say that they didn't have to study because they were having an open-book test. But it takes just as much effort to adequately prepare for this type of test as it does to prepare for a more traditional objective or essay test.

Organization is the key to preparing for open-book exams. You first have to go through the usual preparation steps of predicting, organizing, rehearsing, practicing, and evaluating. But you have to put extra time into organizing. You should mark information that you might use to support points you expect to have to make or pull specific examples from the readings. You will need to have the information you deem important flagged in some way so that it is easy to find. For example, you can tab important passages or pages in your text with self-stick notes. Because you are in a timed situation, you must know where things are and have the information organized so that you can find it quickly.

Take-Home Exams

Take-home exams allow you to have access to your text and notes and put no restrictions on the amount of time you can spend taking the test. The professor gives you the test questions along with some basic instructions, usually reminding you that you can't get outside assistance to answer the questions. Some professors may even have you sign an academic honesty pledge. When professors give take-home exams, they generally expect a very high level of proficiency and thinking. For example, if they give you a take-home essay exam, they would expect your writing to display synthesis, analysis, and critical thought. They would expect extensive support and a paper virtually free of grammatical and spelling errors. Therefore, you usually have to spend a considerable amount of time working on take-home exams.

Even if you know in advance that you will have take-home exams in a course, it is extremely important for you to keep up. Do your reading, attend class, construct rehearsal strategies, and continue to review. Then, when you get your take-home exam from your instructor, you will be ready to organize all the information and spend less time actually taking the test.

ON YOUR OWN

Reflecting on What You Have Read

Think about the most difficult test you have had so far in your college career. Then, write a response to the following questions: What made this test difficult for you? How did you study for the test? Did you feel that you were prepared before taking the test? Why or why not? If you could do it again, what might you do differently?

Real College

Iris

DIRECTIONS: Read the following "Real College" scenario and respond to the questions based on what you learned in this chapter.

Iris had good intentions. And her semester was going quite well—up until this point, that is. Iris had some academic difficulties during her first semester in college, but she had learned from her mistakes, and so far so good. But now it was time for the real test. She knew that an exam was rapidly approaching in Dr. Jameson's history course and she was scared. It was Thursday and the test was the following Tuesday. She had done a decent job of keeping up in her courses this semester—except for Dr. Jameson's, even though she had intended to stay on top of things in history. Somehow she had fallen a little behind. Okay, a lot behind. Now it was time for the first of only two exams in the course and Dr. Jameson's exams had the reputation of being lethal. The most difficult thing was that half of the exam consisted of 30 multiple-choice questions and the other half was 1 essay question. That meant that she had to study in two different ways for the same test, and she hadn't even completed the reading assignments yet. And to make things even worse, she knew that most questions would come from the text and that she would have to pull in text-related information into her essay. Professor Jameson had already been very explicit about that in class.

Given the amount of time she has left to study and the kind of exam that she will have, what recommendations would you give to Iris? How should she prepare for and go about taking her history exam so that she can maximize her grade? If Iris had followed her intentions, what should she have done to prevent her problems?

ADD TO YOUR PORTFOLIO

For your next essay exam, try using the PORPE strategy. Remember, you need to predict the question, organize (using a map, chart, or outline), rehearse, practice, and evaluate its effectiveness. Which parts of the strategy seemed most beneficial to you? What modifications will you make for the next exam?

APPENDIX

Cognition and Intelligence
from *Essentials of Psychology,* Third Edition

ROBERT A. BARON
Rensselaer Polytechnic Institute

Excerpt from Chapter 7, pp. 264–286. Copyright © 2002 Allyn and Bacon. This chapter has been excerpted for inclusion in *College Success Strategies* and does not include many figures and tables mentioned in the text.

Intelligence: Contrasting Views of Its Nature

Intelligence, like love, is one of those concepts that is easier to recognize than to define. We often refer to others' intelligence, describing people as *bright, sharp,* or *quick* on the one hand, or as *slow, dull,* or even *stupid* on the other. And slurs on one's intelligence are often fighting words where children—and even adults—are concerned. But again, what, precisely, *is* intelligence? Psychologists don't entirely agree, but as a working definition we can adopt the wording offered by a distinguished panel of experts (Neisser et al., 1996): The term **intelligence** refers to *individuals' abilities to understand complex ideas, to adapt effectively to the environment, to learn from experience, to engage in various forms of reasoning, to overcome obstacles by careful thought.*

Why do we place so much importance on evaluating others' (and our own) intelligence? Partly because we believe that intelligence is related to many important outcomes: how quickly individuals can master new tasks and adapt to new situations, how successful they will be in school and in various kinds of jobs, and even how well they can get along with others (e.g., Goleman, 1998). To some extent, our common sense ideas in this respect are correct. For instance, the person shown in Figure 7.12 is not acting in a way most of us would describe as intelligent—he is insulting the interviewer! The result? He probably won't get the job. But although intelligence *is* related to important life outcomes, this relationship is far from perfect. Many other factors, too, play a role, so predictions based on intelligence alone can be wrong.

Intelligence: Unitary or Multifaceted?

Is intelligence a single characteristic, or does it involve several different components? In the past, psychologists who studied intelligence often disagreed sharply on this issue. In one camp were scientists who viewed intelligence as a single characteristic or dimension along which people vary. One early supporter of this view was Spearman (1927), who believed that performance on any cognitive task depended on a primary *general* factor (which he termed *g*) and one or more *specific* factors relating to particular tasks. Spearman based this view on the following finding: Although tests of intelligence often contain different kinds of items designed to measure different aspects of intelligence, scores on these items often correlate highly with one another. This fact suggested to him that no matter how intelligence was measured, it was related to a single, primary factor.

In contrast, other researchers believed that intelligence is composed of many separate abilities that operate more or less independently. According to this *multifactor* view, a given person can be high on some components of intelligence but low on others and vice versa. One early supporter of this position was Thurstone (1938), who suggested that intelligence is composed of seven distinct primary mental abilities. Included in his list were *verbal meaning*—understanding of ideas and word meanings; *number*—speed and accuracy in dealing with numbers; and *space*—the ability to visualize objects in three dimensions.

Which of these views of intelligence has prevailed? Most modern theories of intelligence adopt a position somewhere in between these extremes. They recognize that intelligence may involve a general ability to handle a wide range of cognitive tasks and problems, as Spearman suggested, but also that intelligence *is* expressed in many different ways, and that persons can be high on some aspects of intelligence but low on others. As examples of this modern approach, let's briefly consider three influential views of intelligence.

Gardner's Theory of Multiple Intelligences

In formulating their views of intelligence, most researchers have focused primarily on what might be described as "normal" children and adults: persons who neither greatly exceed nor fall far below what most of us would view as "average" levels of intelligence. Howard Gardner (1983) argued that this approach was limiting psychology's view of intelligence. A better tactic, he suggested, would be to study not only persons in the middle of the intelligence dimension, but also ones at the extremes—acclaimed geniuses and those whose cognitive functioning is impaired, as well as experts in various domains and those who might be described as possessing special mental "gifts." For instance, consider the young athletes who compete in the Olympics. Watching these young people, I am often truly amazed by the feats they can perform. Is their ability to execute complex maneuvers like those shown in Figure 7.13 simply the result of extensive training? Or does their performance also show a special kind of intelligence—something very different from the verbal fluency we usually associate with the term *intelligence,* but perhaps just as important?

Gardner would argue strongly for the latter view. In fact, to aspects of intelligence most of us readily recognize, such as the verbal, mathematical, and spatial abilities studied by Thurstone, Gardner added such components as *musical intelligence*—the kind of intelligence shown by one of my friends who, without any formal training, can play virtually any tune on the piano; *bodily-kinesthetic intelligence*—the kind shown by the Olympic athletes shown in Figure 7.13; and *personal intelligence*—for instance, the ability to get along well with others. (I'll return to this latter topic in detail in the discussion of *emotional intelligence.*)

In sum, as its name suggests, Gardner's theory of multiple intelligences proposes that there are several important types of intelligence, and that we must understand each in order to get the big picture where this important human characteristic is concerned.

Sternberg's Triarchic Theory: The Value of Practical Intelligence

Another important modern theory of intelligence is one proposed by Robert Sternberg (Sternberg, 1985; Sternberg et al., 1995). According to this theory, known as the **triarchic theory** of intelligence, there are actually three basic types of human intelligence. The first, called *componential* or *analytic* intelligence, involves the abilities to think critically and analytically. Persons high on this dimension usually excel on standard tests of academic potential and make excellent students. It's a good bet that your professors are high on this aspect of intelligence. The second type of intelligence, *experiential* or *creative* intelligence, emphasizes insight and the ability to formulate new ideas. Persons who rate high on this dimension excel at zeroing in on what information is crucial in a given situation, and at combining seemingly unrelated facts. This is the kind of intelligence shown by many scientific geniuses and inventors, such as Einstein, Newton, and—some would say—Freud. For example, Johannes Gutenberg, inventor of the printing press, combined the mechanisms for producing playing cards, making wine, and minting coins in his invention; thus, he showed a high level of creative intelligence.

Sternberg terms the third type of intelligence *contextual* or **practical intelligence,** and in some ways, it is the most interesting of all. Persons high on this dimension are intelligent in a practical, adaptive sense—they have what many would term "street smarts" and are adept at solving the problems of everyday life (see Figure 7.14). In sum, Sternberg's theory suggests that there is more to intelligence than the verbal, mathematical, and reasoning abilities that are often associated with academic success. Practical intelligence, too, is important and contributes to success in many areas of life.

Cattell's Theory of Fluid and Crystallized Intelligence

In their efforts to determine whether intelligence consists of one or several different components, psychologists in past decades often made use of a statistical technique known as *factor analysis*. This technique identifies clusters of items on a test that seem to be related to one another and so can be viewed as measuring a common underlying *factor*—a specific aspect of intelligence. This technique was used by many researchers; Spearman, for instance, employed it as the basis for his conclusion that there is a general or *g* factor that underlies all the others. Somewhat different conclusions were reached by Cattell (1963), who concluded that two major clusters of mental abilities exist: what he termed *fluid* and *crystallized intelligence*. *Fluid intelligence* refers to our largely inherited abilities to think and reason—in a sense, the hardware of our brains that determines the limits of our information-processing capabilities. In contrast, *crystallized intelligence* refers to accumulated knowledge—information we store over a lifetime of experience, plus the application of skills and knowledge to solving specific problems. In a sense, then, crystallized intelligence is the outcome of experience acting on our fluid intelligence. The speed with which one can analyze information is an example of fluid intelligence, while the breadth of one's vocabulary—how many words one can put to use—illustrates crystallized intelligence.

As I will suggest in Chapter 8, fluid intelligence seems to decrease slowly with age, but crystallized intelligence stays level or even increases (e.g., Baltes, 1987). This is why older, more experienced individuals can sometimes outperform younger ones on cognitive tasks ranging from scientific research to chess: Declines in older persons' fluid intelligence are more than offset by the vast store of knowledge in their crystallized intelligence.

REVIEW QUESTIONS

- What is intelligence?
- What is Gardner's theory of multiple intelligences?
- What is Sternberg's triarchic theory of intelligence?
- What is fluid intelligence? Crystallized intelligence?

Measuring Intelligence

In 1904, when psychology was just emerging as an independent field, members of the Paris school board approached Alfred Binet with an interesting request: Could he develop an objective method for identifying the children who, in the language of that era, were described as being mentally retarded, so that they could be given special education? Binet was already at work on related topics, so he agreed, enlisting the aid of his colleague, Theodore Simon.

In designing this test Binet and Simon were guided by the belief that the items used should be ones children could answer without special training or study. They felt that this was important because the test should measure the ability to handle intellectual tasks—*not* specific knowledge acquired in school. To attain this goal, Binet and Simon decided to use items of two basic types: ones so new or unusual that none of the children would have prior exposure to them, and ones so familiar that almost all youngsters would have encountered them in the past. Children were asked to perform the following tasks: Follow simple commands or imitate simple gestures; name objects shown in pictures; repeat a sentence of fifteen words; tell how two common objects are different; complete sentences begun by the examiner.

The first version of Binet and Simon's test was published in 1905 and contained thirty items. Much to the two authors' pleasure, it was quite effective: With it, schools could readily identify children in need of special help. Encouraged by this success, Binet and Simon broadened the scope of their test to measure variations in intelligence among all children. The revised version, published in 1908, grouped items by age, with six items at each level from three to thirteen years. Items were placed at a particular age level if about 75 percent of children of that age could pass them correctly.

Binet's tests were soon revised and adapted for use in many countries. In the United States, Lewis Terman, a psychologist at Stanford University, developed the **Stanford–Binet test**—a test that was soon put to use in many different settings. Over the years the Stanford–Binet has been revised several times. One of the features of the Stanford–Binet that contributed to its popularity was the fact that it yielded a single score assumed to reflect an individual's level of intelligence—the now famous (some would say *infamous*) IQ.

IQ: Its Meaning Then and Now

Originally, the letters **IQ** stood for *intelligence quotient,* and a "quotient" is precisely what the scores represented. To obtain an IQ score, an examiner divided a student's mental age by his or her chronological age, then multiplied this number by 100. For this computation, mental age was based on the number of items a person passed correctly on the test: Test takers received two months' credit of "mental age" for each item passed. If an individual's mental and chronological ages were equal, an IQ of 100 was obtained; this was considered to be an average score. IQs above 100 indicated that a person's intellectual age was greater than her or his chronological age—in other words, that the individual was more intelligent than typical students of the same age. In contrast, numbers below 100 indicated that the individual was less intelligent than her or his peers.

Perhaps you can already see one obvious problem with this type of IQ score: At some point, mental growth levels off or stops, while chronological age continues to grow. As a result, IQ scores begin to decline after the early teen years!

Partly because of this problem, IQ scores now have a different definition. They simply reflect an individual's performance relative to that of persons of the same age who have taken the same test. Thus, an IQ above 100 indicates that the person has scored higher than the average person in her or his age group, while a score below 100 indicates that the person has scored lower than average.

The Wechsler Scales

As noted earlier, the tests developed by Binet and later adapted by Terman and others remained popular for many years. They do, however, suffer from one major drawback: All are mainly verbal in content. As a result, they pay little attention to the fact that intelligence can be revealed in nonverbal activities as well. For example, an architect who visualizes a majestic design for a new building is demonstrating a high level of intelligence; yet no means for assessing such abilities was included in early versions of the Stanford–Binet test.

To overcome this and other problems, David Wechsler devised a set of tests for both children and adults that include nonverbal, or *performance,* items as well as verbal ones, and that yield separate scores for these two components of intelligence. Thus, Wechsler began with the view that intelligence is *not* a unitary characteristic, shown only through verbal and mathematical reasoning. However, he developed these tests at a time when the multifaceted nature of intelligence was not yet well understood, and it is not clear that Wechsler's various subtests actually do measure different aspects of intelligence. Despite such problems, the Wechsler tests are currently among the most frequently used individual tests of intelligence. (An overview of the subtests that make up one of the Wechsler scales, the *Wechsler Adult Intelligence Scale-Revised* [WAIS-3 for short] is presented in Table 7.4.)

Wechsler believed that differences between scores on the various subtests could be used to diagnose serious psychological disorders (see Chapter 12). However, research on this possibility has yielded mixed results at best.

A Wechsler test for children, the *Wechsler Intelligence Scale for Children* (WISC), has also been developed; it too is in widespread use. Patterns of scores on the subtests of the WISC are sometimes used to identify children suffering from various *learning disabilities.* Some findings indicate that children who score high on certain subtests, such as Picture Completion and Object Assembly, but lower on others, such as Arithmetic, Information, and Vocabulary, are more likely to suffer from learning disabilities than children with other patterns of scores (Aiken, 1991). Once again, however, not all findings point to such conclusions, so the value of the WISC (now in its third revision, WISC-3) for this kind of diagnosis remains somewhat uncertain.

One more point: Tests such as the WAIS are designed to measure the ability to acquire new information or skills, an ability implied by our definition of intelligence. Psychologists describe such tests as **aptitude tests,** and scores on these tests are often used to predict future performance. In contrast, **achievement tests** are designed to measure what you have already learned; for example, the tests you take in this class are designed to be achievement tests. The distinction between these two types of tests is not precise, however. For instance, many aptitude tests (including college entrance examinations) include measures of vocabulary, which, to a degree, reflect past learning. But in general it is useful to think of aptitude tests as ones designed to predict future performance and achievement tests as ones that reflect current performance and the results of past learning.

Group Tests of Intelligence

Both the Stanford–Binet and the Wechsler scales are *individual* tests of intelligence: They are designed for use with one person at a time. Obviously, it would be much more efficient if *group* tests could be administered to large numbers of people at once. The need for such tests was driven home at the start of World War I, when the armed forces in the United States suddenly faced the task of screening several million recruits. In response to this challenge, psychologists such as Arthur Otis developed two tests: *Army Alpha* for persons who could read (remember, this was back in 1917), and *Army Beta* for persons would could not read or who did not speak English. These early group tests proved highly useful. For example, the tests were used to select candidates for officer training school, and they did accurately predict success in such training.

In the succeeding decades many other group tests of intelligence were developed. Among the more popular of these are the *Otis tests,* such as the Otis–Lennon School Ability Test (Otis & Lennon, 1967); the *Henmon–Nelson Tests* (Nelson, Lamke, & French, 1973); and the *Cognitive Abilities Test* (CAT) (Thorndike & Hagen, 1982). All are available in versions that can be administered to large numbers of persons. The advantages offered by such tests soon made them very popular, and they were put to routine use in many school systems—especially in schools in large cities, such as the one I attended. During the 1960s, however, this practice was called into serious question and became the focus of harsh criticism. While there were many reasons for this controversy, the most serious was the charge that such tests were unfair to children from disadvantaged backgrounds—especially youngsters from certain minority groups. We'll return to these objections in a later section. Here, however, we'll pause briefly to address the following question: What are the basic requirements for a useful test of intelligence? For information on this crucial issue, please see the following **Research Methods** section.

The Cognitive Basis of Intelligence: Processing Speed

"Quick study," "quick-witted," "fast learner"—phrases such as these are often used to describe people who are high in intelligence, both academic and practical. They suggest that being intelligent involves being able to process information quickly. Is there any scientific evidence to support this idea? In fact, there is. Psychologists interested in studying intelligence have moved beyond tests such as the Stanford–Binet and Wechsler scales in an attempt to try to identify the basic cognitive mechanisms and processes that underlie intelligence—and that enable people to score high on intelligence tests (e.g., Deary, 1995). This work has led to two major developments. First, several tests have been constructed that are based on the findings of cognitive psychology and on our growing understanding of many aspects of cognition (Naglieri, 1997). Among these the most noteworthy are the *Kaufman Assessment Battery for Children* and the *Kaufman Adult Intelligence Test* (e.g., Kaufman & Kaufman, 1993), and the *Woodcock-Johnson Test of Cognitive Abilities* (Woodcock & Johnson, 1989). The Woodcock–Johnson Test, for instance, attempts to measure important aspects of both fluid and crystallized intelligence.

Second, a growing body of research has focused on the finding that the speed with which individuals perform simple perceptual and cognitive tasks (processing speed) is often correlated with scores on intelligence tests (Neisser et al., 1996; Vernon, 1987). For example, significant correlations (on the order of 2.30 to 2.40) have often been found between various measures of *reaction time* (one measure of processing speed) and scores on intelligence tests (see, e.g., Deary & Stough, 1996; Fry & Hale, 1996).

Another and even more promising cognitive measure of intelligence is a measure known as **inspection time.** This measure reflects the minimum amount of time a particular stimulus must be exposed for individuals to make a judgment about it that meets some preestablished criterion of accuracy. The shorter the duration time necessary for a given individual to attain a given level of accuracy, presumably, the faster the speed of important aspects of that person's cognitive (mental) operations. To measure inspection time, psychologists often use procedures in which individuals are shown simple drawings like the one in Figure 7.17 and are asked to indicate whether the longer side occurs on the left or right. Participants are *not* told to respond as quickly as possible. Rather, they are instructed to take their time and to be accurate. Inspection

FIGURE 7.17 Inspection Time: How It's Measured

To measure inspection time, psychologists ask research participants to indicate whether the long side of a stimulus (left) is on the left or the right. Immediately after a participant sees each stimulus, it is masked by another one in which both sides are long (right). Participants are not told to respond as quickly as possible; rather, they are instructed to take their time and be accurate. Inspection time is measured in terms of the time they require in order to make such decisions at some predetermined level of accuracy.

Stimulus   Mask

time is measured by the time they take to make such decisions at a prespecified level of accuracy—for example, 85 percent.

What does inspection time measure? Presumably, the amount of time individuals require for the intake of new visual information. Supporters of this measure argue that this task—perceiving new information—is basic to all higher-level mental operations in human thought (e.g., Deary, 1995; Deary & Stough, 1996). Further, they note that this measure is closely related to current theories of perception and decision making, theories emphasizing that new visual information is perceived in discrete samples and then combined into judgments such as "I see it" or "I don't see it." Growing evidence indicates that inspection time is indeed closely related to intelligence, as measured by standard tests. In fact, inspection time and scores on such tests correlate 2.50 or more (e.g., Kranzler & Jensen, 1989).

In sum, inspection time appears to be a very promising measure for probing the nature of human intelligence—for understanding the basic cognitive processes that underlie this important characteristic. And since understanding a process is often an essential first step to being able to change it in beneficial ways, this is valuable progress.

The Neural Basis of Intelligence: Intelligence and Neural Efficiency

In Chapter 2, and again in discussing memory in Chapter 6, I noted that everything we do, think, or feel rests, in an ultimate sense, on neurochemical events occurring in our brains. If that is indeed true—and virtually all psychologists believe that it is—then an intriguing possibility arises: Can we trace individual differences in intelligence to differences in neural functioning? The answer suggested by a growing body of evidence is *yes* (e.g., Matarazzo, 1992; Vernon, 1993). Such research suggests, first, that *nerve conduction velocity*—the speed with which nerve impulses are conducted in the visual system—correlates significantly with measures of intelligence (e.g., the Raven Progressive Matrices test) (Reed & Jensen, 1993).

Other, and related, research has examined metabolic activity in the brain during cognitive tasks (e.g., Haier, 1993). Presumably, if intelligence is related to efficient brain functioning, then the more intelligent people are, the less energy their brains should expend while working on various tasks. This prediction has generally been confirmed: The brains of persons scoring highest on written measures of intellectual ability do expend less energy when these individuals perform complex cognitive tasks. The data in these studies have been gathered by means of the PET technique of brain imaging described in Chapters 2 and 6. Using similar imaging technologies, scientists have recently identified an area in the lateral prefrontal cortex of each brain hemisphere that may play an important role in intelligence by providing a global work space for organizing and coordinating information and carrying it back to other parts of the brain as needed (Duncan et al., 2000). Apparently, the relative performance of this "work space" determines how adept a person is at solving cognitive problems—precisely the characteristic that intelligence tests attempt to measure.

Finally, some findings suggest that there is a link between brain structure and intelligence (Andreason et al., 1993). Specifically, scores on standard measures of intelligence such as the Wechsler Adult Intelligence Scale are related to the size of certain portions of the brain, including the left and right temporal lobes and the left and right hippocampus. Moreover, this is true even when corrections are made for individuals' overall physical size.

In sum, it appears that the improved methods now available for studying the brain and nervous system are beginning to establish the kind of links between intelligence and physical structures that psychologists have long suspected to exist. Such research is very recent, so it is still too soon to reach firm conclusions. It does appear, though, that we are on the verge of establishing much firmer links between intelligence—a crucial aspect of mind—and body than has ever been true before.

For a discussion of yet another technique used by psychologists to measure cognitive abilities—and to make important predictions about future success—please see the following **From Science to Practice** section.

FROM SCIENCE TO PRACTICE

Predicting Career Success: Competency Assessment

Earlier, I noted that standard intelligence tests are not very effective in predicting success outside academic circles. They are moderately related to achievement in fields that require skills similar to those needed for success in school (e.g., science, law, medicine) but are quite ineffective in predicting success in other contexts, including the one in which most people spend much of their adult lives: the business world (e.g., Whitla, 1975). Is there a better way to predict success in such settings? Fortunately, there is.

This approach is known as **competency assessment,** and it is based on the following reasoning: If we start with two groups—one known to be highly successful and the other known to be only average in terms of career success—and then search for differences between them, the differences we identify may be useful in predicting success in other groups of persons. But how do we go about identifying the key differences between highly successful and less successful persons? One useful

(continued)

procedure involves what are known as *behavioral-event interviews* (e.g., Spencer & Spencer, 1993). In these interviews persons rated by others who know them well as being outstanding at their jobs, and persons rated as being only average, describe what they said, thought, felt, and did in various work-related situations (e.g., how they reached decisions, how they dealt with sudden emergencies, and so on). Their answers are then carefully examined for patterns of differences. Such differences, when identified, are labeled *competencies:* Presumably, these are the key skills or abilities that distinguish outstanding performers from average ones. Using such interviews, researchers have identified several competencies that seem to play a key role in success in several fields, such as being a business executive. These include skill at several kinds of thinking, such as inductive reasoning and analytical thinking; a strong desire for success; flexibility; wanting to have an impact on others; willingness to take initiative; self-confidence; and good understanding of others (a cluster of skills psychologists often describe as *social skills*).

Are *all* these skills necessary for success? Not necessarily; further studies indicate that being highly successful seems to require only that individuals possess several of them—for instance, five of the competencies listed (e.g., Nygren & Ukeritis, 1993).

Now for the most important question: Does possession of these competencies do a good job of predicting career success? Research findings suggest that they do. For instance, in one major project, McClelland (1998) studied the executives in a large corporation. On the basis of behavioral-event interviews, the researchers classified the executives as being highly qualified or average in potential. They then followed the executives' performance for several years. As expected, those classified as being highly qualified were rated by their bosses as doing a better job, and received significantly higher bonuses, in two different years (see Figure 7.18). Another important finding was this: Although almost half of the executives hired in the usual way by the company quit within a year, none of those hired on the basis of competency assessment (having been rated as outstanding in potential) quit. Hiring and training each new executive cost the company more than $250,000, so by using competency assessment the organization saved more than $4 million in a single year!

In sum, competency assessment appears to provide a useful technique for predicting success in the world of work. So although standard intelligence tests don't seem to do a very good job in this respect, psychologists have used their understanding of human behavior and their knowledge of human cognition and intelligence to devise other, more effective procedures. Clearly, this represents an important contribution by the science of psychology to the solution of important practical problems.

- What was the first individual test of intelligence, and what did scores on it mean?
- What are the Wechsler scales?
- What are standardization, reliability, and validity?
- What is inspection time, and what does it measure?
- What findings suggest that intelligence is related to neural functioning or brain structure?
- What is competency assessment, and how is it used?

Human Intelligence: The Role of Heredity and the Role of Environment

That people differ in intelligence is obvious. *Why* such differences exist is quite another matter. Are they largely a matter of heredity—differences in the genetic materials and codes we inherit from our parents? Or are they primarily the result of environmental factors—conditions in the world around us that affect our intellectual development? I'm sure you know the answer: Both types of factors are involved. Human intelligence is clearly the result of the complex interplay between genetic factors and a wide range of environmental conditions (e.g., Plomin, 1997). Let's now consider some of the evidence pointing to this conclusion.

Evidence for the Influence of Heredity

Several lines of research offer support for the view that heredity plays an important role in human intelligence. First, consider findings with respect to family relationship and measured IQ. If intelligence is indeed determined by heredity, we would expect that the more closely two persons are related, the more similar their IQs will be. This prediction has generally been confirmed (e.g., McGue et al., 1993; Neisser et al., 1996). For example, the IQs of identical twins raised together correlate almost +.90, those of brothers and sisters about +.50, and those of cousins about +.15 (see Figure 7.19). (Remember: Higher correlations indicate stronger relationships between variables.)

Support for the impact of heredity on intelligence is also provided by studies involving adopted children. If intelligence is strongly affected by genetic factors, the IQs of adopted children should resemble those of their biological parents more closely than those of their adoptive parents. In short, the children should be more similar in IQ to the persons from whom they received their genes than to the persons who raised them. This prediction, too, has been confirmed (Jencks, 1972; Munsinger, 1978; Plomin et al., 1997).

Additional evidence for the role of genetic factors in intelligence is provided by recent studies focused on the task of identifying the specific genes that influence intelligence (e.g., Rutter & Plomin, 1997; Sherman et al., 1997). These studies have adopted as a working hypothesis the view that many genes, each exerting relatively small effects, probably play a role in general intelligence—that is, in what many aspects of mental abilities (e.g., verbal, spatial, speed-of-processing, and memory abilities) have in common (e.g., Plomin, 1997). In other words, such research has not attempted to identify *the* gene that influences intelligence, but rather has sought *quantitative trait loci* (QTLs): genes that have relatively small effects and that influence the likelihood of some characteristic in a population. The results of such studies suggest that certain genes are indeed associated with high intelligence (e.g., Chorney et al., 1998).

Finally, evidence for the role of genetic factors in intelligence has been provided by research on identical twins separated as infants (usually, within the first few weeks of life) who were then raised in different homes (e.g., Bouchard et al., 1990). Because such persons have identical genetic inheritance but have been exposed to different environmental conditions—in some cases, sharply contrasting conditions—studying their IQs provides a powerful means for comparing the roles of genetic and environmental factors in human intelligence. The results of such research are clear: The IQs of identical twins reared apart (often from the time they were only a few days old) correlate almost as highly as those of identical twins reared together. Moreover, such individuals are also amazingly similar in many other characteristics, such as physical appearance, preferences in dress, mannerisms, and even personality (see Figure 7.20). Clearly, these findings point to an important role for heredity in intelligence and in many other aspects of psychological functioning.

On the basis of these and other findings, some researchers have estimated that the **heritability** of intelligence—the proportion of the variance in intelligence within a given population that is attributable to genetic factors—ranges from about 35 percent in childhood to as much as 75 percent in adulthood (McGue et al., 1993), and may be about 50 percent overall (Plomin et al., 1997). Why does the contribution of genetic factors to intelligence increase with age? Perhaps because as individuals grow older, their interactions with their environment are shaped less and less by restraints imposed on them by their families or by their social origins and are shaped more and more by the characteristics they bring with them to these environments. In other words, as they grow older, individuals are increasingly able to choose or change their environments so that these permit expression of their genetically determined tendencies and preferences (Neisser et al., 1996). Whatever the precise origin of the increasing heritability of intelligence with age, there is little doubt that genetic factors do indeed play an important role in intelligence throughout life.

Evidence for the Influence of Environmental Factors

Genetic factors are definitely *not* the entire picture where human intelligence is concerned, however. Other findings point to the conclusion that environmental variables, too, are important. One such finding is that performance on IQ tests has risen substantially around the world at all age levels in recent decades. This phenomenon is known as the *Flynn effect* after the psychologist who first reported it (Flynn, 1987, 1996). Such increases have averaged about 3 IQ points per decade worldwide; but, as shown in Figure 7.21 on page 278, in some countries they have been even larger. As a result of these gains in performance, it has been necessary to restandardize widely used tests so that they continue to yield an average IQ of 100; what is termed "average" today is actually a higher level of performance than was true in the past.

What accounts for these increases? It seems unlikely that massive shifts in human heredity occur from one generation to the next. A more reasonable explanation, therefore, focuses on changes in environmental factors. What factors have changed in recent decades? The following variables have been suggested as possible contributors to the continuing rise in IQ (e.g., Flynn, 1999; Williams, 1998): better nutrition, increased urbanization, the advent of television, more and better education, more cognitively demanding jobs, and even exposure to computer games! Many of these changes are real and seem plausible as explanations for the rise in IQ; but, as noted recently by Flynn (1999), there is as yet not sufficient evidence to conclude that any or all of these factors have played a role. In any case, whatever the specific causes involved, the steady rise in performance on IQ tests points to the importance of environmental factors in human intelligence.

Additional evidence for the role of environmental factors in intelligence is provided by the findings of studies of *environmental deprivation* and *environmental enrichment*. With respect to deprivation, some findings suggest that intelligence can be reduced by the absence of key forms of environmental stimulation early in life (Gottfried, 1984). In terms of enrichment, removing children from sterile, restricted environments and placing them in more favorable settings seems to enhance their intellectual growth. For example, in one of the first demonstrations of the beneficial impact on IQ of an enriched environment, Skeels (1938, 1966) removed thirteen children, all about two years old, from an orphanage in which they received virtually no intellectual stimulation—and virtually no contact with adults—and placed them in the care of a group of retarded women living in an institution. After a few years, Skeels noted that the children's IQs had risen dramatically—29 points on average (although later corrections reduced this figure to about 10 to 13 points; Flynn, 1993). Interestingly, Skeels also obtained IQ measures of children who had remained in the orphanage and found that these had actually dropped by 26 points on average—presumably as a result of continued exposure to the impoverished environment at the orphanage. Twenty-five years later, the thirteen children who had experienced the enriched environment were all doing well; most had graduated from high school, found a job, and married. In contrast, those in the original control group either remained institutionalized or were functioning poorly in society.

While more recent—and more carefully controlled—efforts to increase intelligence through environmental interventions have not yielded gains as dramatic as those reported by Skeels (1966), some of these programs *have* produced beneficial results (Bryant & Maxwell, 1997; Guralnick, 1997). However, as noted recently by Ramey and Ramey (1998), such changes are most likely to occur when the following conditions are met: (1) The interventions begin early and continue for a long time; (2) the programs are intense, involving home visits several times per week; (3) the children receive new learning experiences delivered directly to them by experts rather than indirectly though their parents; (4) the interventions are broad in scope, using many different procedures to enhance children's development; (5) the interventions are matched to the needs of individual children; and (6) environmental supports (e.g., excellent schools) are put in place to support and maintain the positive attitudes toward learning the children gain. Needless to say, programs that meet these criteria tend to be expensive. But they can also yield important financial benefits; for instance, one study cited by Ramey and Ramey (1998) suggests that appropriate early intervention programs might have prevented more than 300,000 children in the United States alone from developing IQs that placed them in the "mentally retarded" category (i.e., IQs below 70). Given that such children often require extensive corrective assistance and training, the potential savings to be realized through early enrichment might well be substantial. So there are strong economic arguments, as well as social and humanitarian ones, for instituting the best and most extensive early intervention programs a given society can afford.

Additional support for the role of environmental factors in intelligence is provided by the finding that many biological factors that children encounter while growing up can affect their intelligence. Prolonged malnutrition can adversely affect IQ (e.g., Sigman, 1995), as can exposure to lead—either in the air or in lead-based paint, which young children often eat because it tastes sweet (e.g., Baghurst et al., 1992). We have already examined the adverse effects on the health of developing fetuses of exposure to such factors as alcohol and drugs; here I simply want to add that research findings indicate that these factors can also adversely affect intelligence (e.g., Neisser et al., 1996). In sum, therefore, many forms of evidence support the view that intelligence is determined, at least in part, by environmental factors. Especially when these are extreme, they may slow—or accelerate—children's intellectual growth; and this effect, in turn, can have important implications for the societies in which those children will become adults.

Environment, Heredity, and Intelligence: Summing Up

There is considerable evidence that *both* environmental and genetic factors play a role in intelligence. This is the view accepted by almost all psychologists, and there is little controversy about it. Greater controversy continues to exist, however, concerning the *relative* contribution of each of these factors. Do environmental or genetic factors play a stronger role in shaping intelligence? As I noted earlier, existing evidence seems to favor the view that genetic factors may account for more of the variance in IQ scores within a given population than environmental factors (e.g., Plomin, 1997; Neisser et al., 1996). Many people, including psychologists, are made somewhat uneasy by this conclusion, in part because they assume that characteristics that are heritable—ones that are strongly influenced by genetic factors—cannot readily be changed. *It's important to recognize that this assumption is false.* For instance, consider height: This is a characteristic that is highly heritable—one that is influenced by genetic factors to a greater extent than by environment. Yet despite this fact, average heights have increased in many countries as nutrition has improved (and, perhaps, as young persons have been exposed to the growth hormones used to increase food production). So the fact that a trait is strongly influenced by genetic factors does *not* imply that it cannot also be affected by environmental factors.

The same thing is almost certainly true for intelligence. Yes, existing evidence suggests that it is affected by genetic factors. But this in no way implies that it cannot be influenced by environmental conditions, too—and, as we've seen, it certainly is. The recognition that genetic factors play an important role in intelligence in no way implies that intelligence is etched in stone—and definitely does *not* constitute an excuse for giving up on children who, because of poverty, prejudice, or neglect, are seriously at risk.

REVIEW QUESTIONS

- What evidence suggests that intelligence is influenced by genetic factors?
- What evidence suggests that intelligence is influenced by environmental factors?
- Can characteristics that are highly heritable be influenced by environmental factors? Suppose several genes that influence intelligence are identified. Would it be ethical to alter these genes so as to produce higher levels of intelligence in many persons? What might be the effects on society of doing so?

Group Differences in Intelligence Test Scores: Why They Occur

Earlier, I noted that there are sizable differences among the average IQ scores of various ethnic groups. In the United States and elsewhere, members of some minority groups score lower, on average, than members of the majority group.

Why do such differences occur? This has been a topic of considerable controversy in psychology for many years, and currently there is still no final, universally accepted conclusion. However, it seems fair to say that at present, most psychologists attribute such group differences in performance on standard intelligence tests largely to environmental variables. Let's take a closer look at the evidence that points to this conclusion. I'll then present some findings that argue *against* the view that group differences in intelligence derive from genetic factors. Finally, I'll turn to a different category of group differences in intelligence test scores—gender differences.

Group Differences in IQ Scores: Evidence for the Role of Environmental Factors

I have already referred to one form of evidence suggesting that group differences in performance on intelligence tests stem primarily from environmental factors: the fact that the tests themselves may be biased against test takers from some minority groups. Why? In part because the tests were standardized largely on middle-class white persons; thus, interpreting the test scores of persons from minority groups in terms of these norms is not appropriate. Even worse, some critics have suggested that the tests themselves suffer from **cultural bias:** Items on the tests are ones that are familiar to middle-class white children and so give them an important edge in terms of test performance. Are such concerns valid? Careful examination of the items used on intelligence tests suggests that they may indeed be culturally biased, at least to a degree. Some items do seem to be ones that are less familiar— and therefore more difficult to answer—for minority test takers. To the extent that such cultural bias exists, it is indeed a serious flaw in IQ tests.

On the other hand, though, it's important to note that the tests are generally about as successful in predicting future school performance by children from all groups. So while the tests may be biased in terms of content, this in itself does not make them useless from the point of view of predicting future performance (e.g., Rowe, Vazsonyi, & Flannery, 1994). However, as noted by Steele and Aronson (1996), because minority children find at least some of the items on these tests unfamiliar, they may feel threatened by the tests; and this, in turn, may reduce their scores.

In an effort to eliminate cultural bias from intelligence tests, psychologists have attempted to design *culture-fair* tests. Such tests attempt to include only items to which all groups, regardless of ethnic or racial background, have been exposed. Because many minority children are exposed to languages other than standard English, these tests tend to be nonverbal in nature. One of these, the **Raven Progressive Matrices** (Raven, 1977), is illustrated in Figure 7.22. This test consists of sixty matrices of varying difficulty, each containing a logical pattern or design with a missing part. Individuals select the item that completes the pattern from several different choices. Because the Raven test and ones like it focus primarily on *fluid intelligence*—our basic abilities to form concepts, reason, and identify similarities—these tests seem less likely to be subject to cultural bias than other kinds of intelligence tests. However, it is not clear that these tests, or any others, totally eliminate the problem of subtle built-in bias.

Additional evidence for the role of environmental factors in group differences in test performance has been divided by Flynn (1999), one expert on this issue, into two categories: indirect and direct. *Indirect evidence* is evidence from research in which efforts are made to equate environmental factors for all test takers—for instance, by eliminating the effects of socioeconomic status through statistical techniques. The results of such studies are mixed; some suggest that the gap between minority groups and whites is reduced by such procedures (e.g., Flynn, 1993), but other studies indicate that between-group differences still remain (e.g., Loehlin, Lindzey, & Spuhle, 1975; Lynn, 1996). These findings suggest that while socioeconomic factors contribute to group differences in IQ scores, other factors, as yet unknown, may also play some role.

Direct evidence for environmental factors, in contrast, involves actual life changes that take many minority persons out of the disadvantaged environment they often face and provide them with an environment equivalent to that of other groups. Obtaining such evidence is, of course, very difficult; many minority persons do grow up in environments quite distinct from those of other groups. According to Flynn (1999), however, one compelling piece of direct evidence for the role of environmental factors in group differences does exist. During World War II, African American soldiers fathered thousands of children in Germany (much of which was occupied by U.S. troops after the war). These children have been raised by white mothers in what is essentially a white environment. The result? Their IQs are virtually identical to those of white children matched to them in socioeconomic status (e.g., Flynn, 1980). Given that the fathers of these children scored very similarly to other African American soldiers, these findings suggest that environmental factors are in fact the key to group differences in IQ: When such factors are largely eliminated, differences between the groups, too, disappear.

Group Differences in IQ Scores: Is There Any Evidence for the Role of Genetic Factors?

Now for the other side of the story—the suggestion that group differences in intelligence stem largely from genetic factors. In 1994 this issue was brought into sharp focus by the publication of a highly controversial book entitled *The Bell Curve*. Because the book was written by two well-known psychologists, Richard Herrnstein and Charles Murray, it received immediate attention in the popular press and soon became a best-seller. The book focused on human intelligence and covered many aspects of this topic. The most controversial portions, however, dealt with what is known as the **genetic hypothesis**—the view that group differences in intelligence are due, at least in part, to genetic factors.

In *The Bell Curve* Herrnstein and Murray (1994) voiced strong support for the genetic hypothesis. They noted, for instance, that there are several converging sources of evidence for "a genetic factor in cognitive ethnic differences" (p. 270) between African American and other ethnic groups in the United States. Proceeding from this conclusion, they suggested that intelligence may not be readily modifiable through changes in environmental conditions. They proposed, therefore, that special programs aimed at raising the IQ scores of disadvantaged minorities were probably a waste of effort.

As you can imagine, these suggestions were challenged vigorously by many psychologists (e.g., Sternberg, 1995). These critics argued that much of the reasoning in *The Bell Curve* was flawed and that the book overlooked many important findings. Perhaps the harshest criticism of the book centered on its contention that because individual differences in intelligence are strongly influenced by genetic factors, group differences are, too. Several researchers took strong exception to this logic (e.g., Schultze, Kane, & Dickens, 1996; Sternberg, 1995). They contended that this reasoning would be accurate only if the environments of the various groups being compared were identical. Under those conditions, it could be argued that differences between the groups stemmed, at least in part, from genetic factors. In reality, however, the environments in which the members of various ethnic groups exist are *not* identical. As a result, it is false to assume that group differences with respect to IQ scores stem from genetic factors, even if we know that individual differences in such scores *are* strongly influenced by these factors. (And, as we saw earlier, when environmental differences are removed or minimized, group differences in intelligence, too, disappear.)

So where does all this leave us? With the conclusion that although individual differences in IQ scores are certainly influenced by genetic factors, there are no strong grounds for assuming that such factors also contribute to group differences. While some researchers continue to insist that sufficient evidence exists to conclude that genetic factors play a role (e.g., Rushton, 1997), most take strong exception to this view and contend that the evidence for this view is relatively weak (e.g., Neisser, 1997). As I like to put it, *The Bell Curve* has certainly "rung," at least in an economic sense—the book sold tens of thousands of copies and received a great deal of public attention—but from the standpoint of scientific knowledge, it definitely does *not* ring true.

REVIEW QUESTIONS

- What evidence suggests that group differences in intelligence stem largely from environmental factors?
- Is there any evidence for the role of genetic factors in group differences in intelligence?

Emotional Intelligence: The Feeling Side of Intelligence

When I was in high school, one student stood out as the "superbrain" of our school: Paul Kronen. He was so smart it was scary. Unfortunately, Paul was not very good with people. Many things he did rubbed people the wrong way. First, he was arrogant. He was smart, he knew it, and he made sure that *you* knew it too. In addition, Paul was what I'd now describe as *emotionally unstable.* His moods swung widely and quickly from one extreme to another. Even more important, he seemed incapable of restraining his temper or his impulses: He would get into angry exchanges with teachers because he just didn't know when to quit—when to stop contradicting them and making them look bad in front of the class. Taking all this into account, I was not really surprised to learn that Paul didn't live up to his initial promise. He was brilliant, all right, but only in certain respects; in others, he was truly backward.

These memories of my childhood friend suggest that there is another kind of intelligence, quite distinct from that measured by IQ tests. In fact, one psychologist—Daniel Goleman (1995, 1998)—has argued strongly that this other kind of intelligence is more important for a happy, productive life than IQ. Goleman terms this kind of intelligence **emotional intelligence** (or **EQ** for short) and defines it as a cluster of traits or abilities relating to the emotional side of life. Let's take a closer look at the major components of emotional intelligence and then examine current evidence concerning its existence and effects.

Major Components of Emotional Intelligence

Goleman (1995) suggests that emotional intelligence consists of five major parts: (1) knowing our own emotions, (2) managing our emotions, (3) motivating ourselves, (4) recognizing the emotions of others, and (5) handling relationships. Each of these elements, he contends, plays an important role in shaping the outcomes we experience in life.

Knowing Our Own Emotions

As I noted in Chapter 9, emotions are often powerful reactions, so it would seem at first glance that everyone ought to be able to recognize their own feelings. In fact, however, this is not always the case. Some persons are highly aware of their own emotions and their thoughts about them, but others seem to be almost totally oblivious to these. What are the implications of such differences? First, to the extent individuals are not aware of their own feelings, they cannot make intelligent choices. How can they tell whom to date or marry, what job to take, which house or car to buy, or even what to order in a restaurant? Second, because such persons aren't aware of their own emotions, they are often low in *expressiveness*—they don't show their feelings clearly through facial expressions, body language, or other cues most of use to recognize others' feelings (Malandro, Barker, & Barker, 1994). This can have adverse effects on their interpersonal relationships, because other people find it hard to know how they are feeling or reacting. For these reasons, this first component of emotional intelligence seems to be quite important.

Managing Our Own Emotions

Have you ever lost your temper or cried when you didn't want to show such reactions? Have you ever done something to cheer yourself up when you felt anxious or depressed? If so, you are already aware of the fact that we often try to *manage* our emotions—to regulate their nature, intensity, and expression (e.g., Zillmann, 1996). Doing so is very important both for our own mental health and from the point of view of interacting effectively with others (see Figure 7.23). For instance, consider persons who simply cannot control their temper; are they bound for success and a happy life? No. They will probably be avoided by many people and will *not* get the jobs, promotions, or lovers they want.

Motivating Ourselves

Thomas Edison, the famous inventor, once remarked: "Success is two percent inspiration and ninety-eight percent perspiration." Do you agree? While inspiration or creativity is certainly important (see the next section of this chapter), I'm inclined to believe that Edison was right. By "perspiration," however, I mean more than simply hard work: I also include aspects of emotional intelligence, such as being able to motivate oneself to work long and hard on a task, remaining enthusiastic and optimistic about the final outcome, and being able to delay gratification—to put off receiving small rewards now in order to get larger ones later on (e.g., Shoda, Mischel, & Peake, 1990). Being high in such skills can indeed contribute to success in many different contexts.

Recognizing and Influencing Others' Emotions

Another aspect of emotional intelligence, as described by Goleman, is the ability to "read" others accurately—to recognize the mood they are in and what emotion they are experiencing. This skill is valuable in many practical settings. For instance, if you can accurately gauge another person's current mood, you can tell whether it's the right time to ask her or him for a favor. Similarly, persons who are skilled at generating strong emotions in others are often highly successful in such fields as sales and politics: They can get other people to feel what *they* want them to feel.

Handling Relationships

Some people seem to have a knack for getting along with others: most people who meet these people like them, and as a result they have many friends and often enjoy high levels of success in their careers. In contrast, others seem to make a mess of virtually all their personal relationships. According to Goleman

(1995), such differences are another reflection of differences in emotional intelligence or, as some researchers would phrase it, differences in *interpersonal intelligence* (Hatch, 1990).

What does interpersonal intelligence involve? Such skills as being able to coordinate the efforts of several people and to negotiate solutions to complex interpersonal problems, being good at giving others feedback that doesn't make them angry or resentful (e.g., Baron, 1993a), and being a team player. Again, these skills are clearly distinct from the ones needed for getting good grades or scoring high on tests of intelligence, but they often play a key role in important life outcomes.

Emotional Intelligence: Evidence on Its Existence and Effects

Goleman's (1995, 1998) books on emotional intelligence have been best-sellers, so you may well have heard about the concept before taking this course. Unfortunately, though, most of the evidence Goleman offers concerning the existence and impact of emotional intelligence is anecdotal or indirect in nature. Psychologists, of course, strongly prefer more concrete kinds of evidence. Accordingly, researchers have put the concept of emotional intelligence to the test, trying to determine whether the distinct skills described by Goleman cluster together as a single (if multi-faceted) factor, and whether this factor influences important life outcomes.

With respect to the first of these issues, evidence is mixed. While some researchers (Mayer, Caruso, & Salovey, 1998; Salovey & Mayer, 1994) have reported findings consistent with Goleman's suggestions and with their own, similar definitions of emotional intelligence, others have obtained less encouraging results. For example, in a recent and carefully conducted study, Davies, Stankov, and Roberts (1998) focused on two important questions: (1) Are the methods currently used to measure emotional intelligence adequate—that is, are they reliable and valid? And (2) is emotional intelligence really different from other seemingly related concepts—for instance, social intelligence and several aspects of personality (e.g., empathy)? To answer these basic questions, they conducted several studies in which hundreds of participants varying in age, education, gender, and nationality completed measures designed to assess each aspect of emotional intelligence and several other variables as well. Results indicated that only one of the components emphasized by Goleman and other advocates of emotional intelligence emerged as clear and independent: *emotion perception*—the ability to accurately read others' emotions.

Does this mean that the theory of emotional intelligence is useless and that discussing it has been a waste of time—yours as well as mine? I don't believe so. Another interpretation of existing evidence concerning emotional intelligence is this: At present, we don't have adequate methods for measuring all aspects of emotional intelligence. Further, these components may, in fact, be somewhat independent of each other. Thus, we may not be able to assign individuals a single overall EQ score comparable to the single IQ score yielded by many intelligence tests. In a sense, though, this is not surprising. After all, the more psychologists study intelligence, the more they recognize that it probably consists of a number of distinct components—verbal, spatial, speed-of-processing, and perhaps many others. So the fact that we also possess distinct and perhaps largely independent abilities relating to the emotional side of life simply mirrors this pattern. One point is clear, however: At present, we do not possess fully adequate tests for measuring emotional intelligence. Until we do, we will not be able to fully determine its role in important aspects of our lives.

And yet, having said that, I should add that other research offers support for the view that some of the components included in emotional intelligence—especially emotion perception—can indeed have measurable effects. For instance, in recent studies, Gideon Markman and I (e.g., Baron, 2000; Baron & Markman, 2000) have focused on the following question: Why is it that some entrepreneurs are so successful in starting new businesses, while others fail? This is an important question, because in recent years it is the companies started by entrepreneurs that have created most new jobs around the world (e.g., Shane & Venkataraman, in press). We've used several different methods to study this issue, and what we've found, repeatedly, is this: Entrepreneurs who are adept at "reading" others accurately and who adapt easily to new social situations (what we describe as "social adaptability") are significantly more successful, financially, than entrepreneurs who score lower in these skills. To the extent that these two traits are related to emotional intelligence, our findings can be viewed as offering indirect support for the view that EQ influences the outcomes people experience in practical contexts. But stay tuned: The idea of emotional intelligence is an appealing one with important implications, so it is certain to be the topic of research by psychologists in the years ahead.

REVIEW QUESTIONS

- What is emotional intelligence?
- What does evidence to date suggest about the existence of emotional intelligence? Its effects?

The Nation Divides: The Vietnam War and Social Conflict, 1964–1971

from Created Equal: A Social and Political History of the United States

JACQUELINE JONES
Brandeis University

PETER H. WOOD
Duke University

THOMAS BORSTELMANN
University of Nebraska

ELAINE TYLER MAY
University of Minnesota

VICKY L. RUIZ
University of California at Irvine

Chapter Outline

- Lyndon Johnson and the Apex of Liberalism
- Into War in Vietnam
- The Movement
- The Conservative Response
- Conclusion
- Sites to Visit
- For Further Reading

The soft-spoken black man with the strange Northern accent first showed up in the small town of McComb, Mississippi, in the summer of 1961. Robert Parris Moses had come on a mission of democracy. An organizer for the new Student Nonviolent Coordinating Committee (SNCC), he was there to encourage impoverished African Americans to register to vote. Over the next four years in the Deep South, Bob Moses paid a price for his commitments. Local police imprisoned him, and white supremacists beat him severely and murdered dozens of his fellow activists in the black freedom movement. But Moses remained committed to nonviolence and racial integration. His quiet courage became legendary in the movement. One summer night in 1962, he returned to a deserted SNCC office in Greenwood, Mississippi, that had just been ransacked by a white mob; three other SNCC workers had barely escaped with their lives. Moses looked around, made up a bed in the corner of the devastated main room, and went to sleep. He refused to be intimidated.

During the 1960s, an extraordinary number of idealistic young people became involved in public life in an effort to make real their nation's abstract promises of freedom and justice. The civil rights movement inspired the social movements that followed: for ending the war, for preserving the environment, and for liberating women, Latinos, Indians, and gay men and lesbians. But organizing for change inevitably brought activists up against fierce resistance from what they called "the establishment." Disillusionment and radicalization often followed. Public life became deeply contentious by 1968 as young radicals challenged more conservative citizens on issues of race, war, and gender.

The escalating American war in Southeast Asia loomed over all. Lyndon Johnson brought the nation to its apex of liberal reform with his extensive Great Society legislation. However, the high-flying hopes of Democratic liberals crashed to earth with the destructive war that the Johnson administration waged against seasoned communist revolutionaries in far-off Vietnam. Out of the wreckage of 1968 emerged a Republican president, Richard Nixon, and a growing conservative backlash against the social changes advocated by people of color, the counterculture, the antiwar movement, and the rising tide of women's liberation.

Lyndon Johnson and the Apex of Liberalism

Wealth provided the foundation on which the Great Society was built. American economic expansion since World War II had created history's richest nation by 1960. From 1961 to 1966, the economy accelerated at an annual growth rate of more than 5 percent with very low inflation, stimulated by large tax cuts and extensive military spending. The 41 percent increase in per capita income during the 1960s was not evenly distributed, however. Economist Paul Samuelson explained in 1970, "If we made an income pyramid out of a child's blocks, with each layer portraying $1000 of income, the peak would be far higher than the Eiffel Tower, but almost all of us would be within a yard of the ground." And the distribution of wealth (stocks and real estate) was far more skewed than that of income. U.S. policymakers believed that economic expansion would continue indefinitely and the nation could therefore afford government policies to improve the welfare of less affluent Americans.

The New President

Lyndon Baines Johnson was one of the most remarkable American characters of the twentieth century, both a giant among political leaders and a bully with those who worked for him. Johnson grew up in a family struggling to stay out of poverty in the Texas hill country west of Austin. He entered Democratic politics early as an avid supporter of Franklin Roosevelt and the New Deal, aided by the business savvy and loyalty of his wife, Lady Bird Johnson, who grew wealthy through ownership of TV and radio stations. As First Lady, she became widely known for her leadership in highway beautification. Lyndon Johnson rose like a rocket through Congress to become perhaps the most powerful Senate majority leader ever (1954–1960) and then vice president (1961–1963). Kennedy's assassination catapulted him into the Oval Office as the nation's first Texan president.

Johnson retained Kennedy's cabinet and advisers and used the memory of the fallen young president to rally support for his administration. Johnson turned out to be the more liberal of the two men in part because his early years in Texas had given him a visceral understanding of poverty and discrimination that his predecessor lacked. Johnson's focus was different, too. He retained Kennedy's anticommunist commitments abroad, but his heart remained at home, where he wanted to perfect American society.

First he had to win reelection, because less than a year remained until voters went to the polls in 1964. The Republicans nominated right-wing Senator Barry Goldwater of Arizona, a sign of the party's sharp swing away from its moderate eastern elements toward its fiercely conservative western and southern constituencies. Goldwater believed in unrestricted markets and a minimal role for the federal government in every aspect of American life except the military. He spoke casually about using nuclear weapons against communists abroad. Goldwater declared that "extremism in the defense of liberty is no vice," but Johnson zeroed in on that extremism and swept to the largest electoral majority of any president (61 percent).

The Great Society: Fighting Poverty and Discrimination

In pursuit of what he called the Great Society, Johnson first declared a "War on Poverty." No citizen in the richest nation on earth should live in squalor, he believed. More than one out of five Americans still lived below the conservatively estimated official poverty line ($3,022 for a nonfarm family of four in 1960), and 70 percent of these were white.

The president and a large congressional majority passed several measures to alleviate poverty. They sharply increased the availability of money and food stamps through the Aid to Families with Dependent Children ("welfare") program, and they raised Social Security payments to older Americans. Several programs focused on improving educational opportunities as an avenue out of poverty: Head Start offered preschool education and meals for youngsters, the Elementary and Secondary Education Act sent federal funds to the least affluent school districts, and an expanded system of student loans facilitated access to college. The Job Corps provided employment training, and Volunteers in Service to America (VISTA) served as a domestic Peace Corps, funneling people with education and skills into poor communities to serve as teachers and providers of other social services.

No barrier to opportunity in the early 1960s was higher than the color bar. Both opportunist and idealist, Johnson as president shed his segregationist voting record (necessary for election in Texas before 1960) and became the most vocal proponent of racial equality ever to occupy the Oval Office. Two factors facilitated his change in position. Blatant inequalities for American citizens weakened the United States in its competition with the Soviets and Chinese for the loyalty of the nonwhite Third World majority. Moreover, the African American freedom struggle in the South had reached a boiling point. Black frustration was mounting over white brutality and the seeming indifference or even hostility of the national government.

The Civil Rights Act of 1964 fulfilled the implicit promise of the *Brown v. Board of Education* decision a decade earlier. The 1964 act made desegregation the law of the land as it outlawed discrimination in employment and in public facilities such as restaurants, theaters, and hotels. The Voting Rights Act of 1965 outlawed poll taxes and provided federal voting registrars in states that refused the ballot to African Americans. The single most important legislation of the twentieth century for bringing political democracy to the South, the Voting Rights Act increased the percentage of blacks voting in Mississippi from 7 percent to 60 percent in two years.

The Great Society: Improving the Quality of Life

Johnson's vision of the Great Society extended to the broader quality of life in the United States. Health care was perhaps the most fundamental issue for citizens' sense of personal security. After 1965, the new Medicare system paid for the medical needs of Americans age sixty-five and older, and Medicaid underwrote health care services for the indigent. In 1964, when more than half of adults smoked tobacco, the surgeon-general issued the first government report linking smoking to cancer. Higher federal standards for automotive safety followed a year later. Public pressures also led to the establishment of new requirements for publishing the nutritional values of packaged food. The federally funded Public Broadcasting System (PBS) was established to provide television programs that were more educational than the fare tied to advertising on the three corporate networks (NBC, CBS, and ABC). In fact, most Great Society measures targeted all Americans rather than just the disadvantaged.

TABLE 26.1 The Election of 1964

Candidate	Political Party	Popular Vote (%)	Electoral Vote
Lyndon B. Johnson	Democratic	61.1	486
Barry M. Goldwater	Republican	38.5	52

Nothing more directly threatened the quality of American life than the degradation of the natural environment. The costs of the unrestrained and much-heralded economic growth since World War II showed up in the nation's air, water, and land. The leaded gasoline that fueled products of the booming auto industry created smog, industrial effluents polluted lakes and rivers, and petrochemical wastes poisoned the ground. The products of science that had contributed so much to the production of wealth were turning out to have hidden costs, and a new wave of citizen action to protect the environment began to build.

Growing public awareness prompted the Clean Air Act (1963) and the Clean Waters Act (1966), which set federal guidelines for reducing smog and preserving public drinking sources from bacterial pollution. Even the long dam-building tradition in the American West faced new questions, with the Wild and Scenic Rivers Act enacted in 1968. Meanwhile, Congress passed the Wilderness Act in 1964, setting aside 9 million acres of undeveloped public lands as a place "where man is a visitor who does not remain."

The Liberal Warren Court

The Supreme Court under the leadership of Earl Warren steadily expanded the constitutional definition of individual rights. This shift reached even those deemed to have lost many of their rights: prisoners. *Gideon v. Wainwright* (1963) established the right of indigent prisoners to legal counsel, and *Escobedo v. Illinois* (1964) confirmed the right to counsel during interrogation, a critical hindrance to the use of torture. After *Miranda v. Arizona* (1966), police were required to inform people they arrested of their rights to remain silent and to speak to a lawyer.

The Warren Court bolstered other rights of individuals against potentially coercive community pressures. Decisions in 1962 and 1963 strictly limited the practice of requiring prayers in public schools. In 1963 the Court narrowed standards for the definition of "obscenity," allowing freer expression in the arts but also in pornography. *Griswold v. Connecticut* (1965) established the use of contraceptive devices as a matter of private choice protected by the Constitution. In 1967 the Court heard the case of Mildred Jeter, a black woman, and Richard Loving, a white man, Virginians who had evaded their state's ban on interracial marriage by traveling to Washington, D.C., for their wedding and then returned to Caroline County to live. In the aptly titled *Loving v. Virginia*, the Court declared marriage one of the "basic civil rights of men" and overturned the laws of the last sixteen states restricting interracial unions.

The Supreme Court's interpreting of the Constitution to expand individual rights disturbed many conservative Americans. They saw the Court as another arm of an intrusive national government that was extending its control over matters previously left to local communities. For them, the goal of integration did not justify the busing of school children. Rising crime rates troubled them more than police brutality. Many Roman Catholics were troubled by the legalization of contraceptives. Incensed by the ban on requiring school prayer, Protestant fundamentalists sought redress through political involvement, which they had previously shunned, initiating a grassroots religious conservative movement that helped bring Ronald Reagan to power in 1980.

Into War in Vietnam

The 1960s also marked the culmination of the U.S. government's efforts to control revolutionary political and social change abroad. The Truman Doctrine's logic of containing communism spanned the entire globe, but few imagined that the United States would overreach itself, tragically, in Vietnam. Johnson's accomplishments at home were forever overshadowed by the war he sent Americans to fight in the quiet rice paddies and beautiful highland forests of Southeast Asia. An aggressive U.S. anticommunist policy abroad collided with leftist revolutionaries throughout the Third World, and it was ill fortune for the Vietnamese that this collision struck them hardest of all.

The Vietnamese Revolution and the United States

The conflict in Vietnam began as one of many efforts to end European colonialism. Vietnamese nationalists, varying in ideologies but led by Ho Chi Minh and the Indochinese Communist party, sought since the 1930s to liberate their country from French colonial rule. Japanese advances during World War II put the Vietminh (Vietnamese nationalists) on the same side as the Americans, and Ho worked closely with the U.S. Office of Strategic Services (OSS), precursor to the Central Intelligence Agency (CIA).

After the defeat of Germany and Japan, however, the French wanted to regain control of their colonies in Africa and Asia, including Vietnam. The British provided troop transport ships for French soldiers, and the United States provided most of the funds to support France in its war against the Vietminh (1946-1954). Cold War priorities won out: a weakened France had to be bolstered as the linchpin of a reintegrated, anticommunist western Europe, while the Vietminh were led by Communist party members. The Vietnamese defeated the much more heavily armed French at the battle of Dien Bien Phu in May 1954. Two months later, the Geneva Accords divided the country temporarily at the seventeenth parallel until national elections could be held within two years to reunify Vietnam. Ho's forces solidified their control of the north, the French pulled out entirely, and the Eisenhower administration made a fateful decision to intervene directly to preserve the southern part of Vietnam from communism. The United States created a new government led by the Roman Catholic, anticommunist Ngo Dinh Diem in a new country called "South Vietnam."

The Vietnamese Revolution was only half over, however. The French colonialists withdrew, but the Saigon regime did not hold elections. In the North, the sometimes brutal internal revolution for the creation of a socialist society proceeded with an extensive program of land redistribution. In the South, Diem ruled for eight years with increasing repression of communists and other dissenters. U.S. funding kept him in power. Southern members of the old Vietminh began a sabotage campaign against the Saigon government and formed the National Liberation Front (NLF) in 1960, with the support of North Vietnam. Diem and his American supporters called them Viet Cong or VC, roughly equivalent to the derogatory American term *Commies*. As the struggle to overthrow Diem intensified, several of his own generals assassinated him in November 1963 with the tacit support of U.S. officials in South Vietnam and Washington.

Johnson's War

Lyndon Johnson inherited his predecessors' commitment to preserving a noncommunist South Vietnam. Bolstered by Kennedy's hawkish advisers, he believed that American credibility was at stake. But Johnson faced a swiftly deteriorating military situation. The NLF, which the administration portrayed as merely a tool of North Vietnam, was winning the political war for the South, taking control of the countryside from the demoralized Army of the Republic of Vietnam (ARVN). Faced with the choice of escalating U.S. involvement to prevent an NLF victory or withdrawing entirely from the country, Johnson escalated.

How he did so was crucially important. There was neither a national debate nor a congressional vote to declare war. Johnson did not want to distract Congress from his Great Society agenda, nor did he want to provoke the Soviet Union or China. But he believed he had to preserve a noncommunist South Vietnam or else face a debilitating backlash from Republicans, who would skewer him as McCarthy had done to Truman over the "loss" of China fifteen years earlier. So the president used deception, describing offensive American actions as defensive and opening up a credibility gap between a committed government and a skeptical public.

In August 1964, North Vietnamese ships in the Gulf of Tonkin fired on the U.S. destroyer *Maddox*, which was aiding South Vietnamese sabotage operations against the North. The president portrayed the incident as one of unprovoked communist aggression, and Congress expressed almost unanimous support through its Gulf of Tonkin Resolution. With this substitute for a declaration of war, Johnson ordered American planes to begin bombing North Vietnam, and the first American combat troops splashed ashore at Da Nang in South Vietnam on March 8, 1965. In July the administration made the key decision to add 100,000 more soldiers, with more to follow as necessary.

American strategy had two goals: to limit the war so as not to draw in neighboring China (to avoid a repeat of the Korean War) and to force the

NLF and North Vietnam to give up their struggle to reunify the country under Hanoi's control. The problem was the political nature of the guerrilla war in the South: a contest for the loyalty of the population, in which NLF operatives mingled easily with the citizenry. This kind of war made the enemy difficult to find, as had often been true for the British in fighting the American revolutionaries in the 1770s. The "strategic hamlet" program uprooted rural peasants and concentrated them in fortified towns, creating "free fire zones" in their wake where anything that moved was a target. The U.S. Air Force pounded the South as well as the North, dropping more bombs on this ancient land (smaller than either Germany or Japan) than had been used in all theaters on all sides in World War II. These tactics destabilized and traumatized society in South Vietnam as one-fourth of the population became refugees.

Americans in Southeast Asia

Given America's wealth, size, and superior weaponry, most U.S. soldiers who went to Vietnam in 1965–1966 had no doubt they would win the war. They typically looked down on Asians. Very few knew anything about Vietnamese history or culture, and almost none spoke the Vietnamese language. Although a small number of Americans worked closely with their South Vietnamese allies, most GIs encountered Vietnamese in subservient roles as laundry workers, prostitutes, waitresses, and bartenders. Blinkered by anticommunism and far removed from their own revolutionary roots, Americans from the top brass to the lowest "grunts" marched into a country they did not understand but assumed they could control.

President Johnson spoke of the conflict in Vietnam as a case of one sovereign nation—the North—invading another one—the South. However, few Vietnamese saw the war in those terms. The United States, dismissing the failure of the French before them, had intervened not so much in an international war as in an ongoing revolution that aimed to reunify the country. Few Vietnamese, whatever their opinions of communism, viewed the corrupt Saigon regime as legitimate or democratic. After all, it was kept in place by foreigners, whereas the North was ruled by people who had expelled the French foreigners.

Initial U.S. optimism reflected a grave underestimation of the NLF and the North Vietnamese. Ho Chi Minh was an extremely popular leader, and intervention from the other side of the world only strengthened his position. As the war expanded, NLF recruiting in the South snowballed, and the people of North Vietnam remained loyal to their authoritarian government. Communist forces proved willing to endure fantastic hardship and sacrifices to prevail. Their morale was much higher than that of the ARVN.

Who were the 3 million Americans who went to Vietnam? The initial forces contained experienced soldiers, but as the war escalated, this professional army was diluted with hundreds of thousands of young draftees. Student deferments protected more comfortable Americans, so GIs were predominantly those who lacked money and education. Although 70 percent were white men, black, Hispanic, and Native American enlistees shipped out in disproportionate numbers. In sharp contrast to the motives of the NLF and the North Vietnamese army, these young men (along with 10,000 women who volunteered as nurses) were not in Vietnam to win the war regardless of the cost or duration. They had only to survive twelve months before returning home to the safety of a peacetime society.

North Vietnamese regular army units came South to match the growing number of U.S. forces, and they occasionally engaged the Americans in large set battles, as at Ia Drang Valley in the fall of 1965. U.S. troops fought well in such firefights, making devastating use of their superior weapons and air power. However, the bulk of the fighting consisted of smaller engagements with deceptive enemies on their home turf who faded in and out of the civilian population with ease. Ambushes and unexpected death haunted Americans on patrol, and relentless heat and humidity wore them down.

American soldiers felt mounting frustration and rage over the nature of the war that they were ordered to fight. Lacking a clear battlefront and an understandable strategy for winning the war, they were commanded simply to kill the often mysterious enemy. Yet distinguishing civilians from combatants in a popular guerrilla war was not always easy, especially when so many civilians evidently supported the NLF and so few Americans spoke Vietnamese. Realizing that few of the people they were supposed to be defending actually wanted them there but under orders to produce enemy bodies, U.S. troops on the ground began to slide toward a racial war against all Vietnamese.

Many GIs resisted this logic, sometimes showing real kindness to Vietnamese civilians. But atrocities on both sides inevitably followed from this kind of war. The worst came in the village of My Lai on March 16, 1968, where 105 soldiers from Charlie Company—enraged by the recent deaths of several comrades in ambushes—slaughtered, often after torturing or raping, more than 400 Vietnamese women, children, and old men. The army covered up the massacre for a year and a half, and eventually found only Lieutenant William Calley, the leader of Charlie Company's First Platoon, guilty of murdering Vietnamese civilians.

1968: The Turning Point

In late 1967, the public face of the war effort remained upbeat, as General Westmoreland declared that he could now see "some light at the end of the tunnel." But hopes of an imminent victory were crushed by the startling Tet Offensive (named for the Vietnamese New Year) that began on January 30, 1968. NLF insurgents and North Vietnamese troops attacked U.S. strongholds throughout South Vietnam. The blow to American public confidence in Johnson and his military commanders proved irreversible. Far from being on the verge of defeat, as the administration had been claiming, the communists had shown that they could mount simultaneous attacks around the country.

The Tet Offensive coincided with two other crises in early 1968 to convince American political and business elites that U.S. international commitments had become larger than the nation could afford. First, a week before Tet began, the North Korean navy seized the U.S. intelligence ship *Pueblo* in the Sea of Japan and temporarily imprisoned its crew. U.S. commanders were left scrambling to find enough forces to respond effectively without weakening American commitments in Europe and elsewhere. Second, a British financial collapse devalued the pound and caused the London government to announce its imminent withdrawal from its historic positions east of the Suez Canal, placing new military burdens on the United States in the Middle East. These events reduced international confidence in the U.S. economy, causing a currency crisis in March 1968 as holders of dollars traded them in for gold.

The political career of Lyndon Johnson was a final casualty of these events. His support on the left withered as the antiwar and black power movements expanded. Meanwhile, his more centrist supporters were joining the

MAP 26.2 The American War in Vietnam

Before U.S. combat troops entered Vietnam in 1965, few Americans knew where this Southeast Asian country was. Vietnam's geography and place names quickly became familiar in the United States as hundreds of thousands of young Americans served there and some 58,000 died there. Vietnam's elongated shape, its borders with Cambodia and Laos, and its proximity to China all affected the course of the fighting between 1965 and 1973.

backlash against civil rights, urban violence, and antiwar protesters, peeling off to the Republican party. On March 12, antiwar challenger Senator Eugene McCarthy of Minnesota nearly defeated the incumbent president in the New Hampshire Democratic primary. Johnson's vulnerability was obvious. Senator Robert Kennedy of New York joined the race two weeks later. In a televised speech on March 31 that caught the divided nation by surprise, Johnson announced an end to U.S. escalations in the war, the start of negotiations in Paris with North Vietnam, and an end to his own political career. He would not seek reelection.

The Movement

While national leaders were defending what they called the "frontiers of freedom" abroad, young Americans in the mid- and late 1960s organized to expand what they considered the frontiers of freedom at home. Television for the first time tied the country together in a common culture whose shared images were transmitted simultaneously around the nation. The expanding war in Vietnam radicalized people who had initially been optimistic about reforming American society. Black power, the New Left, the counterculture, women's liberation, and other liberation movements often had quite divergent goals. But participants overlapped extensively and activists spoke of "the Movement" as if it were a unified phenomenon. At the heart of the youth movements of the decade lay a common quest for authenticity—a rejection of hypocrisy and a distrust of traditional authorities—that fused cultural and political protest.

From Civil Rights to Black Power

By 1966 the civil rights movement fractured as it confronted the limits of its success. It had achieved the goals of ending legal discrimination and putting southern African Americans in the voting booth, but it had not brought about a colorblind society. Racial prejudice among white conservatives remained virulent, and white liberals, such as those in the Kennedy and Johnson administrations, revealed themselves as not always trustworthy allies. Expecting only hostility from conservatives, civil rights workers were more disillusioned with what they saw as liberal betrayals.

The Justice Department and the Federal Bureau of Investigation (FBI) did little to restrain the violence of the Ku Klux Klan until the murders of white organizers Michael Schwerner and Andrew Goodman in the summer of 1964—along with black co-worker James Chaney. Two months later, at the national Democratic party convention in Atlantic City, New Jersey, Johnson crushed the effort of the biracial Mississippi Freedom Democratic party to replace the state's regular, all-white Democratic delegates. The president was determined to avoid further alienating white southern voters as he pursued a huge victory margin in the November elections. Outraged at this betrayal, Fannie Lou Hamer—a courageous sharecropper who had been beaten by Mississippi police for her efforts to register black voters—declared in a televised appearance at Atlantic City, "I question America."

The black freedom struggle for centuries had woven together elements of racial separatism with elements of integration into the larger American culture. For many younger African Americans, the pendulum swung toward a need for greater independence from the white majority. They took inspiration from Malcolm X, the fiery and eloquent minister of the Nation of Islam (Black Muslims), who until his murder in 1965 captivated listeners with denunciations of white perfidy and demands for black self-respect. In 1966 SNCC members began to speak of the need for "black power" rather than for the integrated "beloved community" they had initially sought in 1960.

The Black Panther party formed in Oakland, California, in response to police brutality. The heavily armed Panthers engaged in several shootouts with police and were eventually decimated by an FBI campaign against them. White Americans were shocked by the uprisings and riots that swept through black urban communities during the summers of 1964–1968. Triggered by the actions of white police, the riots expressed the fierce frustrations of impoverished people whose lives remained largely untouched by the achievements of the civil rights struggle. The most destructive outbreaks occurred in the Watts district of Los Angeles in 1965 and in Detroit and Newark in 1967.

Black power thrived primarily as a cultural movement that promoted pride in African American and African history and life. The slogan "black is beautiful" captured this spirit: long degraded by their white compatriots as inferior, black Americans in the late 1960s and 1970s reversed this equation to celebrate their cultural heritage. This could be as basic as a hairstyle, the natural Afro replacing hair straightened to look like Caucasian hair. At universities, new departments of African American studies fostered the exploration of black history. Unlearning habits of public deference to whites, most African Americans began referring to themselves as "black" rather than "Negro."

Cultural black power mixed with a different kind of political black power by the late 1960s: the election of black officials. Although militant black power advocates garnered the most media attention, most African Americans supported Lyndon Johnson and used the Voting Rights Act to pursue their goals in the realm of electoral politics. In 1966 Carl Stokes of Cleveland was elected the first black mayor of a major American city, and African Americans won local offices across the South.

The New Left and the Struggle Against the War

In 1962 a group of liberal college activists founded the Students for a Democratic Society (SDS), calling for a rejuvenation of American politics and society to replace the complacency that they saw pervading the country. Racial bigotry and poverty particularly troubled these optimistic young reformers, along with the overarching threat of nuclear destruction (highlighted anew by the missile crisis in Cuba). They hoped to become a kind of "white SNCC," promoting participatory democracy to redeem the promise of Cold War America.

SDS served as the central organization of the New Left. Communism was simply not important to these activists, nor was conservatism, which was then at its lowest point. They focused instead on the behavior of the liberals who ran the U.S. government from 1961 to 1968. They developed a critique of "corporate liberalism" as promoting the interests of the wealthy and the business community far more than providing for the needs of the disadvantaged.

After 1965, SDS's initially broad reform agenda narrowed to stopping the Vietnam War. SDS members organized the first major antiwar protest outside the White House on April 17, 1965, bringing their organization into alliance with the small group of religious and secular pacifists already working against the war. Mainstream Democrats also began abandoning Johnson over the war as it grew. The president had alienated the powerful chair of the Senate Foreign Relations Committee, J. William Fulbright of Arkansas, with his misleading reports during the brief U.S. military intervention in the Dominican Republic in April 1965 to defeat a left-leaning but not communist coup attempt. Fulbright then held televised hearings on the American war in Southeast Asia in January 1966, raising grave doubts about its wisdom. Draft resistance increased: young men moved to Canada, as did SNCC's Bob Moses, or went to jail, as did champion boxer Muhammad Ali.

Antiwar protesters followed the same trajectory of radicalization as black power advocates. Their dismay turned to rage as the Johnson administration continued to expand a war that was destroying much of Vietnam while killing tens of thousands of American soldiers for no reason its opponents considered legitimate. In combination with or in support of black militants, white radicals took over buildings on university campuses in 1968–1969: Columbia, Cornell, Harvard, San Francisco State, and many others. SDS ultimately broke apart in the confusion and exhilaration of its growing demand for revolution against the larger systemic enemies, imperialism and capitalism, not just corporate liberalism. But radical rage could not be understood apart from the ongoing destruction of Vietnam by a government acting in the name of all Americans.

Cultural Rebellion and the Counterculture

While the New Left moved from wanting to reform American society to wanting to overthrow it, the counterculture sought to create an alternative society. Called "hippies" by those who disliked them, these young people were alienated by the materialism, competition, and conformity of American life in the Cold War. They tried to live out alternative values of gentleness, tolerance, and inclusivity. Sporting headbands, long hair, and beads, many identified with traditional Native Americans. In place of junk foods, they promoted health foods;

in place of profit-seeking businesses, they established co-ops. "Do your own thing" was a common slogan.

In reaction against the conformity of mainstream society, members of the counter-culture explored the limitations of consciousness to expand their self-knowledge. They went beyond the nicotine and alcohol that were the common stimulants of their parents' culture to experiment with such mind-altering drugs as marijuana, peyote, hashish, LSD, cocaine, and even heroin. Spirituality was an important path into consciousness for many in the counterculture. Religious traditions associated with Asia, particularly Buddhism, gained numerous adherents, as did the spiritual customs and traditional practices of Native Americans. Others rediscovered the "authentic" Jesus obscured by the institutional structures of the formal Christian church (earning themselves the nickname "Jesus freaks"); Campus Crusade for Christ, InterVarsity, and other evangelical college groups spread across the country. Music served as the most common coin of the countercultural realm, from the political folk sound of Joan Baez and Bob Dylan to the broadly popular Beatles and the more distinctly countercultural rock 'n' roll of the Grateful Dead and Jefferson Airplane.

Older Americans experienced the counterculture largely as spectacle. The mainstream media emphasized the alternative aspects of the hippie lifestyle in its coverage. Viewers were varyingly disgusted by, attracted to, and titillated by the hair, clothing, nudity, and blurred gender distinctions. Meanwhile, entrepreneurs realized that they could market the antimaterialist counterculture profitably. Young Americans eagerly bought up records, clothing, jewelry, and natural foods—a revealing demonstration of how consumer values pervaded American life.

One of the most visible changes of the 1960s was often called the sexual revolution. Changes in Americans' sexual behavior in the 1960s reflected in part the counterculture's goal of living an authentic, honest life in which words matched actions. The sexual revolution removed some of the penalties for the premarital and extramarital sex that had previously been fairly common but unacknowledged. The appearance of the birth control pill in 1960 underpinned the shift to more open sexual relationships by freeing women from the fear of pregnancy. Attitudes toward abortion also became more tolerant. New York passed the first state law legalizing some abortions in 1970, and three years later the Supreme Court established a woman's constitutional right to abortion in the landmark case of *Roe v. Wade*.

Women's Liberation

The movement for women's liberation built on developments earlier in the decade, including Betty Friedan's *The Feminine Mystique* (1963), a widely read book that captured the frustrations of many women who had accepted the role of suburban homemaker after World War II. Friedan and other liberal feminists founded the National Organization for Women (NOW) in 1966 to lobby against sexual discrimination in the public sphere in such areas as employment, wages, education, and jury duty. These challenges had radical implications for women's and men's earnings and thus for responsibilities within families, but NOW did not yet focus on issues inside the private sphere of the home.

The shift to the view that "the personal is political" came from younger, mostly white women who had been active in the civil rights and antiwar struggles. Inspired by the courage and successes of the protest movements in which they figured prominently, these female activists had also learned that traditional gender roles restricted them even in organizations dedicated to participatory democracy. Ironically, radical men could be as patronizing and disrespectful of women's abilities as mainstream men. Younger feminists in 1967 and 1968 agreed with NOW's challenge to discrimination in the public sphere, but they focused even more on the personal politics of women's daily lives, on critical issues such as parenting, child care, housework, and abortion.

The new wave of feminism that washed through American culture at the end of the 1960s triggered fierce debates about the nature of gender. Was there a uniquely feminine way of knowing, seeing, and acting, or were women in essence the same as men, distinguishable ultimately by their individuality? Was womanhood biologically or only culturally constructed? Feminists disagreed sharply in their answers.

However, diversity within the feminist movement did not hide a common commitment to expanding women's possibilities. The women's movement that emerged out of the 1960s permanently transformed women's lives and gender relations in American society, in areas ranging from job and educational opportunities, sexual harassment, and gender-neutral language to family roles, sexual relations, reproductive rights, and athletic facilities.

The Many Fronts of Liberation

Like the women's movement, the Chicano, pan-Indian, and gay liberation movements of the late 1960s were grounded in older organizing efforts within those communities. The struggles for "brown power," "red power," and "gay power" also reflected the newer influence of black power and its determination to take pride in what the dominant American society had denigrated for so long. Activists on college campuses successfully pressured administrations to establish interdisciplinary ethnic studies programs, such as the first Chicano studies program at California State University at Los Angeles in 1968. Ethnic cultural identity went hand in hand with the pursuit of political and economic integration into mainstream American life.

The most prominent push to organize Latinos was the effort led by Cesar Chávez to build a farm workers' union in California and the Southwest. These primarily Mexican American migrant workers harvested most of the hand-picked produce that Americans ate, but their hard work under severe conditions failed to lift them out of poverty. National consumer support for boycotts of table grapes and iceberg lettuce helped win recognition for the United Farm Workers (UFW) union and better pay by 1970. Younger Mexican Americans across the Southwest looked with pride on their Mexican heritage, even appropriating the formerly pejorative term *Chicano*.

Puerto Ricans, the largest Spanish-speaking ethnic group located primarily on the East Coast, experienced a similar growth in militancy and nationalist sentiment during the late 1960s. By the 1960s, more than a million islanders had moved to the East Coast, most to the New York City area. Despite being the only Latino immigrants already holding American citizenship when they arrived, Puerto Ricans experienced similar patterns of both discrimination and opportunity as Mexican Americans.

The most destitute of Americans, Indians also sought to reinvigorate their communities. On the Northwest Coast, they staged "fish-ins" in the mid-1960s to assert treaty rights, and in 1968 urban activists in Minneapolis formed the American Indian Movement (AIM). On November 20, 1969, just days after the largest antiwar march in Washington, seventy-eight Native Americans seized the island of Alcatraz in San Francisco Bay "in the name of all American Indians by right of discovery." For a year and a half, they used their occupation of the former federal prison site to publicize grievances about anti-Indian prejudice and to promote a new pan-Indian identity that reached across traditional tribal divisions. In 1973 armed members of AIM occupied buildings for two months at Wounded Knee, South Dakota, site of the infamous 1890 U.S. Army massacre of unarmed Sioux. Tribal governments sought "red power" in their own quieter way. They asserted greater tribal control of reservation schools across the country.

Although they lacked a unifying ethnic identity, gay men and lesbians also found opportunities to construct coalitions in the more open atmosphere of the late 1960s. Building on the earlier but quieter community organizing of older homosexuals in New York, San Francisco, and Los Angeles, more militant youth began to express openly their anger at the homophobic prejudice and violence prevalent in American society. This demand for tolerance and respect reached the headlines when gay patrons of the Stonewall Bar in New York fought back fiercely against a typically forceful police raid on June 27, 1969. Activists of the new Gay Liberation Front emphasized the importance of "coming out of the closet": proudly acknowledging one's sexual orientation as legitimate and decent.

The Conservative Response

The majority of Americans had mixed feelings about the protests that roiled the nation. They were impressed by the courage of many who stood up against discrimination, and by 1968 they wanted to find a way out of the war in Southeast Asia. But they were alienated by the style and values of others who loudly demanded change in American society. Moderate and conservative citizens and generations of recent European immigrants resented what they saw as a lack of appreciation for the nation's virtues and successes. The political and social upheavals of 1968 opened the door to a Republican return to the White House, and Richard Nixon slipped through.

Backlashes

A backlash developed in response to the increasing assertiveness of people of color. European Americans in every part of the United States had long been accustomed to deference from nonwhites and racial segregation, either by law in the South or by custom elsewhere. Conservatives resented what they considered blacks' ingratitude at the civil rights measures enacted by the federal government, including black power's condemnation of whites as "crackers" and "honkies." Urban riots and escalating rates of violent crime, along with the Supreme Court's expansion of the rights of the accused, deepened their anger. They associated crime with urban African Americans, for although whites were still the majority of criminals, blacks (like any other population with less money) were disproportionately represented in prisons. The rise of often angry nonwhite nationalism dismayed most European Americans. They were troubled by the militancy of Chicanos in the Southwest, Puerto Ricans in the Northeast, Indians on reservations and in cities, and African Americans almost everywhere.

Another backlash developed as a defense of traditional hierarchies against the cultural rebellions of the 1960s. Proud of their lives and values, conservatives rejected a whole array of challenges to American society. Raised to believe in respecting one's elders, they resented the disrespect of many youth, who warned, "Don't trust anyone over 30." A generation that had fought and sacrificed in the "good war" against the Nazis found the absence of patriotism among many protesters unfathomable. The United States remained one of the most religious of industrialized societies, and conservative churchgoers emphasized obedience to authorities. They feared the effects of illegal drugs on their children.

The backlash against the social changes of the 1960s contained elements of class antagonism as well. Working-class whites resented the often affluent campus rebels and the black and Latino poor targeted by some Great Society programs. They believed that their values of hard work, restraint, and respectability were increasingly unappreciated and even mocked. Republican leaders from Goldwater to Nixon to Reagan gave voice to these resentments and drew votes away from Democratic blue-collar strongholds. Democratic governor George Wallace of Alabama also became a spokesperson for the anger of many "forgotten" whites on both sides of the Mason-Dixon line.

The Turmoil of 1968 at Home

The traumas of 1968 brought the conservative backlash to the critical stage. First came the Tet Offensive in Vietnam, creating fears that the war might become an interminable quagmire. Then, on April 4, a gunman named James

Earl Ray assassinated Martin Luther King Jr. in Memphis, where he had gone to support a strike by sanitation workers. King had become more openly radical in his final years, opposing the war and working on class-based organizing of poor people. But he remained the nation's leading apostle of nonviolence, and his murder evoked despair among millions of citizens, especially African Americans. Police battled rioters and arsonists in black neighborhoods of 130 cities across the nation, with forty-six people dying in the clashes.

Summer brought more shocking news. Charismatic senator Robert Kennedy's entry into the presidential campaign had inspired renewed hopes among Democratic liberals. But on the night of his victory in the June 5 California primary, Kennedy was killed by a deranged gunman. Vice President Hubert Humphrey seemed assured of the nomination at the Democratic convention in Chicago in August, despite his association with Johnson's war policies. Some 10,000 antiwar activists, including hundreds of FBI *agents provocateurs* (spies seeking to provoke violence), showed up to engage in protests outside the convention. Chicago's Democratic mayor Richard Daley unleashed thousands of police on protesters, bystanders, and photographers in an orgy of beatings that subsequent investigations called a police riot. Ninety million Americans watched on television as a deeply divided Democratic party appeared helpless before the violence.

Into the vacuum of public anger and alienation that accompanied the liberals' self-destruction in Chicago stepped two men. The spread of the conservative backlash from 1964 to 1968 gave George Wallace a wider constituency for his right-wing populist message of hostility to liberals, blacks, and federal officials. With the national Democratic party committed to racial integration, Wallace ran for president as an independent candidate and won 13.5 percent of the popular vote in November. Republican candidate Richard Nixon campaigned as the candidate of "law and order" and promised that he had a secret plan to end the war in Vietnam. Nixon won the popular vote by less than 1 percent.

The Nixon Administration

A lonely, aloof man of great tenacity and ambition, Richard Nixon had worked hard to remake his public image for 1968. Widely viewed as a somewhat unscrupulous partisan since his early career in Congress, he had refashioned himself as a statesman with a broad vision for reducing international tensions between the great powers. He sounded like a conservative in the campaign against Humphrey, but once in the White House he governed as the most liberal Republican since Theodore Roosevelt, pressed by a Congress still controlled by Democrats.

Nowhere was this clearer than on issues related to natural resources. Much had happened to the environment since Republican Theodore Roosevelt's conservation efforts, little of it for the better. A powerful movement was building to protect natural resources and human health from the effects of air and water

TABLE 26.2 The Election of 1968

Candidate	Political Party	Popular Vote (%)	Electoral Vote
Richard M. Nixon	Republican	43.4	301
Hubert H. Humphrey	Democratic	42.7	191
George Wallace	American Independent	13.5	46

pollution. Biologist Paul Ehrlich's best-selling *The Population Bomb* (1968) warned of the dire consequences of the globe's runaway growth in human population. In 1969 the government banned the carcinogenic pesticide DDT. That same year, a huge oil spill off Santa Barbara fouled 200 miles of pristine California beaches, and the Cuyahoga River in Cleveland, its surface coated with waste and oil, caught fire and burned for days. Environmentalists around the country proclaimed April 22, 1970, as "Earth Day."

Congress responded with legislation that mandated the careful management of the nation's natural resources. The Environmental Protection Agency was established in 1970. Amendments to the Clean Air (1970) and Clean Water (1972) Acts tightened restrictions on harmful emissions from cars and factories. The Endangered Species Act (1973) created for the first time the legal right of nonhuman animals to survive, a major step toward viewing the quality of human life as inextricable from the earth's broader ecology.

What Nixon did care deeply about at home was politics, not policy. Antiwar demonstrations reached their height during Nixon's first two years in the White House (1969–1970). He and Vice President Spiro Agnew loathed the protesters, whom they saw as weakening the nation. The two men pursued what Agnew called "positive polarization": campaigning to further divide the respectable "silent majority," as the president labeled his supporters, from voluble liberal Democrats in Congress and radical activists on the streets, whom they associated with permissiveness and lawlessness. In this broad cultural battle for political supremacy, the president appealed to conservative white southern and northern ethnic Democrats.

Early in his administration, Nixon began wielding the power of the federal government to harass his political opponents. Johnson had used the FBI, the CIA, and military intelligence agencies to infiltrate and thin the ranks of antiwar demonstrators and nonwhite nationalists. Nixon continued those illegal operations, agreeing with his predecessor that radical activists constituted a threat to national security. Nixon went beyond other presidents in assembling an "Enemies List" that included prominent elements of the political mainstream, especially liberals, the press, and his Democratic opponents. The president was particularly concerned about controlling secret information. The Pentagon Papers were a classified Defense Department history of U.S. actions in Vietnam, revealing that the government had been deceiving the American public about the course of the war. When disillusioned former Pentagon official Daniel Ellsberg leaked the study to the *New York Times* for publication in 1971, Nixon was enraged. The White House created a team of covert operatives nicknamed the Plumbers to "plug leaks" by whatever means necessary.

Escalating and De-escalating in Vietnam

Nixon and his national security adviser, Henry Kissinger, had ambitious plans for shifting the relationships of the great powers to America's advantage. To deal with China and the Soviet Union, they first had to reduce the vast U.S. engagement in the small country of Vietnam, which had grown wildly out of proportion to actual U.S. interests there. Under the Nixon Doctrine, the United States would provide military hardware rather than U.S. soldiers to allied governments, which would have to do their own fighting against leftist insurgencies. In South Vietnam, this doctrine required "Vietnamization," or withdrawing American troops so ARVN could shoulder the bulk of the war.

The key to a successful withdrawal from Vietnam for Nixon was to preserve U.S. "credibility." The perception of power could be as important as its actual exercise, and the president wanted other nations, both friend and foe, to continue to respect and fear American military might. There was no immediate pullout but a gradual process that lasted for four years (1969–1973), during which almost half of the total U.S. casualties in Vietnam occurred. Nixon did his utmost to weaken the communist forces during the slow withdrawal. The president ordered the secret bombing and invasion of neighboring Cambodia and Laos, an intensified aerial assault on North Vietnam, and the mining of Haiphong Harbor near Hanoi. Enormous protests rocked the country after the announcement of the Cambodian invasion on April 30, 1970. National Guard troops killed four students at a demonstration at Kent State University in Ohio and two at Jackson State College in Mississippi, deepening the sense of national division.

A majority of Americans now opposed the nation's war effort, a level of dissent unprecedented in U.S. history. Most telling of all was the criticism of some veterans returning from Vietnam. The morale of American soldiers still in Vietnam plummeted as the steady withdrawal of their comrades made clear that they were no longer expected to win the war. Drug abuse and racial conflict increased sharply among GIs. Even "fragging" (killing one's own officers) escalated before the peace accords were signed in Paris and the United States evacuated its last combat troops in 1973.